SHIPWRECKS OF THE LAKES

Told in Story and Picture

SHIPWRECKS OF THE LAKES

Told in Story and Picture

BY

DANA THOMAS BOWEN

Published by
FRESHWATER PRESS, INC.
334, The Arcade, P.O. Box 14009
Cleveland, Ohio 44114

ISBN: 0-912514-21-3

CONTENTS

CONTENTS (Continued)

VIII

CONTENTS (Continued)

CONTENTS (Continued)

ILLUSTRATIONS

XI

ILLUSTRATIONS (Continued)

ILLUSTRATIONS (Continued)

XIII

ILLUSTRATIONS (Continued)

XIV

⚓ ⚓ ⚓ ⚓ ⚓ ⚓ ⚓ ⚓

DEDICATION

TO THE MEMORY OF MY MOTHER

Who always worried when her boy ran off to the docks in Cleveland,

Who always listened attentively to her son tell his ship stories many years ago,

Who took him on his first steamboat ride on the Great Lakes,

Who always encouraged him to write his stories,

Who would have enjoyed so much the reading of this book,

And without whom it could not have been written.

TO PHOEBE ROUND BOWEN
I affectionately dedicate this volume.

Dana T Bowen

XV

PREFACE

Tales of shipwreck have a definite fascination and a universal appeal. They are not only exciting and thrilling but usually contain some element of mystery. They recount the struggle of man to survive, pitting himself and his ship against the elements of destruction, calling forth his utmost skill, his strength and his ingenuity, often with his very life as the high stake. Some men emerge heroes, while others are never heard from again.

It is the author's earnest hope that the tales in this book do not tend to frighten any person away from the glorious wonders of the five Great Lakes. That is far from the intention of this book.

Almost all of the disasters recounted could not have happened even a few years later than they actually did occur. Shipping quickly turns its losses into lessons. Careful study by many separate agencies of each marine disaster always follows. What happened? Why did it happen? If at all possible these answers are found. Then ways and means and laws are made to prevent the same thing from again happening.

A navigator today is bound by certain ironclad regulations made to cover almost every imaginable circumstance. Years ago he was largely on his own.

1

Often he unfortunately guessed wrong, and a shipwreck resulted. There is little need today for guesswork.

The officers of ships today have many fine safeguards. Skippers of yesteryears would indeed marvel at the many safety instruments in the wheelhouse of a modern lake steamer. Hundreds of founderings, collisions, and strandings, and thousands of lives would have consequently been saved, had the old-time masters had modern direction finders, telephones, and radar at their service. When thick weather, fog, heavy rain or snow blotted out the old-timer's vision, he poked along, trusting mostly to luck. Today the ship captain can locate his ship exactly, and can look all about him for many miles, despite bad weather. He can learn the depth of water under his ship by the turn of a button. He has a helpful telephone on his desk, just as any other executive ashore. Reliable and pertinent weather data is always available.

A government book of rules and regulations has been formulated based on marine experiences covering years of navigation. Most marine men believe that if this book is followed to the letter there would be very few major ship disasters, or minor ones either.

It is the author's intent in writing this book to bring out the sterling qualities of the Great Lakes sailor, both the early ones and the present day, also to tell of the hardships and sufferings they sometimes had to endure, and their heroic struggles to carry on when all seemed lost, and their courageous and thrilling rescues made when disaster threatened.

Captains and engineers and their crews do not quit sailing when one of their own is lost. There are many men afloat today who have lost a father, brother, or son, in the business of lake shipping, but still they carry on.

Today the ships of the Great Lakes are the finest and best equipped vessels afloat in the world. Ship builders vie with each other in building the finest and safest ships that sail. Safety of the passengers and crews are the first consideration of ship owners.

Voyages upon the Great Lakes are unsurpassed anywhere. The ports of call are usually large cities, most of them having their beginnings from the lake trade. The great open stretches of fresh water are exhilarating, invigorating, and at the same time restful. Travel the Great Lakes and enjoy for yourself the interesting experiences that await you.

For any writer to attempt to put into a single book the tales of all the shipwrecks of the Great Lakes is sheer folly. Even if it might be possible to obtain or compile just a listing of the names of the wrecked ships, with dates, locations, and causes, it is doubtful that it could be condensed into a single usable book. There have been so very many casualties over the years, especially when the lake commerce was in its infancy, with its wooden sailing vessels and early wooden steamboats.

During the year 1871, for example, it is reported that one thousand one hundred and sixty-seven disasters were recorded. In the two decades between 1878 and 1898, the United States Commissioner of Navigation reported five thousand nine hundred and ninety-nine vessels wrecked on the Great Lakes, and of these one thousand and ninety-three were total losses.

Other interesting statistics from governmental department sources show that during the navigation season of 1905, a particularly bad year on the lakes, there were two hundred seventy-one vessels damaged to a greater or less extent, of which number fifty-four were total losses through stress of weather, and twenty-three through other causes. The 1905 losses were eight times as large as those for the 1904 season.

In this book are told only a selected number of the outstanding shipwrecks of the Great Lakes. Many other wrecks were equally as spectacular. To make the selections was difficult. In previous books of the author will be found the tales of many others.

Accuracy has been of paramount importance in preparing this book. Often the records did not tally, particularly in the number of persons lost and in the dates of the occurrence, especially in the early shipwrecks. It is doubtful that any complete listings were kept of the early passengers that traveled on the lakes ships, and even if kept, the records would most likely be lost with the ship in question. But a reasonable estimate can still be made in such disasters, and herein it is believed that the figures are fairly accurate.

Occasionally the date of the loss of a ship will differ. Many ships perished at a time unknown by anyone on shore. In such cases only an estimate can be given, and some authorities may differ on this point. Aside from these details these accounts are the actual happenings.

In reading the various chapters one cannot help but admire and respect the sailormen of the Great Lakes in their line of duty, from the earliest down to the present. They have been, and still are, a hardy set of men, taking their allotted ships and cargoes where and when duty demands, regardless of personal sacrifice or inconvenience. Bravery on shipboard is as inherent today as it was in the early days. Hard work and heroism go hand in hand on the Great Lakes.

A WORD OF EXPLANATION

This is the third book written by the author on the subject of the Great Lakes. The first was LORE OF THE LAKES, published in 1940, the second, MEMORIES OF THE LAKES, published in 1946.

With the view of avoiding repetition for his readers, the author has herein made no mention of the lake disasters told in his previous works, except for a possible listing. This will explain the omission of such major lake disasters as the *Eastland, Pewabic, Western Reserve, Asia, Waubuno, Kaliyuga, Tashmoo,* the 1905 Blow, the Big Storm of 1913, and the 1940 Armistice Day Storm. Each of these disasters is covered in detail in the two above-mentioned books.

THE TWELVE WORST SHIP DISASTERS IN GREAT LAKES HISTORY

(Based on the number of lives lost)

Steamer	Cause	Location	Date	Number Lives Lost
EASTLAND	Capsized	Chicago Harbor	July 24, 1915	835
LADY ELGIN	Collision	Lake Michigan	Sept. 8, 1860	297
G. P. GRIFFITH	Fire	Lake Erie	June 17, 1850	250 to 295*
MONTREAL	Fire	St. Lawrence River	June 27, 1857	250
PHOENIX	Fire	Lake Michigan	Nov. 21, 1847	190 to 250*
ATLANTIC	Collision	Lake Erie	Aug. 20, 1852	150 to 250*
ERIE	Fire	Lake Erie	Aug. 9, 1841	100 to 175*
PEWABIC	Collision	Lake Huron	Aug. 9, 1865	125
ASIA	Foundered	Georgian Bay	Sept. 15, 1882	123
NORONIC	Fire	Toronto Harbor	Sept. 17, 1949	119
SEABIRD	Fire	Lake Michigan	April 9, 1868	68 to 100*
ALPENA	Foundered	Lake Michigan	Oct. 16, 1880	60 to 101*

*Records vary in exact number lost.

9

⚓ ⚓ ⚓ ⚓ ⚓ ⚓ ⚓ ⚓

CHAPTER ONE

AN EARLY LAKE ERIE HOLOCAUST
—1841—

These lines are being written in the year 1951. Our country was never greater. It has come a long way in the short one hundred seventy-five years since the Declaration of Independence started us off. Wonder upon wonder has unfolded during each decade. We do not pause long to consider the most recent great step forward in our time before another and even greater one seems always to be just around the corner. The years are crowded with great accomplishments.

We seldom look back down the years. Those who do, find themselves richly rewarded. The almost forgotten incidents of the yesteryears present a stirring drama to those who search into our history.

In the early days of our country whole families headed westward, after landing as immigrants upon our eastern shores where cities of considerable size were already growing. In the interior of the country could be found rich land and opportunity that the ambitious settler so fervently prayed for and sought— a country where a man could work and prosper through his efforts.

Reports spread across the land and the oceans that

the country in the region of the Great Lakes of America offered the freedom in which to work, to live, to worship, and to become wealthy. At first the newcomers arrived in trickles. The early way was hard. Waterways offered the easiest mode of travel. Once a man could get his family to the eastern end of the Great Lakes, it was comparatively restful to travel a thousand miles into the rich interior of the country. The early ships of the Great Lakes took care of that. Before long the stream of immigrants increased. Folks flocked from the "Old Country" to settle in America.

At first a fleet of sailing vessels carried the newcomers to their destinations. They usually embarked at Buffalo and unloaded at various ports along the shores of Lake Erie, Lake Huron, and Lake Michigan. Lake Superior came later to the attention of the settler. The ever expanding greatness of this country manifested itself by improving the transportation conditions of the immigrant, and soon the windjammer gave way to the steamboat.

First to ply the upper lakes came the little side-wheeler *Walk-in-the-Water* in the year 1818. Improvement upon improvement crowded into steamboat construction, and by 1841 the Great Lakes traveler enjoyed a large selection of comfortable side-wheel passenger ships traversing the route from Buffalo to Chicago, and making all the ports between.

1841 was an interesting year in the Great Lakes Country—not that anything in particular happened—

interesting in that it continued to expand and develop. Michigan had become a state just four years previously and Chicago had received its first locomotive—from the decks of a lake schooner. Towns were being surveyed and farms settled. Trade was fast growing. It was a time of peaceful prosperity for the territory. The terrible Civil War was not to start for twenty years hence. William Harrison began his term as President in Washington. But it was to be short. He passed away in April and John Tyler, Vice President, was sworn into the high office. Washington had its troubles in 1841 even as it has to this day.

But the trade routes of the lakes churned pleasantly with the steamboats' goings and comings. Eager families sought passage at Buffalo, and as eagerly scrambled ashore at the way ports to begin their new lives.

It was in August, 1841, that painters gave the side-wheel steamboat *Erie* a new and shining finish coating at her dock in Buffalo, New York. The ship was refinished inside and out. Passengers crowded her gangplank on August 9th, the day of her sailing, bound for distant Chicago. Some of the painters even took passage for a short trip to Erie, Pennsylvania. At four that afternoon the *Erie* sailed, her decks and cabins crowded with over two hundred fifty persons and a large load of freight.

The *Erie* was a new ship, this being her fourth season. Captain T. J. Titus was in command. She was owned by a man from Erie, Mr. C. M. Reed, and was

13

considered one of the finest steamboats on the lakes.

A bracing breeze rippled the waters of the lake as the *Erie* cleared Buffalo and headed up the lake for her first port of call, Erie. It was a fine afternoon and from all appearances the ship was off to a good start. Darkness settled over the waters as the *Erie* ploughed onward.

Just before nine that evening a sudden explosion shook the ship, the center of the trouble apparently coming from near the smokestack. It was later learned that the painters had left considerable quantities of turpentine and other inflammable products of their trade stored at the spot where the explosion centered. Either they had neglected to remove their supplies before sailing, or the painters intended to take it to Erie along with them. It is presumed that heat from the stack may have ignited the highly volatile painters' supplies and caused the explosion. No one ever really knew the exact cause.

Clouds of smoke emerged from the scene of the explosion and before anyone could do anything about it, flames licked skyward. The entire ship was built of wood, from keel to trucks, and the freshly painted surfaces fed the flames generously. The same bracing breeze that refreshed the *Erie* upon leaving port now proved to be a devastating enemy. It fanned the flames until within a matter of minutes the *Erie* was on fire from stem to stern. This was before the days of fire protection equipment on shipboard.

14

AN EARLY LAKE ERIE HOLOCAUST

The *Erie* was then about forty miles out of Buffalo, or some six miles off the ports of Silver Creek and Dunkirk, New York. Panic seized the passengers and crew. Captain Titus could do little more than any other individual aboard the *Erie*. Fire drills were unknown. He attempted to issue life preservers to the passengers, but in the confusion on board little was accomplished in the saving of lives. Everyone was more or less on his own.

Reports conflict as to the action of the steamboat. Some say the engines were stopped and the ship allowed to drift. Others state that the wheelsman stayed at his post as long as he was able. He kept the ship turning in large circles with the engines running and finally collapsed from the intense heat.

Many of the passengers jumped into the water rather than face the flames. Of those in the water, many drowned, as there were not enough floating pieces of wreckage to grasp and hold themselves above water. Still others perished in the flames, afraid to leap into the water.

Help arrived about eleven o'clock that night when the steamboat *DeWitt Clinton,* outbound from Dunkirk, sighted the flaming *Erie* and steamed to her aid. She rescued twenty-seven persons. Some of those saved were clinging to the paddle-boxes and under-braces of the *Erie* and some were rescued from the water.

The flames made quick work of the *Erie*. She was

doomed in a short space of time. Passengers and crew scattered, each to his own death or rescue. Two other rescue steamers arrived at the scene of the tragedy, the *Lady* and the *Chatauque*. They managed to get lines on the burning hulk of the *Erie* and towed her toward shore. The remains of the *Erie* sank while the two steamers were in the act of towing her. About four miles off shore she went down with loud hissing noises as the water closed over her burning timbers. She settled in about eleven fathoms.

The death toll was enormous. At least one-half of the passengers lost their lives. Top estimates ran to one hundred seventy-five. A colony of Swiss immigrants numbering around one hundred were all lost. Captain Titus was saved by crawling into a yawl just as the flames scorched his body.

Fifteen years rolled by. Men talked much about the *Erie* holocaust. Reports persisted that the ship carried gold and other valuables. The immigrants were not all poor people. Many were weathly, though they sought a new life in America. They brought their fortunes with them. Salvage-minded lake men wondered if these fortunes might not still be in the hulk of the *Erie,* now resting on the bottom off Silver Creek.

An attempt at raising the wreck proved successful, and once again the *Erie* came above the water. She was towed back to Buffalo and there the hulk was carefully searched. Reports are that the effort paid off very well.

AN EARLY LAKE ERIE HOLOCAUST

Salvagers found much gold and silver specie, reported to be mostly in five franc pieces, totaling nearly two hundred thousand dollars in United States funds.

One man's loss is another man's gain!

⚓ ⚓ ⚓ ⚓ ⚓ ⚓ ⚓ ⚓

CHAPTER TWO

THE BURNING OF THE STEAMER G. P. GRIFFITH
— *1 8 5 0* —

Droves of home-seeking immigrants continued to pour into the United States during the administrations of Zachary Taylor, Millard Fillmore, Franklin Pierce, and James Buchanan, which covered a period from 1849 to 1861. Many of these settlers were headed for the rich farm lands of the middle west. After landing on the east coast of the United States they usually made their way to the Great Lakes. They crowded the steamboat docks at Buffalo seeking transportation to their destinations in Ohio, Michigan, Wisconsin, and Illinois.

Such was the scene on one Sunday morning, June 16, 1850, as the steamer *G. P. Griffith* loaded at her dock in Buffalo. Her passenger list tallied three hundred twenty-six persons aboard, with more than half of them stalwart immigrants from England, Ireland, and Germany. In many cases there were entire families, and with them they brought all their worldly possessions. On their persons they carried considerable specie with which to stake their beginnings in the new world.

BURNING OF THE STEAMER G. P. GRIFFITH

The *G. P. Griffith* cleared Buffalo that same morning, Captain C. C. Roby was in command and traveling with him on this trip was his wife, mother, and two children. The ship was owned by the captain and his brother-in-law of Detroit. Fine June weather prevailed and the *Griffith* plowed her way westward across Lake Erie. Her ultimate destination was to have been far-away Chicago. Many stops were scheduled enroute.

Between three and four the next morning the mate reported smoke coming from the hold of the steamer, where were stored the goods of the passengers and some freight. Captain Roby ordered his ship to be headed toward the shore immediately. They were then some five miles out in the lake and about off the small town of Willoughby, Ohio, some twenty miles east of Cleveland. Attempts were made to fight the fire, but the hold was crowded with freight. The smoke grew more dense and soon flames were leaping from the hold. By the time the *G. P. Griffith* was within three miles of shore, the flames had reached her main deck. Desperately the crew tried to crowd steam in the boilers in order to reach shallow water before the flames would envelop the entire vessel. This action proved to be unwise as it increased the drafts throughout the steamer, which fanned up the flames all the more. All the passengers were aroused hurriedly from their berths and they stood huddled in the more protected places away from the searing heat.

Captain Roby might have won his desperate race

with the fire and reached the shore line before his ship was entirely destroyed, except that fate intervened. The *G. P. Griffith* was only a half mile away and all hopes of those aboard were high, when the prow struck a sandbar with a sickening lurch. The flaming vessel was held fast on the bar, and the fire raged anew.

As were all the steamboats of that day, the *G. P. Griffith* was built entirely of wood. There was no escape from the heat. The passengers became panic-stricken and many leaped into the lake. Little wreckage floated, and the plunge meant death for most of them. Some chose to stay aboard the craft until the flames ended their hopes. Only the best of the swimmers were saved. The mate swam to shore and found a small boat with which he returned to the burning ship and saved some of those struggling in the water.

Captain Roby saw that his ship was doomed. In one tragic decision he grabbed his wife and threw her into the water. Then his mother, and his two children, and lastly the wife of the barber. Then he leaped in after them. He and his family all perished. Every woman and child that was aboard the steamer lost their lives, except the barber's wife, who was miraculously saved. The ship continued to burn until the flames reached the very water's edge. Only about thirty men, and the lone woman, lived to tell of their horrible experiences aboard the immigrant-laden steamboat.

The limited facilities of the country around which

the wreck occurred were in no manner adequate to prepare the bodies that washed ashore for proper burial. So a huge trench was dug near the water's edge, and the dead, many without any means of identification, and all without coffins, were laid to rest along the shore of the lake that had claimed their lives. It has been reported that this burial ground has since been washed into Lake Erie by the continual erosion taking place along the shore.

Sometime after the disaster, the steamer *Delaware,* cruising in the vicinity of the *G. P. Griffith* wreck, pulled the hulk off the fatal sandbar on which she grounded at the height of the fire, and pushed it onto shore at a nearby deep-water spot, where it eventually fell apart.

The appalling disaster caused great consternation among the public. Cleveland, the largest settlement near the wreck, held open meetings in an effort to have proper regulations and inspections for vessels of the Great Lakes, especially those carrying passengers. Progress was also made toward the licensing of the navigators of these ships. There is no force as powerful as the public aroused. Far-off Washington felt the reverberations of these lake-town meetings. By August, 1859, the Congress had passed navigation laws providing for the inspection of hulls and boilers, and other precautionary measures. Thus, the dead of the *G. P. Griffith* had not died in vain.

It was estimated that, in the decade from 1840

through 1850, one thousand lives had been lost by fire and explosions on lake steamboats and for many years thereafter the *Griffith* disaster stood at the head of the list of Great Lakes casualties.

Chapter Three

THE PROPELLER IN THE PARK

— 1 8 5 3 —

Probably no other spot on the Upper Peninsula of the State of Michigan draws as many visitors during a normal shipping season on the Great Lakes as do the famous locks at Sault Ste. Marie. Thousands upon thousands of interested tourists gather around the walls of the four great American locks (there is one lock on the Canadian side also) and watch with astonishment as the heavily-laden giant lake freighters are lifted or lowered some twenty-two feet in about as many minutes. The St. Marys Falls Ship Canal, as it is officially known, is the busiest canal in the world in point of tonnage. There is no charge for this great outdoor show, nor is there any charge for the ships using the locks, and the show continues constantly, day and night, around the clock, as long as the shipping season operates.

People have come to watch the ships lock through, ever since that afternoon of the eighteenth day of June in 1855, when Captain "Jack" Wilson stood on the bridge of the old sidewheeler *Illinois* and locked her through, westbound, the first ship to use the canal.

23

SHIPWRECKS OF THE LAKES

Adjoining the locks is an attractive small park with large shade trees. Iron benches are placed on the well-kept grass to accommodate the throngs of visitors to the locks. Concrete walks make a pattern of criss-cross paths, and almost in the center, stands a queer old iron propeller. It looks more like a small modern tractor wheel of today than what it really is—a ship's propeller. Many folks pass by it wondering just what it is and why it rests there. The old wheel is a true relic of bygone Great Lakes shipping, and it has an interesting story behind it. Government engineers placed it in the park years ago after it was retrieved from the bottom of the St. Marys River. Other engineers have cared for it since then, and so it is that today it still stands in the little park. The old wheel once had a twin, but the years have separated the two propellers, and now only this one remains in the region of its actual working. This old propeller came from the early lake steamer *Independence,* the first steamship to travel over the blue deep waters of Lake Superior.

But to begin at the beginning, the scene shifts to a small shipping office along the waterfront in Chicago in 1843. Here one Mr. J. M. Averill, an Englishman, sat smoking. His mind was upon his newest business venture, a fine steamboat. It was to be launched within a fortnight, built of stout wood from the nearby forests. Possibly his fortune and business fame were to be assured. He would load this ship with grain from the Chicago area and float it across the Atlantic to England, where he hoped to sell it at a good price. England in those days was a long way off, but a steamboat should be able to cross the miles of watery waste rather quickly, he reasoned. Then on the return trip he would load her with British-made products to sell in the new country. He felt certain that the new vessel would bring him financial independence, and so it was that he named her the *Independence.*

Shipbuilders in those days, in and about Chicago, were just good carpenters, not skilled engineers. They could tell what a ship would do only after it was launched and put into trade. The *Independence* was outfitted with a propeller, a strictly new device for powering a ship. The first such steamboat to try one of these contraptions on the Great Lakes was the *Vandalia,* and this had been only three years previous. Reports from Oswego, New York, were that the *Vandalia* was a success. Mr. Averill was sure that the propeller was an improvement over the sidewheel type of ship then in use on the Great Lakes. He reasoned, as did most of the other marine men, that the propeller would remain in the water better than the side wheels, and would therefore take the large ocean waves better.

But Mr. Averill was sadly disappointed when the *Independence* came out. In the first place she was exasperatingly slow. A man could walk as fast as the steamboat could travel. Then there was the item of fuel. Whether she used wood or coal for her boiler, Mr. Averill figured that if she were loaded entirely with either fuel, she would consume it all before she reached

25

British shores, probably in mid-Atlantic. Thus there would be no room for her "pay" cargo.

Mr. Averill was not a man to be easily discouraged. He talked the situation over with his son, Albert J. Obviously, another field must be found for the *Independence*. The Averills liked the prospects of the Lake Superior country. Iron and copper ores had been discovered near the shores of the big lake a year or so previously; fur trading was thriving; settlers were talking about the fortunes to be made in this wild country.

One huge obstacle loomed in their way of getting the *Independence* onto Lake Superior. That was the shoal rapids in the St. Marys River that flowed from Lake Superior into Lake Huron. The water in the rapids was deep enough for only the small boats of the fur trappers and Indians. True, there were rumors of a canal and lock to be built, but that prospect was still in the dim future.

The Averills decided that Albert would pilot the *Independence* into Lake Superior. He would sail her up to the foot of the Sault Rapids and then take her ashore and, like moving a house, would portage her overland to a point above the rapids, where he would again launch her, this time into deep water that would carry her into the great lake.

The Averills then began to put the *Independence* into shape for her days in the north country. First of all her engines were changed. This time she had two rotary engines installed, connected to shafts that turned her two propellers. She carried one mast to augment her steam power, with foresail, mainsail and jib. A new invention, a steam whistle, was placed near her smokestack. Her hull was painted a jet black.

It was late summer of 1845 before the *Independence* was ready to leave Chicago for her new territory. She was loaded with all the materials and tools that would be required to portage her overland, together with the men who were hired to do the manual part of the big job. Young Albert J. Averill was the captain.

With her sails set and her two propellers churning, the little one hundred sixty-two ton *Independence* could make a scant four miles an hour going up Lake Michigan. She successfully navigated the Straits of Mackinac and entered the mouth of the St. Marys River at Detour Passage. Then began the tortuous run up the river to the town of Sault Ste. Marie, Michigan. As they tied up their steamboat at a dock below the treacherous Rapids of St. Marys a chill wind of the north country made the men aboard the *Independence* feel that fall was not far off.

A small sailing craft, the fore-and-after, *Ocean,* had just made the portage around the Rapids, and a larger sailing vessel, the *Merchant,* was half the way over when the *Independence* arrived at Sault Ste. Marie. The arrival of a steamboat in the little settlement caused great excitement, especially when it was learned that she was to be portaged.

Without further delay work was begun on hauling the steamer out of the water below the Rapids. It was no easy matter to keep the craft upright and to move her forward over the uneven ground at the same time. The task of moving the ship was accomplished by the use of wooden rollers and the motive power was the lowly horse. The men comprising her complement ate their meals and slept aboard the ship as she made the passage overland. No particular accidents occurred although it required seven weeks to make the portage of approximately one mile. It was late October by the time she was launched in the river above the Rapids.

As the *Independence* lay at her new dock preparing to proceed to the mining towns on Lake Superior, many people requested passage on the steamboat, and it was doubtful if she could handle all the freight that was offered. It appeared that this new venture of the *Independence* was to be a success.

Lewis Marvill, the steward of the steamer, has left his account of this, the first trip on Lake Superior. He mentions that, due to the lateness of the season, some doubt was expressed that she would be able to make the trip. However, manned by a crew of fourteen experienced sailors, she cleared from the Sault and across Whitefish Bay into Lake Superior. The first port of call was Fort Wilkins, or Copper Harbor, as it is known today. Then the *Independence* continued on to Eagle Harbor. Some freight and passengers were left at each port. Eagle River was the third call, and here she ran into difficulty. While unloading her freight, a violent

28

northwest wind sprang up and the ship was forced to weigh anchor and seek shelter, with some fifty kegs of powder still to put ashore. Things grew steadily worse aboard the little pioneer ship as she steamed toward the Apostle Islands for protection. The wind whipped up into a gale and the *Independence* was tossed about by the huge seas. Her heating stoves broke loose from their fastenings and began to slide about the cabin. All hands worked feverishly to put out the live embers scattered about by the moving stoves. Finally shelter was reached and the imminent danger aboard the vessel was greatly lessened. She laid to in this shelter for several days until the gale blew itself out. The crew busied themselves by gathering wood for fuel from the forests on shore, and rowing it out to the anchored steamer in small boats.

When the storm abated the *Independence* again resumed her voyage, calling at La Pointe, Wisconsin, and unloading the balance of her cargo. She then returned to the Sault with no further difficulty, and was laid up there for the winter. Thus was the first trip made by a steamer on Lake Superior.

For the following few years one hears little about the *Independence*. She continued sailing on Lake Superior, serving the new mining towns which were springing up along the shore. Other captains took over her command as the years passed. Other steamboats were taken across the portage at the Sault and competed with the veteran *Independence* for the trade. One such vessel was the *Julia Palmer,* a sidewheel craft, which was the second steamboat to sail on Lake Superior. She was portaged in 1846. On one occasion the *Julia Palmer* was caught in a violent storm and was given up as lost with all hands, but after three weeks she returned to her home port, much to the surprise and satisfaction of all concerned. Records indicate that the *Julia Palmer* sailed only a season or two, and was then laid up.

Sailing vessels also traded on Lake Superior along with the few steamboats. This fleet did much to relieve the suffering of the pioneers in the northland and brought them such delicacies as fresh beef and fruits. It was not an unusual sight in the autumn, when the weather was cold, to see one of these ships come into a Lake Superior settlement with sides of beef and carcasses of sheep hanging from their rigging.

It was while making her last trip of the 1853 season, on November 22nd, that the *Independence* ended her days. She had finished loading her passengers and freight at her dock above the Rapids, having an unusually large complement of both. This trip was important in that the steamer carried winter provisions for the settlers living in the isolated mining towns of the Upper Peninsula of Michigan. Soon freezing temperatures would form ice that would hold them prisoners in their little settlements until the coming of spring. The last trip of any steamer on Lake Superior is an event, even to this day.

THE PROPELLER IN THE PARK

About midnight the lines were cast off and the *Independence* slowly swung her nose away from the dock. Her two propellers began churning the clear cold water of the Upper St. Marys River. Captain John McKay was on the bridge scanning the river ahead, watching for the shores to widen into lower Whitefish Bay. The chief engineer had just received the "full speed ahead" signal from the bridge, and had so set his engines. When she was about one mile above the Rapids, without any warning, a terrific explosion occurred. Her boiler had exploded! The *Independence* was torn apart. Her cabins were reduced to kindling wood. Cargo and ship were blown sky high.

Nothing was left of the little pioneer steamboat but about twenty-five feet of her bow and a small piece of her boiler. Nothing remained of her engines. Her two thousand seven hundred barrel cargo was scattered in every direction.

Four men, an engineer, two firemen, and one passenger lost their lives in the disaster. Many were injured. Some thirty persons escaped safely. Two of those who lived to tell of their experiences later became famous local characters, making their homes in Sault Ste. Marie. One of them, Jonas W. Watson, was the ship's clerk. Everyone marveled at the level-headedness of Mr. Watson. When he was fished out on the bank of the river, he astonished his rescuers by producing the important papers of his ship.

The second man was Amos Stiles. He became

31

known after the disaster as "the man who never smiled." Mr. Stiles is reported as having been blown skyward in the explosion. While in the air he came in contact with a bale of hay. Clinging desperately to this, he landed in the river and used the bale as a life-raft, climbing upon it as it gathered speed in the rushing current of the river. Mr. Stiles, riding his bale of hay, was "shot" down the raging St. Marys Rapids, a very dangerous feat usually accomplished only by the experienced Indians in their canoes. He was rescued at the foot of the Rapids. It is believed that the shock was so great that his facial nerves were effected so that he never was known to smile again. He later served for many years as a watchman on the Falls Canal.

For eighty years the remains of the *Independence* lay on the bottom of the St. Marys River in deep cold water. Above her much was happening. Within two years of the explosion, the first State Lock at the Sault was opened. Ships could then travel between Lake Superior and the lower lakes without having to be portaged overland. Later, larger and faster locks were built, and ship traffic above the wreck increased to astonishing proportions.

Then came the day in 1933, when the United States Engineers began to dredge the channels where the *Independence* remains lay forgotten. Their equipment caught hold of parts of the hulk of the old steamboat. The twin propellers were hoisted once again into clear air and sunshine. Other parts of the old vessel were made into canes, checker boards and such souvenirs for the marine-minded.

So it is that for the intervening years the old propeller of the old steamboat *Independence* has lain in the park around the locks of Sault Ste. Marie, where the many thousands pass by it and wonder what it is and why it is there.

NOTE—The other propeller from the *Independence* is now on permanent display at the Mariners' Museum in Newport News, Virginia.

⚓ ⚓ ⚓ ⚓ ⚓ ⚓ ⚓ ⚓

Chapter Four

THE OCEAN WAVE

—1853—

Another of the early passenger ship fires occurred aboard the steamer *Ocean Wave* as she was enroute westward, or upbound, on Lake Ontario, out of the port of Kingston, Ontario. While this lake has had its full share of the ordinary vessel losses, it has, fortunately, had fewer of the larger and more serious catastrophies, the recent *Noronic* disaster being the exception.

The business of transportation by vessel on the Great Lakes began upon Lake Ontario. Its little wind-jammers were floating from port to port, doing a fairly thriving business before the upper lakes were ready for such commerce. This lake, smallest in water area of all of the five Great Lakes, can boast of armed schooners and brigs, as early as the French and Indian War. The British built several ships of war on Lake Ontario during the year 1755.

Commerce therefore developed and kept pace with the rapidly growing transportation demands on this lake, and by the year 1853 there were many established passenger and freight lines doing business in that region.

34

THE OCEAN WAVE

One fine upper-cabin passenger steamer of this era was the *Ocean Wave,* built in Montreal, Quebec, during the year 1851. She traded between Ogdensburg, New York, and Hamilton, Ontario, and like all the passenger vessels of her day, she made stops at most of the ports along the route.

Fat pine was the fuel used under the boilers of the steamships of those days. The supply was easily available and cheap. The logs, full of inflammable sap, gave quick and plentiful heat to keep up the steam pressure required by the ships' engines. But when piled on the open deck these same logs presented considerable fire hazard.

The *Ocean Wave* had been painted and readied for the 1853 season. By April 30th of that year she was already in operation, and had called at the Canadian port of Kingston. There, after taking care of her passengers and freight, she loaded cord wood for her boiler fuel. She sailed some time before midnight, bound up the lake.

Around one in the morning the steamer was twenty-three miles out of Kingston, just about two miles off the Duck Islands, when the purser was notified of a fire aboard the ship. In no time the only exit from the lounge was blocked by the flames. Hurriedly grabbing an axe, he chopped a hole through the cabin wall in the after end, through which the passengers trapped in the cabin escaped. This afforded these unfortunate victims

35

only temporary relief, as the flames, whipped by a strong northwest breeze, ate rapidly into the open decks.

Captain Wright soon saw that his ship was doomed, and turned all his efforts to saving the lives of his passengers and crew. So quickly did the fire spread that it was impossible for the crew to launch the life boats, which were carried on the deck above the burning cabins. The water buckets, placed aboard for just such an emergency, could not be reached as the flames devoured the entire cabin walls upon which the fire buckets hung. Within twenty minutes the ship's cabins were a flaming furnace. The burning ship lighted the sky for miles around, and folks living on the nearby Duck Islands reported they could read by the light from the flaming ship. The vessel's freshly painted wooden surfaces furnished the tinder and the cord wood piled on the deck fed the inferno. How it started was never definitely learned. It is thought that quantities of inflammable freight stowed on board may have been set off by spontaneous combustion, or a carelessly tossed spark.

Two schooners, one the *Emblem* under Captain Belyea of Bronte, and the other the *Georgina* under Captain Henderson of Port Dover, were out on Lake Ontario that night, in the vicinity of the burning *Ocean Wave*. The schooners' crews were attracted to the steamer's plight by the brightly lighted sky and they hurried over to the disaster scene.

THE OCEAN WAVE

Several rescues were made by both schooners in daring runs toward the blazing *Ocean Wave*. The survivors, twenty-one persons in all, were returned to Kingston aboard the *Georgina*. But the twenty-eight dead, thirteen passengers and fifteen crew, were left behind, either in the charred ruins of the ill-fated steamboat or drowned in Lake Ontario.

After the conflagration had raged some thirty minutes the ship lost its bouyancy and sank. It was a fast and furious ending to a fine and almost new steamer. Besides the loss of life the *Ocean Wave* was a total loss, along with her cargo consisting of three thousand barrels of flour, several hundred bags of seed grain, three hundred kegs of butter, sixty barrels of potash, a large number of hams, as well as some general package freight. The total loss, both in lives and property, presented a staggering blow to the Lake Ontario marine shipping interests of those days, but the disaster did pave the way for safer navigation in the days to come.

CHAPTER FIVE

THE WRECK OF THE LADY ELGIN

— 1860 —

For more than half a century the ill-fated steamer *Lady Elgin* held the ignominious record of being the number one disaster of the Great Lakes. Even as this is written this ship can lay claim to being the second worst tragedy on these waters. Only the terrible *Eastland* disaster, which occurred less than twenty miles from the scene of the *Lady Elgin* calamity, exceeds her record for loss of life.

The story of the *Lady Elgin* wreck is one of collision at sea in the blackness of the night, between a loaded passenger steamer and a heavily-laden freight schooner, with the steamer being struck a fatal blow; of high winds and high seas and heavy rains; of those aboard the *Lady Elgin* being plunged into the water to sink or swim; of bodies and wreckage being washed ashore; and of tales of heroism and sadness.

The year of the wreck was 1860; the month September; and the date the eighth, just a little over a half year before the start of the Civil War; the time of day very early morning, between two and three; the scene,

38

THE WRECK OF THE LADY ELGIN

Lake Michigan some ten miles off Winnetka, Illinois.

The *Lady Elgin* was named for the wife of Lord Elgin, who was at that time Governor General of Canada. The steamer was one of the fine lake liners of her day, a favorite among travelers, and her furnishings were considered elegant. Built in Buffalo in 1851, she was of wood construction throughout, hull, cabins and all. Large paddle wheels on each side of the ship sent her moving swiftly over the water. She was three hundred feet long and had huge arches fitted longitudinally to strengthen her against the stress and strain of heavy seas. The *Lady Elgin* carried as life-saving equipment four yawls, three lifeboats and four hundred life preserver floats which were made of two-inch planks, twelve to eighteen inches wide and five feet long, with rope at each end, capable of supporting one person.

Early in her career she traded between Northern Canadian lake ports. Upon the completion of the Grand Trunk Railroad she was purchased by Gordon S. Hubbard and Company of Chicago. For the four years prior to her disaster she operated between that city and Lake Superior, and she called at ports between the two terminals.

The master of the *Lady Elgin* was Captain John Wilson, a capable and popular skipper. Records indicate that she was manned by a well-trained crew, among the officers listed were Fred Rice, the steward, and a man named Caryl, the clerk.

39

SHIPWRECKS OF THE LAKES

On the run to Chicago the *Lady Elgin* had put into Milwaukee and had picked up about three hundred members of the Union Guards, a military organization, and their friends for an excursion to Chicago and return. They were on the return trip when the disaster occurred.

On Friday, September seventh, the *Lady Elgin* lay at her dock in Chicago, between Clark and La Salle Streets, loading her passengers and freight for the upper lake ports. Besides the Union Guards she had fifty other passengers and a crew of forty-five. She also had the usual amount of freight and mail.

At about half past eleven that night she cast off her lines and headed out of Chicago Harbor, bound for Lake Superior, with Milwaukee as her first port of call. Dozens of well-trimmed and well-polished kerosene lamps illuminated her social hall where the ship's orchestra was playing for dancing.

The weather was ominous; the sky was overcast, but still could not be termed stormy as the *Lady Elgin* entered Lake Michigan. Hardly had her engines settled down into their rythmic steadiness of full speed ahead when the elements changed. First the wind shifted to the northeast and rain began to fall. It was very dark on the open lake. Captain Wilson continued on duty, standing watch with the second mate.

The course of the ship after clearing Chicago took her somewhat along the shore line on her port side with the land gradually receding. At two in the morning of the eighth, the *Lady Elgin* was between Waukegan and Winnetka ten miles off shore. Some of the passengers were still on the dance floor, but many of them had retired to their staterooms. It was possible for the men in the pilot house to pick up an occasional light when the rain squalls ceased for a spell. All the essential lights aboard the *Lady Elgin* were burning, and from her cabin windows shafts of light from within pierced the blackness of the night. The wind increased and the steamer began to roll.

Suddenly out of the darkness loomed the sharp prow of a heavily-laden schooner under full sail. The force of the impact was terrific as it thrust itself far into the port side of the passenger ship, just aft of the wheel, cutting it nearly half way through below the water line. The schooner carried no lights. The offending vessel was the *Augusta of Oswego,* owned in Detroit, with a cargo of lumber for Chicago and under the command of Captain D. M. Malott.

After the crash the schooner, with her bow badly stove in, drifted away from the steamer and was soon carried by the wind away from the scene. She made no attempt to come about, but continued on her course to Chicago. Upon reaching that port, while passing through a drawbridge, Captain Malott megaphoned to the bridge tender that they had struck a steamer near Waukegan.

The elegant steamer *Lady Elgin* had received her

fatal blow. Captain Wilson ordered men into one of the small boats to attempt to cover the gaping hole with canvas. This was not successful as the small boat was unable to hold its position alongside the fast-sinking steamer and was quickly carried far astern by the seas. Cattle were pushed overboard in the hope of lightening the ship, but this helped little. Captain Wilson headed his stricken ship toward shore, but the inrushing water soon put out the fires under her boilers, and she was helpless.

The *Lady Elgin* began to settle deeper, then took on a list. Lightning flashed across the skies, affording the stricken passengers a short look at their sorry plight. Within thirty minutes the ship took her final plunge to the bottom of Lake Michigan. Just as she went down a huge wave struck her and tore loose her upper cabin deck. This afforded many of the passengers a life raft and they crawled up on the teetering protection. The sea soon broke this up into smaller sections which drifted about in the storm with many humans clinging desperately for their lives. The surface of the water was a mass of wreckage and kindling with human forms struggling to gain a hold on anything that would support them. Many went down. One or two of the ship's boats got away with people, but came to difficulty when they reached the high surf near the shore and capsized.

Throughout the catastrophe Captain Wilson did his utmost to rescue his passengers. Many times he helped a struggling person to gain a firmer grasp on a bit of floating wreckage. He shouted encouragement to those in the water. At last he himself gained a hold on a floating cabin door, and on this he was carried toward shore. As he neared land he saw two women and a child on a section of cabin roof. Only one of the women appeared to be alive. As he watched helplessly, all three were washed off their raft. Captain Wilson, then nearly exhausted, left his float to rescue the women and child. He reached them, but in attempting to get them back on the raft they all drowned. His body was found several days later, and was buried near his former home at Coldwater, Michigan.

It was five in the morning before the townspeople of Winnetka learned of the tragedy and hurried to the lake shore to assist the struggling shipwrecked persons safely to land. The wreckage drifted toward shore, only to be hit by the first breaker of the surf and turned completely over, sending its victims into the water and drowning many of them. Many perished within sight of the would-be rescuers on the beach. Several stout swimmers tied ropes around their bodies and, with one end held by a man on shore, they plunged into the roaring surf to attempt to save as many as possible.

Many herioc rescues were made by a dozen young men from Northwestern University and The Garrett Biblical Institute who came to the scene of the disaster to assist in the rescue work. One of them, Edward W. Spencer, a ministerial student at Garrett, gained much fame for his fine efforts. He alone saved seventeen people from drowning. Time and time again he plunged into the cold surf and brought struggling humans to a safe place on the beach, until he finally succumbed to exhaustion himself. In his delirium he kept crying out, "Did I do my best?"

Spencer never became a minister. He so over-exerted himself in the rescue work that he was forced to abandon his college career. Although he lived to the ripe age of eighty-one years, he was never after robust of health. It is interesting to note that many inspiring sermons have been preached in pulpits based on Edward W. Spencer's words that morning on the beach after he collapsed from weariness in saving the lives of seventeen souls, "Did I do my best?"

By two that afternoon the last struggling survivor had been taken from the water, and only the broken wreckage was left to slosh about in the quieting surf. A tally of the records showed that two hundred ninety-seven persons had lost their lives in the *Lady Elgin* disaster.

As in all great catastrophies, an inquiry was conducted. The one in this case was held by the United States Steamboat Inspectors, with Messrs. R. Prindville and Thomas C. James hearing the testimony. Captain Malott was arrested and ordered to appear for questioning before the board. Many other witnesses were heard. The final outcome was that Malott was not held at fault, even though his officers testified that they had plainly seen the lights of the *Lady Elgin* in sufficient time to avoid a collision, but did not alter their course.

THE WRECK OF THE LADY ELGIN

The captain of the *Lady Elgin* and his ship were found not to blame, inasmuch as the steamer was perfectly sound and seaworthy and was being navigated with all caution at the time of the accident. It was held impossible for her officers to have sighted the schooner without lights in the blackness of the night.

The law of the sea was held to blame. A laxity in the navigation rules permitted the *Augusta* to be operated without lights, as was the current custom among sailing vessels. The prevailing law made it incumbent upon the steamers to keep out of the way of sailing vessels under all circumstances. The regulations were subsequently changed to remedy such situations by requiring sailing vessels to carry proper lights.

A stigma followed the *Augusta*. Her name was changed to *Colonel Cook* and as such she sailed the Great Lakes for several years, but sailors avoided her, making it difficult to get crews. She was finally wrecked near Cleveland in 1894. Captain Malott and his crew changed ships, going into the schooner *Mahor*. Bad luck still continued to follow the men however, as they were all lost when the *Mahor* was wrecked a few years folowing the *Lady Elgin* disaster.

For many days after the unfortunate collision the tug *McQueen* searched that section of Lake Michigan for bodies and valuable wreckage. She located the entire forward section of the *Lady Elgin,* partially submerged and riding at anchor, her upper decks gone. Her engines had slipped out of the vessel so that the wreck had risen toward the surface and was held there by her anchor and chains. That was the last that men saw of what was once the elegant side-wheel steamer *Lady Elgin*.

♣ ♣ ♣ ♣ ♣ ♣ ♣ ♣

CHAPTER SIX

THE SEABIRD FIRE

—*1868*—

It was early in the morning and still very dark. Passengers were asleep in their staterooms. A white-coated porter, coal scuttle in hand, tended the stove in the after cabin. He shoveled the hot ashes into a container, then he walked through the companionway, pushed open a door leading to the promenade deck, and vigorously threw the ashes into Lake Michigan. Because of this routine act, within a short time, he was to die. Also to perish with him were the captain, all the officers, the chief engineer, and all but three of the passengers. They had not long to wait.

A vessel has two definite sides as related to the wind. One is called windward, and is that side facing the wind. The other, known as leeward, is the side facing away from the wind. One of the first and most important lessons any sailor learns as soon as he puts foot on a deck is that when throwing things overboard, he should always go to the leeward side of the ship. The force of the wind will then carry the material thrown overboard clear of the ship. Many a landlubber aboard ship has unknowingly violated this fixed rule of the sea, and has tossed objects overboard to windward, only to have them promptly slapped right back at him by the wind.

The unwitting porter had carelessly thrown the ashes to windward. The strong wind shot them all back upon the ship. Freight was stowed on the deck below, among which were some new freshly varnished wooden tubs carefully packed with straw. In a flash the straw caught fire, and quickly ignited the varnished wooden tubs. The strong breeze spread the flames to the deck houses and cabins.

It is believed that only one man and the porter were about in that section of the ship. The two worked frantically to put out the flames as they shouted for help. Too many were asleep. Soon the flames shot skyward from the ship and lighted the entire craft in that cold predawn of April 9th, 1868. The wooden steamer *Seabird* was doomed!

Many of the details of this tragedy are lost or have been confused and distorted. But the main facts are that the *Seabird* was a passenger ship of the famous Goodrich Line, which operated steamers upon Lake Michigan, out of Chicago, for many years. She had been built originally for the Ward Line to run out of Detroit, but misfortune had struck her and sent her on the beach, a wreck, four years previously. She subsequently had been salvaged, refloated and rebuilt, and then she entered the Goodrich service.

THE SEABIRD FIRE

Records show that the *Seabird* had wintered at Manitowoc, Wisconsin, during the winter of 1867-68, and that her disasterous fire occurred on her first trip to Chicago. She had made calls at Sheboygan and Milwaukee, and was headed for Chicago when the fiery misfortune struck. Her master was Captain John Morris and the Chief Engineer was Thomas Honahan. The records vary somewhat as to the number of persons aboard, all the way from sixty-eight to one hundred and three.

Even the number of survivors is questioned, some records claiming two persons, and others state three. Your author has been able to find three persons, all passengers, definitely named as surviving the holocaust, C. A. Chamberlain, Edwin Hanneberry and James H. Leonard. The latter jumped into the water as the flames seared the ship. He was a hardy man and an excellent swimmer. In the water he managed to clamber onto some wreckage which he rode throughout the day. The wind carried him away from the burning ship, and after drifting an estimated fifteen miles he came ashore three miles north of Evanston, Illinois. He was near death from exhaustion when found, but revived later and told of the fatal burning of the *Seabird*. He told of being one of twenty or more persons who jumped into the water, some of whom sank almost at once, while others swam about for some time, only to perish eventually.

The first mentioned two survivors were rescued by the schooner *Cordelia,* under Captain Yates. When the

Cordelia was off Waukegan, Illinois, the burning steamer had been sighted four or five miles away, and immediately she headed for her. The schooner arrived very late at the fiery scene, but still in time to rescue one man from among the wreckage in the water and another clinging to the side of the burning *Seabird*. No other life was to be seen. The helm of the doomed steamer had evidently been lashed hard-a-port, as she continued to move in large circles as long as her engines kept operating. The *Cordelia* stood by the wreck searching for more survivors. When she did finally leave the scene the *Seabird* had burned down to the water's edge.

Thus it was that the elegant side-wheel steamer *Seabird* became the eleventh worst disaster in number of lives lost upon the Great Lakes. Controlled fire helps man in many ways and without it he could not exist, but fire uncontrolled is man's great peril.

The tragic scene closed as the charred and waterlogged hull of the *Seabird* drifted ashore near Lake Forest, Illinois, a total wreck. Sixty-eight, or possibly one hundred souls aboard had perished!

⚓ ⚓ ⚓ ⚓ ⚓ ⚓ ⚓ ⚓

CHAPTER SEVEN

THE MORNING STAR AND THE COURTLANDT

— *1868* —

These lines are being written in mid-May, 1951. Today at the foot of Third Avenue in Detroit and also at the foot of East Ninth Street in Cleveland are two very complete passenger terminal ticket offices and waiting rooms, heavily locked and barred. Spacious freight sheds and warehouses stand empty and bare. Shore dirt and grime are gathering. The stillness of the buildings is appalling. These are the offices and docks of the Detroit & Cleveland Navigation Company.

This year the company has suspended operation of all its five passenger steamers. For approximately a century, passenger ships have been operated between Cleveland and Detroit. Most of the runs were made overnight, though for many years a daylight trip was also made. Lake shore and riverside dwellers set their clocks by the passing of the trim side-wheelers. From the day that the ice permitted in the spring, until it froze over again in early winter, the D & C steamers moved across Lake Erie and up the Detroit River, carrying thousands of passengers and thousands of tons of freight on the one hundred and eight mile cruise.

51

The D & C steamers were a tradition. Today they await a somewhat dubious future. Time alone holds the answer. Many ships and many men have worn out together on this old time-honored route. It is the story similar to many other passenger steamer lines in North America. They are bowing out gracefully in favor of more expedient transportation mediums. One hundred years is a long time.

Whenever and wherever things move, there is risk. Everytime a ship sailed a potential danger prevailed. But the D & C line was remarkably free of trouble throughout all of its years of operation. This can be credited to many men: owners, shipbuilders, officers and crews, lighthouse keepers, government inspectors, and many others. Only one serious shipwreck resulted in the century of operation of passenger ships on the D & C route between Detroit and Cleveland. That occurred many years ago, on the dark and windy night of Saturday, June 20, 1868, almost eighty-three years ago.

Captain E. R. Viger commanded the side-wheel passenger steamer *Morning Star* on the Detroit-Cleveland run that year. The ship had been built but five years previously, entirely of wood as was the custom, and had made for herself an enviable reputation during that time. Captain Viger's record was equal in all respects to that of his vessel, except of course, for longer service. He had sailed the lakes since boyhood, and had risen from cabin boy to master by hard work.

It was exactly ten-thirty in the evening of that

twentieth day of June, when Captain Viger piloted his steamer *Morning Star* out of the harbor of Cleveland on her regular run to Detroit. There were aboard forty-four first-class passengers and seven immigrants, in addition to a freight cargo consisting of: one hundred tons of bar iron, several hundred kegs of nails, forty-five boxes of glass, twenty-five boxes of cheese, sixty-five tons of chill metal, thirty-three mowing machines, seven barrels of oil, four tons of stone, and one hundred thirty-seven kegs and boxes of various package freight.

Sailing vessels were numerous on the lakes in those days. In majestic silence they floated heavy cargoes of iron ore from the upper lakes to the ports on Lake Erie. One of these was the bark *Courtlandt* (sometimes spelled *Cortland*) with Captain G. W. Lawton in command. He had reached Lake Erie on his downbound voyage and had set his course for Cleveland where his cargo of iron ore was consigned. Thus, the *Courtlandt* and the *Morning Star* were meeting on the same course.

The night was chilly, with a brisk wind out of the north, which whipped up a big sea along the course of both vessels. Captain Viger remained on the bridge of the *Morning Star* after they had cleared Cleveland; most of the passengers had retired. Several sailing vessels were sighted and passed, presumably headed for Cleveland. Midnight arrived and a dark night was noted on the log. Their position was off Black River, now the city of Lorain, Ohio. Just forty-five minutes later, while the passenger ship was proceeding at full speed ahead, she crashed into the bark *Courtlandt* with a terrific ripping of timbers, her bow piercing the hull of the wooden sailing ship about three-quarters the way back.

The only warning of impending danger that the officers of the *Morning Star* had, was the ringing of the bell on the windjammer a few seconds before the crash. Then it was too late! They claimed that the bark carried no lights. Captain Lawton of the *Courtlandt* stoutly defended his situation by later stating, "I had just as good lights as ever were carried. I saw the steamer and kept on my course. I rang my bell three times and put my wheel hard up just before they struck."

The sharp prow of the steamer had cut almost through the bark. The force of the impact had torn the steamer's two bow anchors loose from their moorings, and hurled them forward. One of them slid entirely across the deck of the *Courtlandt* and into the water on the far side. The anchor chain then bound the two ships together, locked in a death struggle. Both vessels began to take in water fast.

Captain Viger called through his megaphone, "What vessel are you?"

"Bark *Courtlandt* with ore for Cleveland," came the reply, "we are sinking. Can you take our men aboard your ship?" asked the master of the sailing ship.

"We are sinking too," replied Captain Viger.

54

The lights of one or two ships could be seen out over the lake, but their attention could not be attracted. In the rough seas the windjammer swung about and crashed broadside into the side of the steamer, smashing her paddle-wheel. The two ships were grinding to pieces as the waves beat them together. It was futile to even attempt to save either craft, so every effort was bent on rescuing the passengers.

On board the *Morning Star* all was confusion, although the officers stood by their stations. Chief Engineer Watson was at his post in the engine room. He was thrown violently against his engine controls and rendered unconscious. He came to later and found himself struggling in the cold water, from which he was eventually rescued.

Captain Viger went to the main salon of his stricken steamer and tried to quiet his passengers by telling them that there was little danger. He sought the assistance of another lake captain whom he knew was on his passenger list, Captain Hackett of Detroit. The *Morning Star's* purser, James Morton, located him in his stateroom helping his wife into a life preserver and otherwise preparing for the worst.

Upon learning that Captain Viger needed his services, Captain Hackett asked the purser to continue to help Mrs. Hackett and he left for the steamer's bridge. Both Mrs. Hackett and Purser Morton lost their lives. Captain Hackett survived. The life boats, reported to be but two in number, were swung out and were quickly filled, mostly by the crew, although a few passengers managed to get into them before they were lowered away.

The *Courtlandt* managed to loosen herself from the *Morning Star's* anchor chains, and she drifted one half mile to the southwest before the waves rolled over her. Within a very few minutes both ships had sunk beneath the waves in seventy feet of water.

The hurricane deck was torn loose from the *Morning Star* as she sank and it was the means of saving fourteen of the steamer's passengers and crew, Captain Viger included. Many perished as the last floating section of the steamer went down beneath their feet. Bits of wreckage floated about and covered the scene of the tragedy.

At three that morning the shivering survivors were heartened by the sighting of the lights of an oncoming passenger steamer. As it neared them they all shouted with all the human effort they could muster. They were sighted! The steamer began heading directly toward them and the mass of floating debris.

It was the *R. N. Rice*, sister ship of the *Morning Star* making the opposite trip from Detroit, Captain William McKay in command. As quickly as possible the crew of the *R. N. Rice* hauled out of the water the weary survivors of the ship collision. The officers and crew of the *Courtlandt* with the exception of two, were

rescued by the *Rice*. Captain Viger and his party clinging to the wreckage were also saved.

Another rescue was made that was a bit unusual.
This was a lone man passenger who exhibited great
calmness about the entire matter. Upon finding himself
in the water he crawled onto a portion of deck that
floated by. Soon a chair came within his reach. He
dragged it onto his improvised raft and proceeded to sit
on it. And lastly there drifted along a large metal
cracker box, which he also brought aboard his temporary haven. When rescued he was sitting on the chair
with his feet propped up on the cracker box.

The *R. N. Rice* continued her search for survivors
until well after daybreak; then she headed for Cleveland, taking the rescued with her. She left behind her
in the waters the dead, estimated from twenty-three
to thirty-two. Many of the bodies were later located;
others were never seen after the disaster.

But the business of lake passenger transportation
was very vital in those days. The owners promptly
replaced the ill-fated *Morning Star* with another fine
side-wheeler, the *Northwest,* with Captain Viger as
her commander.

NOTE—Among his many papers and documents of lake shipping, Mr.
William A. McDonald of Detroit, has in his possession an interesting signed
statement of a survivor of the *Courtlandt,* the lookout, written after the
tragedy. The paper states that just prior to the collision he had informed
the mate that their starboard light was burning very dimly. The lamp was,
of course, oil-fueled.

The schooner's mate then took down the light and cleaned off the
accumulation of soot and trimmed the wick. He was in the act of replacing
the cleaned lantern when the Steamer *Morning Star* struck the *Courtlandt.*
The mate was crushed in the collision and killed.

57

⚓ ⚓ ⚓ ⚓ ⚓ ⚓ ⚓ ⚓

CHAPTER EIGHT

AN OLD LADY REMINISCES

— *1869* —

The gravity of a shipwreck naturely depends entirely upon how close you are to those aboard the distressed vessel. Normally no one passes over such calamities lightly, but to the families left ashore by shipwrecked men, that wreck stands out comparable to the worst marine disaster ever to occur. And rightly so, for to them it has taken away that which can never be replaced. It usually changes the course of their entire lives. From that day henceforth the world will never be quite the same for them.

A kindly old Canadian grandmother, considerably past her eightieth birthday, knows the full import of the above paragraph. Her world changed for her when the sailing vessel *Kate Bully* capsized on Lake Michigan in a wild squall on October 4th, 1869. That wreck left her, then a baby, without a father. Also sharing her fate were her four sisters and brothers. The family faced a dubious future when Captain Henry Leonard Mac-Glashan perished with his ship. No other shipwreck can hold the import of tragedy for that kindly old woman that the wreck of the *Kate Bully* does. That is easily understandable. But to the rest of the busy world it did not cause any great concern.

Not much is known today regarding the lost schooner *Kate Bully*; there are apparently no photographs or drawings of her; her name does not appear in government listings. The reason for these omissions lies undoubtedly in the fact that the windjammer did not last long enough; she never completed her first voyage!

But to turn back to her actual beginning. Around 1860 John Bailey opened a blacksmith forge in Corunna, Ontario, close by the St. Clair River. He constructed and repaired wagons. Later he followed with a saw mill and a grist mill, and then the St. Clair River attracted him with its heavy-laden passing ships. He built a dock at Corunna. The new dock attracted ships trading in that vicinity, and soon John Bailey was busy repairing the various vessels that made his dock a port of call. In some manner, and without explanation, his name became Bully, and he was henceforth known by that name. A daughter was born to the Bullys and she was given the name of Kate.

John Bully was a forward looking man, and now he set his sights on owning a ship. The wood for its construction grew close at hand. He had his own saw mill and blacksmith shop and local dock. He began to sort out the timber for his new ship. Soon the keel was laid, for what turned out to be Corunna's only shipbuilding venture. The new craft was named in honor of his daughter, *Kate Bully*. As the vessel neared completion it was apparent that Bully intended her to be used mainly in the lumber trade. Into her transom were built swinging ports to permit the handy loading of long square timbers.

From the very beginning the *Kate Bully* was a cantankerous craft. On the day of her launching she stuck on the ways. No amount of coaxing by shipbuilders could budge her. In desperation they called a river tug to help. With the concentrated effort of all hands, the *Kate Bully* at last slid into the St. Clair River—only to run aground. After much delay she was brought back to Bully's dock.

Throughout the building of the schooner, John Bully was assisted by the MacGlashans, father and son. They were both sea captains and had salt water voyages to their credit before coming to Canada to settle. The son, Captain Henry MacGlashan was appointed master of the *Kate Bully,* and a crew of men was selected from around the dock and mills at Corunna.

The cargo was placed aboard the vessel at Sarnia, Ontario, a few miles up the river from her launching spot. Some freshly cut hardwood timbers were loaded, and a large number of railroad ties, together with some ordinary lumber. The elder MacGlashan, Captain Charles, eyed with much concern the heavily laden schooner, her hull deep in the water. But all his remonstrations were of no avail, and the *Kate Bully* slipped away from her Sarnia dock, bound for Chicago, on the morning of September 28th, 1869. John Bully's ship had put to sea!

Evidently the schooner made slow progress with her heavy cargo. It required several days for her to sail up Lake Huron, through the Straits of Mackinac, and into Lake Michigan. Here she began the long southward trek to Chicago. The weather began to cloud up, the wind freshened, and some long rollers swept over the deck of the *Kate Bully*. But she shook them off and continued on her course. The further she sailed the worse the weather grew.

Monday, October 4th, about dark, found the little schooner a few miles off Manistee, Michigan. She was still riding the waves in fair fashion. Shortly Captain MacGlashan discovered that his ship was taking in water. By half-past eight that evening it was necessary to call all hands to man the pumps as the water was coming into the hull at an alarming rate. Part of the crew was ordered to drop the cargo overboard. This was a slow and laborious process. After some thirty minutes of such strenuous work a sudden wind squall struck the *Kate Bully* and, without further warning she capsized. As she turned on her beam-ends everything on her deck slid into the water.

The mate who was steering the vessel was tossed off into the waves and was not seen again, and a seaman was also lost overboard. The other members of the crew and Captain MacGlashan managed to retain their holds on the schooner. Most of them lashed themselves to the various parts of the ship that remained above the water.

The cargo below deck being of green hardwood offered no buoyancy to the stricken *Kate Bully,* as some other lumber might have done. This cargo was like steel; it did not float. Captain MacGlashan did not attempt to save himself by lashing his body to any part of the ship. Instead he groped about over the wreck shouting words of encouragement to his crew.

One of the sailors attempted to assist the woman cook to hang on, but he was struck with a swinging boom and his arm and side were bady crushed. He was forced to let go of the woman and she was swept away. Her terrifying screams as she sank beneath the waves chilled the blood of the men remaining on the wreck.

At this point, possibly in an effort to aid the unfortunate cook, Captain MacGlashan loosened his grip on the bulwark and was lost in the stormy waters. Several others of the crew still clung precariously to whatever parts of the schooner remained above the water. As the long night wore on some of them were unable to hold on longer and silently slipped away.

Reports vary as to the number that clung to the waterlogged wreck for nearly forty hours. Some say three and others four. Finally, help did reach the benumbed seamen with the arrival of the schooner *Black*

AN OLD LADY REMINISCES

Hawk, late in the day of Wednsday, October 6th. The rescued were taken to the port of Manistee and all of them lived to tell of their harrowing experiences.

The kindly old Canadian grandmother still lives close to the banks of the St. Clair River. Sailing vessels have given way to steamers, and she has watched these grow in size until now her father's schooner *Kate Bully* would make a small shadow on one of their hulls.

Strangely, the passing ships still hold a charm for the gentle old lady. The fact that one of their kind robbed her of a father causes her no resentment. She is the last living child of Captain Henry MacGlashan's five children. In her veins still runs the blood of hardy sailormen such as her father, who had the courage and pioneer spirit to sail the early schooners of the great fresh-water seas of America.

CHAPTER NINE

THE SCHOONER SOUVENIR

—1872—

The townspeople of Pentwater, Michigan, were stunned by the news of the wreck of the locally owned and locally manned schooner *Souvenir*. It was a sad blow to the little community. All hands aboard were lost. The *Souvenir* had sailed from Pentwater, in company with the schooner *Minnie Corlett,* loaded with lumber and bound for Chicago. The following day she lay a wreck on the beach with a dead man at her wheel and the balance of her crew gone forever.

It was in the blackness of the night of November 26, 1872, that the two sailing schooners cleared Pentwater for Chicago. The weather was good, wind favorable and temperature warmer than normal. On board the *Souvenir* was a fine cargo of eight hundred thousand wooden shingles. The *Minnie Corlett* had her hold filled with lumber and on her deck she carried big square timbers. Captain Charles Craine was in command of the *Souvenir,* with Frank Whitcomb as mate, John Perry as steward, and four seamen.

Shortly before midnight the wind sprang up from

the northwest and soon the two schooners found themselves in a terrific gale, accompanied with blinding swirling snow. The thermometer plummeted to zero. All that wild night the crews battled against the elements to keep their vessels afloat and right side up.

At daylight the *Souvenir* was sighted near the Claybanks, south of Ludington, Michigan. She was headed toward the shore, grounding on a bar. Only one man could be seen, and he was at the wheel. The vessel itself was a shambles. The rigging was gone, except for some spars that had fallen aft and still could be seen on deck. The shingles that she had carried on deck were nowhere to be seen.

There was no life-saving crew to call upon for help. The waves were too high for a row boat to attempt a rescue from shore. Watchers on the beach tried to signal to the man at the wheel to tie a line about his body and let the other end float ashore.

No one will ever know what Frank Whitcomb, the mate—for it was he who was clinging to the schooner's wheel—thought about as he looked stolidly toward the shore. He made a motion of hopelessness or despair that was seen by the men on shore.

However, about noontime the wind abated and the waves lessened their pounding. Lighthouse Keeper Girard of Ludington, volunteered to go out to the *Souvenir* in his small boat with any of the persons on the shore. No one dared to make the trip. Girard went alone. Luck was with the plucky lightkeeper and after a perilous trip, he reached the side of the stranded schooner.

He clambered up on to the wrecked deck and hurried aft to Whitcomb who still clutched the wheel. Only a faint spark of life remained in the mate's body. He was unable to speak, and he died while Girard was attempting to comfort him. No one else of the crew was on board amid the tangled wreckage.

Fate was kinder to the *Minnie Corlett*. Maybe it was her scow-shaped hull which helped. She was washed high upon the beach not far from the wrecked *Souvenir*. Several of her crew were badly injured, or had frozen hands or feet, but all lived to tell of the horrors of that furious night on Lake Michigan off Pentwater.

Chapter Ten

THE ALPENA STORM

— *1880* —

"This is terrible. The steamer is breaking up fast. I am aboard from Grand Haven to Chicago," read a water-soaked note that had been quickly scrawled and then tucked behind a piece of the molding in the cabin of the steamer *Alpena,* back in 1880. It was signed by George Conner, although the name may have been Connell, as it was barely legible.

The note had been found by a beach-combing college professor who was searching through wreckage that was washing ashore from Lake Michigan near Holland. Its writer did not live through the shipwreck! Not a single soul aboard that ill-fated Goodrich passenger liner came through alive! The records today vary greatly as to the number of persons that were aboard, making the trip from Grand Haven, Michigan, to Chicago. The smallest number reported lost is placed at sixty, while the maximum is one hundred and one. Either figure would place the tragedy as one of major importance upon the Great Lakes.

Friday, the fifteenth of October, 1880, began as a

67

fine warm and sunny day on Lake Michigan. Mariners, ever watchful of their barometers, noted a quick fall. All concerned prepared for a blow. The storm began with gentle breezes, then intensified and grew steadily stronger. By nine that night the winds had reached gale velocity and Lake Michigan was being whipped into a frenzy. Heavy, low hanging clouds tore across the heavens. The winds were in conflict, seemingly blowing from all points of the compass in great gusts.

As the night wore on, the storm increased in its fury. Giant waves beat upon the shores and undermined huge trees, crashing the entire mass of soil, grass and tree, into the lake. The following day, Saturday, the sixteenth, saw the storm at its height. The angry lake was a sight to behold. Lake Michigan bore the brunt of the gale, although Lake Huron suffered also. Ninety ships caught out on the open waters, and some believed safe in harbors, were wrecked by the enraged seas. A lightkeeper on Pilot Island reported that the water of Lake Michigan was white for a week after the storm. His theory was that the storm had ground together so many of the limestone rocks, which abound on the bottom of the lake, that it formed a white lime powder which was held in suspension by the swirling water for many days afterwards.

Sailors named this the Alpena Storm. The reason being that the outstanding loss during the blow was the steamer *Alpena*. This unfortunate vessel had picked up passengers and freight at Muskegon and Grand

Haven, both ports on the east shore of Lake Michigan. Early on the evening of the fifteenth she cleared the last named city, bound for Chicago, one hundred and eight watery miles across the lake to the southwest.

Captain Nelson W. Napier, master of the *Alpena,* evidently did not consider that the oncoming storm would reach any such proportions as later developed. He was rated as an experienced navigator, having previously commanded several passenger steamers on the Great Lakes. The *Alpena* was fifteen years old at the time of the blow, but had been rebuilt several years before. She measured one hundred seventy-five feet in length and thirty-five feet breadth, with twelve feet depth, and was considered a fine ship of six hundred fifty-three tons.

The *Alpena* was sighted during the evening by another ship, but was in no particular difficulty at that time. That was the last seen of her. Sometime between that midnight and dawn, she vanished. The storm was then at its peak and marine men are certain that the *Alpena* foundered, though they can but guess at the actual cause.

By morning of the nineteenth, a Tuesday, the wreckage of the *Alpena* began to wash ashore. Great quantities floated up in the vicinity of Holland, Michigan. There was no difficulty in establishing its identity. There were fire buckets with the name of the ship stencilled on them, a piano with the lid torn off, part of a stairway, cabin doors, life preservers, even the bodies of a few of the passengers. The wreckage was eventually strewn along the shore to the northward as far as Grand Haven. Apples, of which the *Alpena* carried several carloads, bobbed about in the restless surf. Some two weeks later the five-by-ten foot flag, with the name *Alpena* in large letters, was found on the beach near White Lake Channel, many miles from where it is believed the steamer went down. Sixty years later this flag was placed on public display, and may today be a prized possession of some ardent lake ship fan.

But aside from a few silent relics, the steamer *Alpena* with her entire compliment of living souls, has been almost forgotten. As this is written it has been over three score and ten years—the normal span of human life—since Captain Napier sailed the *Alpena* out of Grand Haven and into Eternity.

⚓ ⚓ ⚓ ⚓ ⚓ ⚓ ⚓ ⚓

CHAPTER ELEVEN

TUGBOAT RIVALRY

—*1880*—

The era of the sailing vessel on the Great Lakes brought about the era of the steam tugboat. Each ship was necessary to the other. The schooners could carry the cargoes from one port to another after they were out in the open water of the lakes, but they were not able by themselves to navigate the congested harbors and narrow twisting rivers that make up so many of the lake ports. That was where the steam tug entered the scene. It would scurry out into the lake to meet an incoming schooner and escort it cleverly to the proper dock. The windjammer captains of the Great Lakes came to depend a great deal on the stout, seaworthy, and powerful steam tugs.

The tug business prospered on the lakes. Like all successful businesses, competition began to develop. Sometimes tugs of rival lines would leave port at the same time to meet an inbound sailing vessel. Then a race was on to reach the schooner first. Usually the sailing captain would accept the first tug that reached his ship. So it was that the competition brought about faster and larger tugs. A fine fleet of steam tugs oper-

71

ated out of most of the lake ports, especially along the Detroit and St. Clair Rivers. Old-timers tell about the famous Grummond Fleet of tugboats that operated out of Detroit. In this fleet were the tugs *Champion, Sweepstakes, Swan, Moore, Winslow, Oswego, Crusader,* and *Owen.*

There were also many other tugs like the *Samson,* that were operated by smaller owners, and were equally good vessels. These little ships were very powerful and often would tow five or six loaded sailing ships through the Detroit and St. Clair Rivers in the same tow.

Many nefarious tricks were resorted to by the tug crews in order to obtain business. One old stunt was to sneak aboard a rival tug when the crew were not aboard and, with a saw, cut almost but not quite through the wooden handles of the firemen's shovels. The result was that when the fireman would grab his shovel to throw some coal into the firebox, as the tug was racing off to meet an incoming ship, the shovel handle would snap in two. Without the proper tools with which to heave in the coal, the steam pressure would soon lessen, and the scheming rival tug would be the first to reach the incoming windjammer.

Another old ruse that the tug men were said to have employed when cruising in open waters after dark, awaiting the arrival of an inbound ship, was to reverse their riding lights. All steam vessels underway at night carry a red light on their port side forward, and a green light on their starboard side. When another ship sights them it can be ascertained at a glance in what direction the craft is headed. Thus by switching their lights, a rival tug would not know without constant watching, in which direction its competitor was moving. This practice was, of course, strictly against the navigation laws and would subject the captain to severe penalty if caught. But seventy or eighty years ago the marine laws were not as rigidly enforced as they are today.

Every lake port of any consequence had its fleet of towing tugs. A small port might enjoy a monopoly and have but a single tug if business weren't too heavy. A large port might have as many as twenty or more.

Old-time sailors from Pentwater, Michigan, can recall the tragic rivalry between two tugs from that Lake Michigan port many years ago. It is coupled with a steamboat race — a race in which the loser never returned.

Quite a few sailing schooners traded into Pentwater in the 1880's carrying lumber to Chicago. Two tugs, the *Messenger* and the *George Lamont,* both owned by the Lamont family, had been enjoying freedom from competition in the harbor towing business in Pentwater. But this happy situation was not to last.

One day a rival tug, the *Gem,* steamed into the serene little harbor and set about to share the towing business with the two Lamont tugs already there. The *Gem* was considerably larger than the other tugs, being around ten tons burden, while the *George Lamont* was only about five. Naturally an intense rivalry quickly sprang up between the newcomer *Gem* and the established *Lamont*. It began with the owners and crews of the two craft, and soon spread throughout the water front and even into the town. The crews led the bantering. Strange stories of the unseaworthiness of the two tugs were circulated around the town.

The upshot of all this antagonism came with an offer of a race over a stated course on Lake Michigan off Pentwater. All hands were quick to grasp the sporting significance of such an event. Sailors bet heavily on their favorite tug. Even up in the town, wagers were made amongst the merchants and townspeople. It rapidly became a local major sporting event. Both tug owners welcomed the speed trial, and they set Sunday, March 14th—the year was 1880—for the date of the big race. Local excitement ran high and the town was agog with side bets and wagers.

Lake Michigan was in a bad mood on the morning of the race. Heavy seas were rolling into the river; crested white caps dotted the dull gray surface of the lake. It was definitely not a good day for the race, but this did not daunt the skippers of the *Gem* or the *George Lamont*. They both had been out on the lake in worse storms before. The high pitch of enthusiasm over the race was not to be let down. Both captains were anxious to get going.

TUGBOAT RIVALRY

Captain Charles Lamont of the *George Lamont* took with him Palmer Hill, as engineer and crew, and Georgie Lamont, his son, a lad of about twelve. Captain Lamont was also an excellent steam mechanic, and he had the tug engine working perfectly. He had checked over everything on the *George Lamont* and was confident that his tug would win.

Three persons also made up the crew of the *Gem*. They were Captain P. H. Adams, John Millidge and Moore Hardway. The *Gem* had also been given a careful checking over and her backers were equally confident that their tug would win.

Out they sailed onto stormy Lake Michigan and side by side, they began the course of the race. The shore of the lake was lined with onlookers who had brought binoculars and various glasses with which to follow the racers. The first leg of the race angled out into the lake away from the shore.

Supporters of the *George Lamont* were disheartened early in the race when they saw their favorite being outdistanced by the *Gem*. The gap continued to widen between the racing tugs. It appeared that the *George Lamont* was no match for the *Gem* in such a sea. As the tugs moved into the distance the onlookers left their stations. A light fall of snow blotted out the racing tugs, and a strong wind began to whirl it in all directions. The snow increased quickly and soon nothing could be seen from the shore of the lake.

SHIPWRECKS OF THE LAKES

The men in the pilot house of the racing *Gem* were elated with their lead, but still they had to admire the pluck and seamanship of the losing tug. In spite of falling behind in the race the *George Lamont* continued to plow along through the huge waves in a futile attempt to win. Then came the snow which obscured everything on the big lake.

It was nearly four o'clock that afternoon when the *Gem* returned to Pentwater. The snow had stopped falling, but the lake was still thrashing angrily. Captain Adams' first inquiry upon coming ashore was of the whereabouts of the *George Lamont*. In a short lull in the falling snow out on the lake, he believed he had seen the *Lamont* turning about. He presumed she was returning to Pentwater and abandoning the race. Then the snow laid down another curtain. The *Gem* completed the assigned race course as well as she could under the difficult conditions.

Nothing was to be seen of the gallant little *George Lamont*. She had not returned to port. There was only one answer. She had gone down with all hands!

Beach searching parties were immediately organized, and they scoured the lake front to the north and to the south. At last the party that went north sent back word that they had found wreckage of the ill-fated *George Lamont*. There was no sign of life.

There have been many famous steamboat races

upon the waters of the oceans, the Great Lakes, and the Mississippi River and its tributaries, but it fell to the lot of the humble little steam tug *George Lamont* to be the only racing contestant vessel to disappear entirely with all hands during this all but forgotten race. Pentwater was indeed saddened by the tragic results of the sporting event it had so looked forward to.

The bodies of Captain Charles Lamont, his son Georgie, and Palmer Hill, came ashore a few days later and were buried in the nearby village cemetery.

The following Pictorial Section is a collection by the author of photographs of various wrecked ships or ones that later figured in shipwrecks.

Obviously, the entire collection is the result of the efforts of many people and comes from greatly varied sources. Where origin of the photograph is known it is so mentioned, also the collection from which it has been presented or loaned.

SHIPWRECKS OF THE LAKES

One of a pair of early propellers from the steamer *Independence* which
sank in the St. Marys River, Nov. 22, 1853. After eighty years on the
bottom, it was salvaged and mounted in concrete in the park adjoining
the locks at Sault Ste. Marie, Michigan.

Loudon Wilson Studio

An artist's conception of the burning of the steamer *Seabird* on Lake
Michigan, off Evanston, early in the morning of April 9, 1868.

SHIPWRECKS OF THE LAKES

A photograph of a painting depicting the scene of the burning of the early Great Lakes steamer *Erie* in August, 1841, on Lake Erie off Dunkirk, N. Y.

From a woodcut in Frank Leslie's Illustrated Newspaper of September 22, 1860

Schooner *Augusta* at dock in Chicago with her bow stove in, after colliding with steamer *Lady Elgin* on Lake Michigan, September 8, 1860.

Steamer *Lady Elgin* at Chicago, from a photograph taken the day before her fatal collision with the schooner *Augusta* on Lake Michigan, September 8, 1860. Inset shows Captain John "Jack" Wilson master of the *Lady Elgin* at the time of her disaster.

From a woodcut in Frank Leslie's Illustrated Newspaper of September 22, 1860

SHIPWRECKS OF THE LAKES

Side-wheel steamer *Alpena* which disappeared in a violent gale on Lake Michigan, October 16, 1880. Wreckage came ashore for several weeks in the vicinity of Holland, Michigan. There were no survivors.

Canadian propeller steamer *Algoma*, built in Scotland and wrecked during her second season on the Great Lakes by striking on Isle Royale in a blinding snowstorm on November 7, 1885.

SHIPWRECKS OF THE LAKES

The early bulk freight steamer *Brunswick* lasted but a few months on the Great Lakes. She sank in Lake Erie, off Dunkirk, N. Y., on November 12, 1881, in a night collision with the schooner *Carlingford*.

The early passenger and freight steamer *Winslow of Erie,* afire in Duluth Harbor, October, 1891. She burned to a total loss.

Lake Michigan wooden passenger and freight steamer *Chicora* disappeared on January 21, 1895, between Milwaukee and St. Joseph—Benton Harbor. All hands lost.

SHIPWRECKS OF THE LAKES

Early wooden freight steamer *Tecumseh* being raised from the bottom of the harbor at Marquette, Michigan, June 29, 1898.

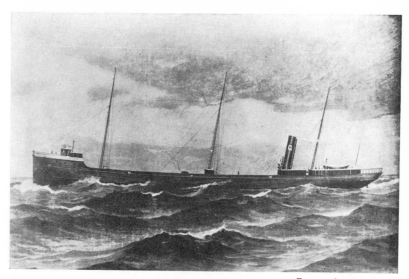

From a drawing

Two year old steel bulk freight steamer *W. H. Gilcher* disappeared in Lake Michigan near North Manitou Island on October 28, 1892.

SHIPWRECKS OF THE LAKES

Unidentified remains of a wooden lake steamer ashore on Isle Royale, Lake Superior .

Battered wreck of an unidentified wooden schooner on a Lake Michigan beach about 1894.

Schooners *Moonlight* and *Kent* ashore on Chocolay Beach, near Marquette, Michigan, wrecked on September 29, 1895. Both ships were later salvaged and returned to service. Their towing steamer, *C. J. Kershaw*, was a total loss.

SHIPWRECKS OF THE LAKES

Wooden steamer *Idaho,* built at Cleveland in 1863, was lost in a gale on Lake Erie, November 5, 1897, with her entire crew except two who clung to the mast until rescued by a passing freighter.

Glander Studios

Typical of the freight vessels trading between Lake Michigan ports at the turn of the century is the schooner *Lydia,* built at Manitowoc, Wisconsin, in 1874, shown here wrecked on the beach near Manistee, Michigan.

SHIPWRECKS OF THE LAKES

Young Photo

Wooden bulk freight steamer *John B. Lyon,* built in 1881 at Cleveland, Ohio, foundered in Lake Erie, September 11, 1900.

Hansen Studio

Rescuing a man by life line from an early Pere Marquette steamer over the icy waters of Lake Michigan near Ludington, Michigan.

SHIPWRECKS OF THE LAKES

Wooden freighter *William F. Sauber,* built in 1891 at West Bay City, Michigan, foundered October 25, 1903, off Whitefish Point, Lake Superior. Inset shows Captain William E. Morris who chose to perish with his ship.

Kamera Shop

Wooden freighter *George G. Hadley* on the bottom near Duluth, Minnesota.

Buffalo Harbor scene about 1906. Both ships in foreground met with disaster. At left is package freighter *Clarion* which burned off Southeast Shoal in Lake Erie, on December 8, 1909, with loss of fifteen of her crew. In center is steel freighter *D. R. Hanna* lost by collision on Lake Huron, May 16, 1919, with no loss of life. Passenger steamers *Juniata* and *Japan* are in center background.

SHIPWRECKS OF THE LAKES

Steamer *Sevona* with her upper works encased in ice. Inset picture of Capt. Donald S. McDonald, lost with his ship during a gale on Lake Superior, September 2, 1905.

Abandoned wreck of steamer *Sevona* on the rocks between Sand Island and Raspberry Island of the Apostle group in Lake Superior.

SHIPWRECKS OF THE LAKES

Glander Studio

Two-masted schooner *Josephine Dresden* ashore in the sand dune section of Lake Michigan, following a gale.

J. W. Bald Studio

Bradley freighter *Joseph S. Fay,* built in 1871 at Cleveland, Ohio, and wrecked on Lake Huron near Rogers City, Michigan, October 19, 1902, with the loss of one life.

Twenty-five day old steel freighter *Cyprus* disappeared October 11, 1907, in Lake Superior, off Deer Park, Michigan. Only one man of her crew survived.

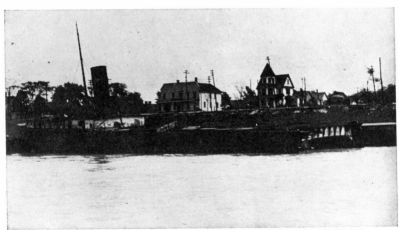

Captain Frank E. Hamilton Collection

The after half of steamer *W. C. Moreland*, wrecked in Lake Superior October 18, 1910. Her forward half was lost. This after half made a round trip as such between upper and lower lakes and was subsequently attached to a new forward half, becoming a regulation freighter. She is now the *Gene C. Hutchinson*.

Canadian wooden passenger steamer *Cambria* aground after running into
log rafts, thereby disabling her machinery and steering apparatus.

Wm. A. McDonald Collection

Lumber steamer *N. J. Nessen* on the bottom near Manitowoc, Wisconsin.
Sister ship *F. W. Fletcher* standing by. The sunken ship was raised and
returned to service. She finally foundered in Lake Erie on October 23,
1929, with the loss of 13 lives.

SHIPWRECKS OF THE LAKES

Two-masted schooner *Mars,* wrecked on South Fox Island, Lake Michigan, November 19, 1903.

Canadian steel passenger and freight steamer *Huronic* on the rocks of Lucille Island, Lake Superior, August 6 to 16, 1928. Ship was subsequently refloated and did many years of service on the Great Lakes.

SHIPWRECKS OF THE LAKES

Steel passenger and car ferry steamer *Pere Marquette 18,* built at
Cleveland in 1902, lost in Lake Michigan between Ludington and Milwaukee on September 9, 1910.

Pilot house and forward cabins of the sunken freighter *John Plank-
ington* show above the surface of the Detroit River. The steamer went
to the bottom in a collision in 1917.

Steel freight steamer *Benjamin Noble* ready for launching at Wyandotte, Michigan, in 1909. She disappeared with all hands in Lake Superior during a storm on April 27, 1914.

Pesha Photo

Composite freight steamer *John Owen,* built at Wyandotte, Michigan, in 1889, disappeared with all hands in Lake Superior near Caribou Island.

SHIPWRECKS OF THE LAKES

Ship fire at Ecorse, Michigan on February 21, 1929. Steamer in center is side-wheel passenger ship *Erie*, originally *Pennsylvania* and later *Owana*. Behind her is side-wheel passenger steamer *Dover*, formerly *Frank E. Kirby* and *Silver Spray*, which was not completely burned. In near foreground is the hull of the old Detroit River ferry *Sappho*, which burned almost to the water's edge. All ships had been laid up for the winter.

British ocean freighter *William Brewster* rests on her side on the bottom of the St. Clair River near Algonac, after a collision June 15, 1943. Built at Superior, Wisconsin, she was on her first trip, after loading wheat at the lakehead for Great Britain.

Wooden lumber steamer *Myron*, built at Grand Haven, Michigan, in 1888, foundered November 23, 1919, in Lake Superior near Whitefish Point. One man survived.

Wooden lumber steamer *H. E. Runnels*, built at Port Huron, Michigan, in 1893, was lost in Lake Superior, off Grand Marais, Michigan, on November 14, 1919.

A terrific explosion aboard the passenger ferry steamer *Omar D. Conger* at Port Huron, Michigan, on March 26, 1922, reduced the ship to this debris.

Richard Gordon Wendt Collection

Starboard quarter view of the side-wheel passenger steamer *Arrow* after a devastating fire while the ship was at dock at Put-in-Bay, Ohio, in the fall of 1922. There were no casualties. The ship was rebuilt and saw many years of service.

SHIPWRECKS OF THE LAKES

J. W. Bald Studio

Canadian freighter *Maplehurst* lies a wreck in Lake Superior, off the West Entrance of Keweenaw Waterway. She foundered November 30, 1922, with a loss of eleven members of her crew. Nine were rescued by the U. S. Life Savers in a stirring action.

CDR. A. F. Glaza U. S. Coast Guard (Ret.) Photo

Steamer *Turret Chief* with her bow driven hard on the shore of Keweenaw Peninsula on November 8, 1913. Picture taken six months after her mishap. Ship was later salvaged and returned to service.

SHIPWRECKS OF THE LAKES

All photos by CDR. A. F. Glaza, U. S. Coast Guard (Ret.)

TOP—Steamer *City of Bangor* as she looked three months after her stranding.

CENTER—Clearing deck of snow and ice to remove the remaining 230 Chrysler autos (18 having been lost overboard).

BOTTOM—As the wrecked ship appeared January 25, 1927.

SHIPWRECKS OF THE LAKES

STR. "ALTADOC" 1928.
WRECKED DEC. 8,1927.
KEWEENAW POINT.
A.F.G.

Wrecked Str. "Altadoc" Keweenaw Point,
Storm of December 8-10, 1927.
Photo
A F Glaza

Top and bottom photos by CDR. A. F. Glaza, U. S. Coast Guard (Ret.)

Steel freighter *Altadoc* wrecked on Keweenaw Point, Lake Superior, December 8, 1927.

TOP—Port-side view of stranded *Altadoc* the following spring.

CENTER—Pilot house of wrecked steamer placed on shore at Keweenaw Point.

BOTTOM—Starboard view of wrecked ship the following spring.

SHIPWRECKS OF THE LAKES

Canadian steel freighter *Novadoc* lies a broken wreck in Lake Michigan, near Pentwater, where she stranded and became a total loss on November 11, 1940. Two lives lost; balance of crew removed by fishermen.

Sandsucker steamer *Hydro* on the bottom of Cuyahoga River in Cleveland, where she settled while taking a cargo up river on September 12, 1939. She was later salvaged and returned to service.

SHIPWRECKS OF THE LAKES

Passengers awaiting rescue stand on the side of the capsized steamer *Eastland* when she rolled over in Chicago on July 24, 1915. This disaster is the worst in the annals of lake shipping, based on number of lives lost—835.

Canadian wooden package freight steamer *St. Magnus* capsized in the Cuyahoga River at Cleveland, Ohio, on June 7, 1895, with no loss of life.

TOP—Passenger steamer *Lakeland*, formerly the freighter *Cambria*, entering Milwaukee harbor on one of her regular trips. Lost Dec. 3, 1924.
Edwin Wilson Photo

CENTER—Detroit's famous excursion steamer *Tashmoo* resting on the bottom of the Detroit River where she sank June 18, 1936, after hitting an obstruction which tore a hole in her hull. Her passengers were safely landed at Amherstburg, Ontario. She was later dismantled.

BOTTOM—Passenger steamer *George M. Cox,* formerly *Puritan,* aground on Rock of Ages Reef, Isle Royale, Lake Superior, May 27, 1933.
Captain H. C. Inches Collection

SHIPWRECKS OF THE LAKES

Captain W. J. Taylor Photo

Canadian passenger and freight steamer *Hamonic,* which for thirty-six years plied the upper Great Lakes, giving enjoyment to thousands of vacationists and commercial travelers.

Fire which spread from a dock destroyed the fine steamer *Hamonic* at Point Edward, Ontario, near Sarnia on July 17, 1945, with no fatalities.

Captain W. J. Taylor Photo

Passenger and freight steamer *Noronic,* built at Port Arthur, Ontario, in 1913, was the flagship of Northern Navigation Division of the Canada Steamship Lines.

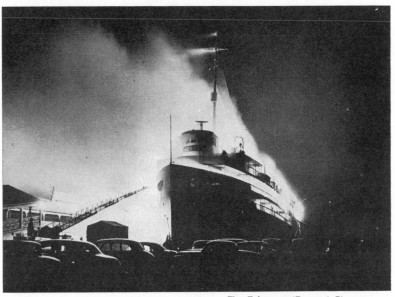

The Telegram (Toronto) Photo

The end of the *Noronic.* She was destroyed by fire while tied to her dock in Toronto, Ontario, on September 17, 1949.

Large photo by Young Studio
Inset from W. A. McDonald Collection

Big ore carriers *J. P. Morgan, Jr.,* (large picture) and *Crete* (lower inset) damaged in collision in a dense fog on Lake Superior near Devil's Island, June 23, 1948. Both ships were promptly repaired and returned to service.

⚓ ⚓ ⚓ ⚓ ⚓ ⚓ ⚓ ⚓

CHAPTER TWELVE

THE CARLINGFORD AND THE BRUNSWICK

— 1 8 8 1 —

Skippers of windjammers and steamers sailing in the easterly end of Lake Erie during the years from 1882 to 1887 reported a strange spar sticking out of the water. This interesting piece of wood was observed between Point Abino and Port Colborne, near the Canadian shore. It puzzled the authorities and old-timers alike. What could it be? Some late comers argued that it was the wreck of the schooner *G. M. Case*. Officials however quickly settled that by pointing out that the *Case* wreck had occurred during the fall of 1886 and had been located and identified. Still the strange spar remained unknown.

The mystery continued to vex lake mariners. So one fine day in June, 1887, Captain McKenzie of the United States Lighthouse Service supply steamer *Hazen* set out to settle once and for all the identity of the hull that most likely lay under the water at the base of that protruding mast. With him went the newly appointed Lighthouse Service Inspector for the district, Captain Charles Vernon Gridley, U. S. N., who was later to be made famous by that cryptic order of Admiral George

Dewey at the Battle of Manila, "You may fire when ready, Gridley."

The records show that on June 24th, 1887, the *Hazen* sailed into Buffalo Harbor with the answer to the lake mystery. It was the spar of the schooner *Carlingford,* which had been lost in collision with the steamer *Brunswick,* twelve miles off Dunkirk, New York, nearly six years previously! How the *Carlingford* had arrived on the Canadian side of the lake, and at least twelve miles beyond the scene of her collision, neither Captain Gridley nor Captain McKenzie could explain. The *Carlingford* still flauntingly continued to vex the men of the lakes.

The only logical explanation seemed to lie in the guess that she may have floated longer than her crew supposed, after abandoning ship. In the darkness of the night the schooner may have drifted, slowly settling deeper in the water as she went along. At last, possibly her bottom may have touched Canadian sand somewhere between Port Colborne and Point Abino. Then there were the theorists who reasoned that the sunken wooden schooner, with her cargo of grain trapped in her hold, may have retained some degree of bouyancy even after her keel scraped the bottom of Lake Erie. They figured that in this condition she may have slowly slipped along with the water currents until she grounded in the more shallow water near the Canadian shore. No one really knows.

The tale of the wreck of the two lake vessels is interesting. There was in 1881, as there is today, the ever present danger of collision between ships at sea, though mariners of today have far more instruments to guide them than did the sailors of the nineteenth century, who relied mostly on their eyes and ears and a couple of feeble oil lamps.

The good ship *Carlingford,* typical Great Lakes wooden schooner of her day, had loaded wheat at Duluth until the precious grain completely filled her hold. The hatches were fastened carefully in place over the cargo, and then heavy tarpaulins were securely battened over the covers for extra protection. Wheat is easily ruined by water, and the *Carlingford* had three of the five Great Lakes to traverse, a distance of nearly one thousand miles, before she would be relieved of her burden at Buffalo. Only the best of the wind-jammers could carry grain and keep it dry. The *Carlingford* was a stout vessel and well-kept. She was twelve years old at this time, having been built at Port Huron, Michigan, in 1869 and was owned by Captain Oscar B. Smith of Huron, Ohio, and others.

And so she sailed from Duluth, Minnesota, early in the treacherous month of November, 1881. Late season sailing, even to the present day, is no pleasure cruise on the Great Lakes. November and December are dangerous months. But the wind-borne *Carlingford* successfully negotiated Lake Superior, then Lake Huron, and on to Lake Erie. The weather had been kind to her and she had made good time. On November twelfth the schooner was on the very last lap of her voyage, at the eastern end of Lake Erie as darkness settled. The night was nothing unusual for November weather. Around ten o'clock there was a snow flurry which cleared about eleven. The wind was east-southeast about seven miles per hour. The visibility after the snow squall was fair. The *Carlingford* was by this time some twelve miles off the harbor lights of Dunkirk, New York.

The scene now shifts to another vessel, the new iron steamer *Brunswick,* then only a few months old. Captain Chamberlain stood in her wheel house and piloted his ship out of the harbor of Buffalo. As she cleared the outer light the captain made the notation in the log—that the time was ten P. M.; that it was snowing and that the visibility was a little thick. The *Brunswick* had a cargo of anthracite coal and was bound for Duluth.

The captain remained in the pilot house for two hours after his ship had cleared the Buffalo lights. Then, at midnight, the watch changed, and First Mate John Fraser assumed charge of the freighter. The snow had stopped falling. As the captain left the pilot house, he noted their position was some twelve miles off Dunkirk Light, which he could see dimly in the distance.

He clumped aft to the dining cabin. Once inside he removed his heavy overcoat and boots. The oil lamps gleamed in the comfortable cabin. The captain ordered a lunch, pulled up his chair to the table, and proceeded to enjoy the midnight snack. The lunch finished, he pulled his chair nearer to a steam pipe heater, then another chair for his feet to rest upon, and the ship master relaxed while he smoked his pipe.

When his pipe had burned out, Captain Chamberlain decided to turn in. His room was up forward, so he again donned his boots and, as he struggled into his overcoat, he felt the ship give a severe jolt and he heard the pilot house signal the engine room to stop, and then to back up. He rushed to the bridge. Another hard jolt was felt as he reached the bridge.

"What's wrong, Mr. Fraser?" demanded the captain.

"We've struck a loaded schooner, sir," answered the mate.

"That's a bad job, Mr. Fraser," retorted Captain Chamberlain.

"Yes, it is, sir, I'm afraid," said the mate.

By this time the second mate appeared on the bridge, roused also by the collision. He was promptly dispatched to inspect the hold and report the damage, if any. The captain rushed to the bow to see what had happened there.

He found that his steamer had struck the schooner *Carlingford* on the latter's port side, about opposite the foremast, and that she was about to sink. In the dark-

117

ness he could make out the crew of the sailing vessel taking to their yawl boat, and he felt relieved that they were able to take care of themselves. His own ship had stove in her bows.

The second mate now arrived back on the bridge just as the captain opened the pilot house door.

"Captain, we're sinking!" he bellowed.

At the moment the captain did not realize that the *Brunswick* was in any such serious situation, so he hurried off to the hold to see for himself. He soon learned that the second mate was indeed correct. Water was rushing into the hold from somewhere along the bottom of the steamer. He raced back to the bridge.

"Steer for the shore," he ordered, "and tell the engineer to start the pumps at once."

The *Brunswick* slowly pulled away from the stricken *Carlingford* and headed toward Dunkirk Light.

Meanwhile aboard the schooner the situation was equally desperate. A great hole had been stove in her side, and the water was gushing in at a terrific rate. The *Carlingford* was doomed. Her crew below were quickly roused out and all hands took to the small boat. Just as the skiff was about to shove off from the schooner, one crewman asked to be allowed to go back to his bunk. He rushed into the forecastle just as the *Carlingford* went down bow first. He never came out.

The small boat reluctantly pulled away, and it too headed toward the nearest land.

Chief Engineer Francomb of the *Brunswick* was urging his ship on with all possible speed. It was hoped that she would reach the shore before sinking. But that was not to be. Forty-five minutes after she had collided with the *Carlingford,* she sank to the bottom of Lake Erie. The crew of fifteen had donned life jackets, with the exception of Captain Chamberlain, who refused the proffered help. As the freighter settled, the men attempted to launch their two lifeboats.

The captain took command of one of the boats and the chief engineer the other. The engineer's boat was the first to lower away, but in the confusion of the launching, Francomb lost his hold on the small craft and he fell into the water and was never seen again. The rest of the men in the boat came through all right.

But the captain's boat never left the *Brunswick.* As it was being loaded and ready to cut loose from the steamer, the captain unfastened the lines at the stern end, but the man at the bow was unable to loosen his end, and the small boat was carried down along with the steamer as she sank. Those in the boat were dumped out, all except two cooks, and were picked up by the engineer's boat.

The captain fully expected that the lifeboat would break off from the steamer as she sank, and he planned to hold on to the small boat as it went down, believing that he would be all right when it broke off and came up. He called to the two cooks to hang on to their seats. They clamped their arms tightly to the seats as the boat sank. That was the last that Captain Chamberlain, or anyone else, ever saw of them.

The captain himself hung on as the lifeboat went down with the ship. Down, down, it went, until it became apparent that it was not going to break loose. Then the captain let go his hold. He thought that he would never again see the top of the water. But he did. As his head appeared out of the water he was near the other lifeboat, and was quickly hauled aboard. Hours later they made Dunkirk, and Captain Chamberlain was carried ashore completely exhausted. He eventually recovered.

From records of the testimony of the survivors of the collision, it appears that the lack of understanding proper passing signals was responsible for the disaster. Each vessel changed her course twice or more in frenzied efforts to avoid a collision, much the same as when one pedestrian will quickly sidestep another, only to see the other one quickly change his course also. Thus a collision is often inevitable.

And so it was with the schooner *Carlingford* and the steamer *Brunswick*. Their collision seemed inevitable. Three men drowned from the steamer and one from the schooner. Mr. Charles Bewick, owner of the steamer, lost a brand new ship worth a fortune, and the loss of the *Carlingford* to Captain Oscar B. Smith, her owner, was also a staggering financial blow. Captain Smith had previously sailed the *Carlingford* himself, but turned the command over to another captain during his absence while on a trip to California.

⚓ ⚓ ⚓ ⚓ ⚓ ⚓ ⚓ ⚓

CHAPTER THIRTEEN

THE ALGOMA

—1885—

Saturday, November 7th, 1885, stands out prominently in the history of the far-flung Canadian Pacific Railroad. On that day the Honorable Donald Smith drove the last spike in the construction of the trans-Canadian railroad, joining the eastern rails with those from the west, high in the Canadian Rocky Mountains at the small wayside station of Craigellachie, in the Eagle Pass. Historians record that the famous spike was just an ordinary one, not like the gold and silver ones used on similar occasions in the United States, but it answered exactly the same purpose. Likewise, only a modest celebration on the spot marked the joining of the rails which signified the successful completion of a long and most difficult railroad construction project.

Fate balanced the account with the Canadian Pacific on that same day before dawn, by striking down one of its new lake liners, the steamer *Algoma,* within some sixty feet of solid land! It was a day of strange contrasts for the owners: on the one hand a great triumph, and on the other, a dreadful tragedy!

THE ALGOMA

The *Algoma*, despite the fact that she was but two years old, had an interesting background. She, along with two sister ships, the *Athabasca* and the *Alberta*, had been built on the Clyde River, at Whiteinch, Scotland, and had sailed, each under her own power, across the wide Atlantic Ocean and into the St. Lawrence River to the port of Montreal, Quebec. The *Algoma* was probably the first steamer to bring the Plimsoll mark on her hull into the Great Lakes. Samuel Plimsoll had recently persuaded the British Parliament to adopt such markings on vessels as a safety precaution when loading. A glance at the Plimsoll mark on a vessel would tell how deeply, and consequently how safely, she was loaded. These markings are carried on the ships of all nations to this day, and are regarded as a necessary safeguard by navigators around the world.

Montreal water-front folk marveled at the splendid lines of the new propeller-type *Algoma*. Her white cabins made a sharp contrast to her glistening black hull. She had a substantial smokestack and two high masts, capable of carrying considerable sail. She stretched two hundred seventy feet long with a beam of thirty-eight feet, while her depth was twenty-three feet and three inches.

At a shipyard in Montreal the three ships, *Algoma*, *Athabasca*, and *Alberta*, were cut in two amidships, to enable them to be towed through the canals of the St. Lawrence River and the old Welland Canal between Lake Ontario and Lake Erie. It was a treacherous trip, as the two halves of each ship were unwieldy, and much depended on the weather.

The half steamers made the voyage successfully and were safely brought into port at Buffalo, New York, to once more be joined together. From there they sailed to Port Colborne, Ontario, where they were outfitted completely. It was early May, 1884, when the three vessels cleared the Welland Canal port for the upper lakes to begin their regular runs between Owen Sound on Georgian Bay, and Port Arthur on Lake Superior.

It was a big day in Owen Sound that tenth day of May, 1884, when the sleek new steamer *Algoma* arrived in port. She was the finest ship yet to dock there, and immediately lifted the standard of the business of water transportation to a new high level. The *Alberta* followed, arriving the next day, and the *Athabasca* steamed in on the 13th. All three ships then entered upon their scheduled runs providing tri-weekly service to the Canadian lakehead. That season of 1884 was a big success. Many immigrants were heading for the great spaces of middle and western Canada, and the freight often taxed the capacity of the three ships to their limits.

After this noteworthy sailing season, the three new steamers spent their first winter ice-locked in Great Lakes harbors. The following spring found them with steam up and sails ready, and as soon as the ice left the waters, the ships began their careers of 1885. As previously mentioned, the transcontinental rails were not yet in complete operation, and travel on the three sisters was heavy. Great quantities of supplies for the new railroad provided much of the freight, and the influx of the immigrants provided well-filled cabins aboard the ships.

The season was nearing a close; it was the fifth of November, when the *Algoma* cleared her home port of Owen Sound for the regular run up to Port Arthur. Passenger trade was greatly reduced so late in the season—she carried only eleven, five first class and six steerage—but her freight cargo totaled some five hundred and thirty tons of various supplies and merchandise.

Captain John I. Moore of Owen Sound, Ontario, was the master of the *Algoma*. He navigated his vessel through the locks at Sault Ste. Marie without incident —just a usual late season trip. After leaving the locks and upon entering Lake Superior, Captain Moore ordered full sail spread. A stiff wind astern quickly filled the sails, and with her steam engines full speed ahead, the *Algoma* raced across Lake Superior at the spanking rate of sixteen knots.

All through the night of Friday, November 6th, the *Algoma* sped along, running with the wind. In this position she did not roll badly, and to those aboard she was not particularly uncomfortable, even after the wind increased. An icy rain began to fall and froze the sails and ropes stiff. Soon it turned into snow squalls and the wind increased to gale force. Visibility at times was zero, and at best was only a ship's length or two. But still the sail-assisted steamer scurried onward.

By four o'clock Saturday morning, the seventh, the captain took stock of his situation carefully. He believed that his ship then stood some fifteen miles off rocky Isle Royale, past which he must sail on his course to his destination, Port Arthur. After passing Rock Harbor on Isle Royale, the *Algoma* would have to clip off just twenty-seven miles more, before entering the safety of Thunder Bay, where another hours run would put the ship alongside the dock, and the stormy voyage would be over.

But Captain Moore did not like the idea of running the dangers of entering Thunder Bay with his sails all swelling to the gale. He ordered them taken down. This was very difficult for his crew to perform, as the sails were frozen and the tackles and lines ice-encrusted. But in a half hour down came the sails in spite of the handicaps. Only the small trysail remained on her foremast.

Then he unknowingly gave the order that wrecked his ship, "Put the wheel hard over to starboard." He had decided to turn about and to remain in the open waters of Lake Superior, rather than chance the treacherous rock-bound course that he well knew but could not see. His decision was sound; the fatal error was that his order came too late.

Just as the ship came about and began to head

126

outward, the storm caught her and tossed her violently. Her stern was flung onto a huge rock, and her stout steel rudder crumpled like so much tin. Her propeller was also severly damaged. The *Algoma* instantly became unmanageable. She was suddenly at the entire mercy of the storm. But there was to be no mercy for the stricken steamer. Giant waves lifted the stern high in the air and then quickly dropped it, pounding it hard upon the solid rocks. The seas swept over her, wrecking everything in their path.

The *Algoma* was quickly doomed. No ship could stand such terrific pounding on rugged rocks. Each time the vessel struck on the bottom she loosened some of her plates and frames. Her captain frantically ordered her sea cocks opened, believing that this would settle her securely on the bottom and thus prevent the awful pounding. The storm was now the real master. The steam was let out of the boilers to prevent a possible explosion as the ship settled deeper in the icy waters.

The officers believed that their vessel had struck upon a shelf of rock. The after half was banging itself to pieces while the forward half did not hit, indicating to them that it overhung a ledge into deep water. This caused an intense strain on the hull amidships, and soon it was feared that the entire forward half of the steamer would break off and sink in the deep water. All hands were called aft as the plates began to separate. At least

127

there was a bottom under the after end which likely would prevent it from sinking.

The howling tempest soon claimed the forward half of the stricken *Algoma*. Possibly she split open where she had been cut through for the passage through the canals on her way into the lakes. No one knows. With a terrible rending of steel that could be heard above the storm, the forward end sank beneath the waves. It was hoped that all aboard the sunken half of the ship had gotten aft. That too, will never be known.

The break in the steamer loosened the cabins of the after end which now rested more easily on the rocks beneath her keel. In the wild confusion the captain tried his utmost to save his passengers and crew. He ordered life lines of stout rope strung along the remaining deck, and instructed all hands to cling fast, hoping thereby to prevent their being washed overboard by the huge combers which surged over the wreck, but many persons were swept into oblivion.

Captain Moore was everywhere on the wreck encouraging the living to hold fast until daylight, when he was certain help would arrive. While doing this a section of the loosened cabin came crashing down upon him, pinning him to the deck and injuring him painfully. Many others lost their grip on the cabin rails and were washed overboard. Some were destined to find solid ground, but the majority were lost.

It was a tragic moment aboard the wreck. Faint

gray could be seen in the eastern sky. The deck was covered with water, slush, snow and ice, and wreckage of all sorts. The injured captain summoned about him all that could hear his voice. He asked them to kneel and he would pray. Upon that storm-swept deck they knelt and heard Captain Moore pray for their safety. They could not hear all the words that came from the stricken shipmaster, but they knew that his thoughts were for their safety. No man could then do more.

Daylight came at last. Land was not over sixty feet away! But in the raging maelstrom it was a most difficult passage. Numerous rocks lay between, around which the seas surged angrily. Corpses floated in the water between the ship and the shore. The storm was subsiding, but it would take a long time for the enraged waters to calm. Several of the crew decided to strike out for the small bit of nearby land. They launched the remaining lifeboat and managed to get into it. Immediately it capsized and they were thrown into the sucking waters. Some managed to get a grasp upon the boat which remained afloat and thus they reached the little island almost exhausted. A shivering few chose to remain on the wreck.

Saturday passed, a day of utter desolation and intense suffering. All that night those of the passengers and crew that remained alive huddled together in whatever shelter they could find, some aboard the wreck and a few on the island. The wind quieted and very slowly the action of the waves followed.

By daylight Sunday morning the unfortunate survivors began to take steps to improve their situation. Those on the island scattered about searching for possible inhabitants. Fortunately they located several fishermen who at once did everything possible to help the shipwrecked people. A life line was rigged from the wreck to the shore, but there was no tackle for further rescue work.

With great effort those still aboard the *Algoma* constructed a light raft from wreckage of the cabins. Standing on this and holding themselves upright by the life line, they ferried across the now calmer waters from the wreck to the shore. Fear was rising that the remaining after half of the *Algoma* might slide off the rock upon which she rested, and go down in the deep water which had claimed the forward half of the steamer. All hands made the crossing safely during Sunday morning and the *Algoma* was abandoned. The survivors learned that they were wrecked on a rock called Greenstone within one mile of the Rock Harbor Light, which marks a harbor, deep and rockbound, near the eastern tip of Isle Royale, on the side toward Lake Superior. Many rocks, large and small, rise from the lake floor; some peer out of the water while others remain hidden below the surface. Such was the water that had claimed the *Algoma* during the stormy darkness.

Sunday night was spent ashore by the survivors. The air was damp and chilly off the lake and grim despair gripped most of them. The fishermen provisioned a small tug used in their trade and it left Monday morning in search of help. The storm by then had completely blown itself out.

A careful check of the survivors counted fourteen; including the injured Captain Moore. Thirty-seven were lost. Their bodies were still floating ashore, many were entwined in the nets of the fishermen; nets that had been set before the storm and now torn and wrecked, they lay amongst the rocks and on the shore line.

The hopes of the fourteen survivors heightened as they watched the tiny fish tug chug its way in the direction of Port Arthur. In the distance and possibly coming toward them and on the same course that the tug was sailing, appeared the smoke of a steamer. Gradually the lines of the on-coming ship took shape. Hope of rescue quickened fourteen hearts on the rocky island, for the oncoming ship was none other than the sister ship of the *Algoma,* the CPR steamer *Athabasca!* She had left Port Arthur bound down the lake for Owen Sound on her return trip. It was a heartening sight for the weary shipwrecked souls. Warmth, food, a place to rest and dry their clothes, the *Athabasca* brought all this and more. Life could now go on for them.

The fish tug hailed and pulled alongside the passenger ship and the officers of the *Athabasca* were told of the loss of the *Algoma.* The survivors had built a large bonfire on the shore, hoping also to attract the attention of the passing ship. The *Athabasca's* engines were stopped and a boat was quickly lowered and headed for the wrecked *Algoma,* whose after half still rested upon the fatal Greenstone. The rescue steamer returned to Port Arthur with the survivors and a shocked world learned of the wrecking of the fine steamer *Algoma.*

What causes one ship to be wrecked and another to sail on is always a mystery. Sometimes it is faulty judgment, then again just plain bad luck has caused many a wreck. One interesting angle of the *Algoma* disaster is that at the same time the *Algoma* was pounding her heart out on Greenstone, her sister ship, the *Alberta,* cruised past her not very far off and on the same course, but heading in the opposite direction, bound down the lake. The men in her pilot house were watching for the *Algoma* as they neared Rock Harbor Light, but they reported the snow storm rendered visibility to hardly a ship's length. The down bound *Alberta* had actually steamed right past the *Algoma* during the height of the storm and had never seen her sorry plight.

The following summer the wreck lay as it had crashed during the storm. Salvage wreckers arrived and removed the engines and boilers from the *Algoma* and took them to Owen Sound. They were subsequently placed in the new steamer *Manitoba,* which was built there in 1889 to replace the lost *Algoma.* This machinery served well in the good ship *Manitoba,* lasting until that ship was dismantled in Hamilton, Ontario, during the summer of 1950.

⚓ ⚓ ⚓ ⚓ ⚓ ⚓ ⚓ ⚓

THE CITY OF GREEN BAY—HAVANA—CALIFORNIA
—1887—

We stood on a fine, clean, sandy beach and Lake Michigan made a background of sparkling blue. Beautiful Evergreen Bluff rose boldly from the shining beach a mile or two from where we were, and farther to the northward lay the harbor of South Haven, Michigan.

Our interest was centered just a few feet out from the water's edge. Here the playful wavelets splashed around some darkened pieces of sturdy oak, their bottom ends buried deep in the sands.

"That's all that's left of her now," pointed out Allen Chesebro, our host and guide. Allen was born on Evergreen Bluff sixty-eight years previously, and his father had settled there years before that. The Chesebro family really knew that section of the Lake Michigan coast.

We were looking at all there was left of the big three-masted cargo schooner, *City of Green Bay*; that is, all there was left of it still in the water. A moderate-sized building still stands near the golf course high on the bluff, built from the spars of the wrecked ship.

"She fetched up here during the historic storm of 1887, on October third," Chesebro related, "and she was a fine old ship, so they say. She even sailed the Atlantic Ocean. Made trips from Chicago to Boston and then to Scotland. Back then to Montreal and down to South America. Then to Liverpool, and so on for two years, when she returned to the Great Lakes. But it took old Lake Michigan to end up her days. And right here on this spot. I was only five years old at the time of the wreck and so I can't actually remember it much, but my father often talked about it."

He took from his pocket a well worn card in his own handwriting.

"Here are some notes I copied from Father's diary, written on the day of the disaster," he said, and then he read from the card, "A three-master went on the bar off C's place at seven this morning, and by ten o'clock it had gone all to pieces. Six men were drowned but one was saved."

October arrived on the Great Lakes in 1887 with a roar. The gale hit Lake Michigan from the northeast, and churned the surface into a maelstrom. It caught the sturdy schooner *City of Green Bay* bound out of Escanaba, Michigan, to Saint Joseph, Michigan, with a heavy cargo of some seven hundred tons of iron ore beneath her hatches. Captain P. W. Costello ordered the sails trimmed in order to ride along with the storm. The *City of Green Bay* scudded through the giant waves, which soon were breaking over her bows and crashing along her decks.

There was no shelter for the storm-tossed wind-jammer. She was caught out on the broad waters of the lake and forced to ride out the gale. Many other more fortunate vessels had sought shelter behind many of the islands that dot the upper half of Lake Michigan. But for the *City of Green Bay* there were no islands. That protection was many miles astern.

By midnight of Sunday, October second, the wind had shifted to the west and increased in violence into a howling gale. All six members of the crew, and the captain, were standing duty. The harbor lights of South Haven, Michigan, were sighted, and the ship was brought nearer the shore. The fifteen year old vessel began to leak; the terrific strain opened her seams below the water line. The crew turned to the pumps, but in spite of their efforts the water in the hold rose faster than it could be expelled. Captain Costello knew his ship was in a very dangerous situation. When the *City of Green Bay* was some four miles off shore, and southward of the lights of South Haven, he ordered both anchors down and distress signals hoisted.

Throughout the remaining hours of darkness the heavily-laden schooner continued to roll, strain and pitch, and the water in her hold continued to rise. The crew could no longer work the pumps, as one by one they quit from sheer exhaustion. Just as a faint glow of daylight appeared in the eastern sky, Captain Costello realized that his ship was doomed and would shortly sink beneath the angry waves. He then ordered the anchors slipped, in one last desperate hope of putting the ship on the beach before she went down.

Freed from her restraining anchors, the *City of Green Bay* leaped before the wind and plunged headlong through the stormy seas toward the land, carrying only a close-reefed foresail. A few minutes before seven on that Monday morning of October third, the schooner *City of Green Bay* struck the outer bar with a wrenching thud. A giant wave struck her and carried her over the bar and swung her broadside to the shore, which she hit with a tremendous crash. Then a continual pounding of the seas began. Mountainous seas of green-white water swept over her decks and she rolled like a giant mortally wounded. Her crew and captain scrambled into the rigging, where with great difficulty they clung hoping help would come now that daylight was at hand.

Help was already on its way. The lookout at the South Haven Life-saving Station had sighted the distress signals of the schooner and had notified the keeper of the station. By eight o'clock Monday morning, the life-saving crew were on the beach opposite the wrecked schooner, trying to rescue the men they could see clinging in the rigging. The rescuers did not believe that the schooner could stand up under the terrific pounding of the surf. They were correct. While they watched, the mainmast went over the side, carrying with it the three or four men who had climbed up on it for safety, drowning all of them. One of the bodies was later found, that of Captain Costello.

The rescue crew worked feverishly at their task, but it appeared that all their efforts were in vain. Their shot lines parted, their ammunition for the Lyle gun ran out, and finally their tackle became hopelessly tangled. They then attempted to launch a surfboat, but the high seas and floating wreckage banged down upon them, and try as they would, they could not get the surfboat under way.

Some of the schooner's crew, seeing the quick fate of their fellow sailors who were clinging to the mainmast, decided to come down and take their chances on the deck. They were washed off and drowned. A few remained on the foremast. It began to loosen and soon went crashing over the side, throwing the men on it into the water and drowning them.

One lone deck hand was rescued. Somehow he managed to ride a large piece of wreckage toward the shore. He was hauled into the rescuers' surfboat after a terrific struggle. By ten o'clock that same morning, the schooner *City of Green Bay* was a total wreck, and most of it was scattered along that same sandy beach near the foot of Everygreen Bluff. Only the stout oak timbers remained. Today they silently tell the observant beachcomber of that wild night on Lake Michigan sixty-three years ago when the wooden schooner *City of Green Bay* perished, along with all but one of her valiant crew.

At almost the same hour that the *City of Green Bay* was breaking up on the east coast of Lake Michigan, another wooden sailing schooner, the *Havana,* was also wrecked on the same coast not many miles away. The two shipwrecks were similiar in many details; they both carried the same cargo material, iron ore; they both loaded at the same port, Escanaba, Michigan; and both were consigned to unload at the same port, Saint Joseph, Michigan; they both sailed on the same day. So it was inevitable that they both were struck by the same gale.

The experiences of the *Havana* were much the same as those of the *City of Green Bay*. Hit by the storm in mid-lake, she battled her way until she foundered just six miles short of her destination, Saint Joseph. As the ship began to take water faster than the men could pump it out, the crew similarly took to the rigging. Captain John Curran tried to beach his vessel when he found that she was in a sinking condition. Three-quarters of a mile off shore, the *Havana* with her six hundred ton cargo of iron ore wallowed beneath the roaring waves. A tremendous lurch of the vessel tore the mainmast loose and it crashed into the sea, killing the captain, steward, and one sailor. One of the other masts proved more sturdy, and it remained upright until help arrived. Thus four men were saved.

SHIPWRECKS OF THE LAKES

Still another lake ship ended her career in that same early October storm on Lake Michigan. She was the wooden Canadian propeller *California* under the command of Captain John V. Trowell. The *California* loaded various package freight, mostly corn and pork, at Chicago. Late Saturday night, October first, she sailed, bound for Montreal. She carried a crew of twenty-two and five passengers. Her trip was uneventful down Lake Michigan until she was between the Manitou Islands and the Fox Islands. Here the fateful gale began to strike. By the time the *California* was abreast of Beaver Island she was in the midst of the storm. Huge seas swept over the steamboat, thoroughly drenching everything. It was early Monday morning, the third, when the wheelsman reported difficulty in steering the ship. The gigantic waves had evidently damaged her rudder, and soon the *California* was unmanageable; she then fell an easy victim to the gale.

Water began to rise in her hold. Some of the crew threw overboard her cargo of pork and corn hoping to lighten the ship, while others manned the pumps. But it was of little use. At eleven that night, after a terrible day of battering, the *California* had been pushed about to a spot abreast of St. Helena Island in the Straits of Mackinac. It was here that a giant sea broke through the ship's gangway and a rush of water put out the fires under her boilers. That appeared to be a signal for the vessel to begin breaking up. The elements had won, and the *California* was doomed.

140

Captain Trowell went to the passengers' cabins and herded those unfortunates toward the lifeboats. Imagine their horror when they saw that the lifeboat gear was so battered that it was not possible to launch a boat, and that the mate and several of the crew had got away in the only lifeboat that could be put over the side. Soon the shivering passengers and captain were swept into the lake.

By dint of great strength and courage, young Captain Trowell struggled onto a section of the wreck which still held one of the unlaunched lifeboats. With the help of a sailor he managed to cut it free. Then they manned it and went about picking up the passengers and crew that were still in the water. Fate relented then and sent the lifeboat drifting alongside the steamer *A. Folsom* which had sought shelter behind St. Helena Island during the storm.

Statistics vary as to the number saved; some say thirteen persons lived to tell the tale; others, seventeen. As to the number that perished, reports vary from nine to fourteen. Captain Trowell was among those rescued. He continued to command Canadian passenger and freight ships upon the Great Lakes for many years, and lived to a fine old age.

The waterlogged hulk of the *California* drifted in the Straits of Mackinac to about a mile from shore at Mackinaw City. Her masts were gone and her cabins stood on end, as the sullen waters sent crashing waves for several days over the derelict.

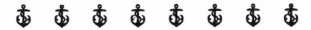

CHAPTER FIFTEEN

THE QUINTE FIRE

—*1889*—

Tucked away in the northeast section of Lake Ontario is the Bay of Quinte. It lies not far from where the mighty Saint Lawrence River begins. Bay of Quinte is a long and comparatively narrow body of water lying between Prince Edward County and Amherst Island on the south, and the Canadian mainland to the north. Its total length is about seventy-five miles. Several rivers flow into it from the north.

Today there are but small light-draft vessels plying its waters, mostly pleasure craft. But back in the year 1889 the Bay of Quinte had numerous passenger and freight steamers touching at several ports along its shores.

Probably the finest of these Bay of Quinte steamers was the *Quinte,* flagship of the Deseronto Navigation Company. She was built in 1886 entirely of wood and expressly for these waters. Her equipment was of the finest and she was the most popular excursion steamer on the bay. Her summer of 1889 had been singularly successful and by October of that year she was about to close the season, making only a light schedule of the regular ports of call. There was still considerable freight, mostly lumber, to be carried.

It was five-thirty in the afternoon of October twenty-third, when Captain Duncan B. Christie, then in his early thirties, sailed the *Quinte* out of Deseronto, Ontario, bound for Picton, Ontario, thirteen miles southward on the Bay of Quinte. Among his passengers were his mother and twelve year old brother. Other passengers included Colonel Strong, the United States Counsel stationed in Belleville, Ontario; and Miss Asulia Kellar, an officer in the Salvation Army stationed at Picton. The weather was chilly, and the passengers were at tea in the dining hall as the *Quinte* left Deseronto harbor.

When the steamer was about three miles from her dock, a deckhand burst into the engine room shouting that the ship was on fire. He had discovered the smoke and flames on the freight deck. Chief Engineer Thomas Short immediately started the pumps and notified the captain.

The flames, whipped by a fresh breeze, had such a start on the fire fighters that it was soon apparent that the *Quinte* was in a serious situation. Captain Christie ordered the ship headed for the nearest shore which was Grassy Point on the island of Prince Edward County. The mate and wheelsman felt the keel of the *Quinte* strike the beach before they left their posts in the pilot house. By that time the flames were all about them, but they managed to escape the inferno.

Captain Christie remained in the midst of the excitement and managed to land all his passengers on shore as quickly as his ship touched the Point. His mother and brother fell victims of the fire, despite the fact that in his efforts to rescue them, he severely burned his hands, permanently crippling them.

Two other persons aboard the *Quinte* perished, totaling four casualties in all. They were a cook's helper and her little son. Much credit for averting greater loss of life was due to the heroic efforts of the captain and his crew, as well as to Colonel Strong and the Salvation Army lass. Through their combined efforts there was no panic, although several were burned and a fireman was scalded.

The flaming *Quinte* could be seen from Deseronto, from where the ship had so recently sailed. Small boats hurried from there to the scene and a steam yacht, the *Ripple,* managed to save many lives. The survivors were returned to Deseronto aboard the *Ripple.*

Captain Christie continued in his marine career until his retirement, after which he engaged as pilot for the occasional oil tanker that traversed the Bay of Quinte. It is reported that the charred remains of the *Quinte* still rest in the shallow water on the edge of Grassy Point.

⚓ ⚓ ⚓ ⚓ ⚓ ⚓ ⚓ ⚓

NASHUA — W. H. GILCHER — OSTRICH
— 1892 —

Today it is somewhat difficult to fully appreciate the dire situation of the shipwrecked mariner of yester-years. Today within a few moments a shipmaster can communicate with capable help on shore, or afloat, or in the air, and receive quick assistance, be his trouble a total shipwreck or merely the infected finger of a deck hand. The captain of today has many instruments to aid and guide him in his responsibilities of navigating a vessel. A direction finder will tell him his exact location on the Great Lakes, regardless of daylight or dark, rain, snow, or fog. Sounding instruments will tell him how deep the water is under his ship. The radar will allow him to look all around for many miles, no matter how thick the weather may be. And his telephone is almost as reliable as its counterpart on shore, and is equal in scope.

Picture then the vulnerable position of the skippers of years gone by, years when there were few safety instruments for them to use in their work. Nor were their ships the sturdy vessels of today. The scientist and the shipbuilder have done much throughout the years for the sailor of today.

Captain Decatur (Dick) Millen commanded the one hundred thirty-four foot propeller steamer *Nashua* in 1890, which he and one or two other men had purchased from a passenger line going out of business and had refitted her for the lumber trade on the Great Lakes. Up to that time she had sailed for twenty-two seasons, but her wooden hull was still considered in good condition. At one time sails had augmented her steam power, but these were subsequently abandoned.

Captain Millen came from a prominent lake sailing family and was regarded as a competent and fearless shipmaster. He had sailed through many storms while other more cautious men had sought shelter.

During the last few days of September, 1892, the *Nashua* lay peacefully loading lumber at a dock in a Georgian Bay port. This was a slow job, and the fifteen people comprising the ship's company, including the wives of the captain and the steward, enjoyed going ashore in the quaint Canadian port while the cargo was being placed aboard.

It was early October when the loading was completed and the *Nashua* was ready to sail. Her hold was filled and her deck was piled high with the pungent fresh-cut lumber. Heavy chains held the deck load down to prevent it from sliding. Captain Millen, stand-

146

ing on the bridge, ordered the lines cast off; the engines began to turn. The *Nashua* was underway, bound for Toledo, Ohio. The course was set for Flowerpot Island Light, around which the ship must sail before she turned into large Lake Huron. The weather was ideal for autumn, clear and crisp, with chilly nights. The keeper of the light on Flowerpot Island watched the *Nashua* steam past until only a thin line of her smoke was visible on the horizon, as she headed toward Lake Huron.

The next man to see the *Nashua* was the captain of the tug *Howard,* then eight miles off Bayfield, Ontario, on Lake Huron. The *Nashua* was then floating on the lake, bottom side up, with the boilers and engine gone, and no sign of life about the wreck! This he reported when he docked at Harbor Beach, Michigan, (then known as Sand Beach) on October seventh. The *Nashua* had encountered a terrific storm and had lost. Not a soul survived to tell what had happened aboard the steamer out there on deep Lake Huron early that fall.

Lake men had feared the worst for the *Nashua* when she was unreported and long overdue at Port Huron. The storm had struck Lake Huron right along the path of the unlucky steamboat. Word from the *Howard* confirmed their fears.

Next word of the wreck came from the schooner *Ontario* which put into Goderich, Canada. She reported passing through great quantities of wreckage floating in the lake some twelve miles off that port. The wind was off the lake, so a volunteer beach patrol was organized and a close watch was kept along the Canadian shore for survivors and signs of jetsam or flotsam.

By the next day, Saturday, October eighth, all hope for the safety of the persons aboard the *Nashua* was definitely abandoned. Nothing came ashore all that day. Life could not be sustained very long on that tempestuous water; exposure and exhaustion must be reckoned with.

On Monday, October tenth, men patrolling the beach reported the hulk of the *Nashua* washing ashore three miles south of Bayfield. Her starboard side, from fifty feet aft of amidships, was completely carried away. It was supposed that the boilers broke loose from their fastenings and, as the ship pitched, they crashed through the side, leaving a great opening. Large quantities of loose wreckage also drifted ashore that day; among the debris were four life jackets with the name of the ship stencilled on them. The following day the body of the wife of the steward floated ashore three miles south of Goderich.

It was surmised that the ill-fated lumber laden freighter had met her doom by capsizing or foundering during the height of the storm on October fourth, 1892, somewhere on Lake Huron, probably off Bayfield or Goderich. Without any means of communicating his plight to the shore or other ships, Captain Millen had to face the situation alone and as best he could. What occurred will, of course, never be known.

The name of the ship *Nashua* was added to that long list of Great Lakes ships to sail away, never to make port. Lake Huron still retains the mystery.

Shipping circles in the lake ports were still discussing the sad fate of the *Nashua,* when not quite a month later they received another and even greater shock. Newspapers throughout the country came out with startling headlines on Wednesday, November second, 1892, "SHIP BELIEVED FOUNDERED! FEARED ALL ON BOARD ARE LOST! BIG LAKE FREIGHTER MISSING!"

The steel bulk freighter *W. H. Gilcher* was long overdue at Milwaukee. She had a cargo of coal loaded at Buffalo, and was last seen as she steamed westward through the Straits of Mackinac at two-twenty on Friday afternoon, October twenty-eighth. Strong winds were blowing, and many smaller vessels were seeking shelter. The *W. H. Gilcher* was a new ship, having been launched at Cleveland in December, 1890. She had therefore only one whole season of sailing to her credit, and so was considered entirely staunch and seaworthy.

Several outstanding facts were the boast of the *W. H. Gilcher*. She was the largest ship ever built in Cleveland, being three hundred eighteen feet over-all length, forty-one feet beam, and twenty-five feet molded depth; she had carried a record cargo of grain, one hundred and one thousand bushels, from Chicago to Buffalo; she was an exact duplicate of the steamer *Western Reserve* which foundered on Lake Superior some sixty days earlier.

Captain Leeds H. Weeks of Vermilion, Ohio, was in command of the *W. H. Gilcher,* and her chief engineer was Sidney B. Jones of Marine City, Michigan. All her crew of twenty were carefully chosen men, mostly from the captain's home town. The opportunity to work aboard the *Gilcher* was a prize berth for a sailor.

There is little to report on the *Gilcher* after she passed upbound through Mackinac Straits. The storm developed into a gale as early darkness settled over restless Lake Michigan. It is presumed that she continued on her way until at least nine that night. Wreckage picked up later by Captain Jenks of the steamer *White and Friant* bore this scribbled notation, "James Rider—9 PM." It was evidently scrawled hastily by a member of her crew, upon the handrail of the pilot house as the ship was lurching in the heavy seas. It is believed that the *Gilcher* would have been off the Manitou Islands at that time. The exact hour of her sinking will, of course, never be known.

Another doomed vessel, the wooden schooner

Ostrich, was also battling her way through the stormy lake off the Manitous that same night. Captain John McKay was both the master and the owner of the *Ostrich.* Aboard with him on that fateful trip was a crew of seven, including a woman cook. The schooner was light, and had left Milwaukee bound for Torch Lake to load hemlock lumber for Milwaukee.

In the whistling blackness of that night, it is thought that the *Gilcher* and the *Ostrich* may have collided, and that both vessels had sustained fatal wounds, sending them to the deep bottom of Lake Michigan. Wreckage found later indicated that the crew of the *Gilcher* had chopped away the fastenings of the lifeboats, denoting there was little time to launch them in an orderly manner.

The storm raged for several days. When at last it subsided, the more fortunate ships that were in shelter began to nose their way out onto the open lake. On Tuesday, the first of November, the steamer *Paunee* docked at Chicago and reported sighting wreckage north of North Manitou Island. The wreckage consisted of furniture, bedding, stanchions, and loose boards, but was not definitely identified.

By the next day, the captain of the steamer *St. Lawrence* reported sighting much wreckage near the Manitous, and shortly thereafter he passed the hull of a schooner floating bottom-side up, but he could not make out its name.

All hope for the crews and ships involved was given up by Friday, November fourth. Furniture and wreckage had come ashore on North Manitou Island with the name *W. H. Gilcher* painted on it. Nearby other wreckage bore the name of *Ostrich*. What happened to those two vessels on Lake Michigan to cause them to founder, is still an unsolved mystery.

October, however, was yet to wreak more havoc with lake shipping. On the very last day of the month, the schooner *Zach Chandler* foundered in a blow on Lake Superior, four miles east of Deer Park, Michigan. She carried one of her crew to his death. The *Zach Chandler* had a cargo of lumber from Ashland, Wisconsin, for the lower lakes, and was in tow of the steamer *John Mitchell* when her ill luck befell her.

♆ ♆ ♆ ♆ ♆ ♆ ♆ ♆

THE NEW AND THE OLD

— 1 8 9 5 —

Like a shot out of a gun a sleek ship of the air, a DC-4 plane, roared down the take-off at Willow Run, the airport for Detroit. It was very early in the morning, not much after midnight; the year was 1950; the month, June, the date the twenty-fourth; and the new day was a Saturday. Fifty-eight persons were aboard, including the crew of three.

The take-off was uneventful and the plane, after rising, squared away on its regular course for Minneapolis, Minnesota. Its lights were quickly lost to the sight of the few men on the field at Willow Run. That was the last seen of the airship.

Within a few short hours authorities were searching for the ship for many miles along the plane's course! It had completely vanished! The last reportedly heard from the pilot was a radio message requesting permission to come to a lower ceiling. This request was reported as denied the airman, as other ships were in the suggested area. No word of trouble, at least nothing much out of routine; not a hint of imminent disaster.

The searchers did not know where to look for the plane.

Only Lake Michigan knew the answer! The DC-4 had to cross that lake. An electrical storm sputtered over the waters in the path of the plane. What happened aboard that ship of the air will never be known. A day or so later Coast Guard craft searching the waters picked up a blanket with the name of the airline on it. Other bits of wreckage were retrieved from the waters. The plane had dived to the bottom of Lake Michigan! That much was now certain.

Historians of the air ways recorded the crash as our nation's worst commercial airline disaster to date. They estimated the plane went down some twelve to fifteen miles northwest of the city of Saint Joseph, Michigan.

Lake Michigan had done it again! And almost on the same spot! Fifty-five years previously it had swallowed up a crack lake liner and had left few crumbs. Today it is entirely possible that the wreckage of the ill-fated DC-4 and the battered hull of the passenger ship *Chicora* lie close together on the bottom of the lake. It is not likely that the lake will ever give up its secret.

The tale of the lost *Chicora* is one of the most often told of the shipwrecks of the Great Lakes and consequently is well remembered. It centers around an all important message, delivered just a few minutes too late, and the subsequent vanishing of an almost new steamship with its entire complement of human beings and its cargo.

The *Chicora* was busy doing what later on no ordinary passenger ship considered good business—running during the winter months. At the time of our story she was only three years old. Her stout wooden hull had been designed for use as a "winter ship" and was protected at the water line by heavy iron sheets intended to keep the ice from gouging at her wooden planking as she rammed her way into ice fields. Her dimensions were: length two hundred seventeen feet over all; breadth, forty feet over all; and depth of thirteen feet six inches. She was of the propeller type. Her cabins could accommodate two hundred overnight passengers. She was rated as a first class ship in every respect.

During the winter of 1895 she was operating between her home port of Saint Joseph, and Milwaukee, almost one hundred miles diagonally across Lake Michigan. While the passenger traffic was practically nothing at that time of year, there was always a goodly amount of freight to be carried, and the *Chicora* had just loaded a cargo of sacked flour at Milwaukee. She carried a crew of twenty-three, most of whom came from Saint Joseph and Benton Harbor, and had a passenger list of but one man. The crew generally referred to the run over to Milwaukee from Saint Joseph as outward bound, and returning was considered as coming home.

A stroke of luck befell the second mate of the *Chicora,* in that a temporary illness confined him to his bed. In his stead went the son of the master. Captain Edward Stines was proud of his son, Bennie, and was grooming him for the job of a captain aboard one of the future passenger ships of the Great Lakes. He may have hoped for a berth for him in the same fleet as the *Chicora,* that of the Graham & Morton Line. That business had great possibilities in those days and that particular company was destined to be one of the major passenger and freight lines on Lake Michigan.

January twenty-first, 1895, began like a spring day. Fishermen tended their nets and considered themselves lucky, but shook their heads wisely and remarked that such spells were but "weather-breeders" and that it would likely change very quickly for the worse. In the five o'clock pre-dawn darkness, Captain Stines was standing on the bridge of the *Chicora* ordering the lines cast off. They were sailing back home to the twin ports of Saint Joseph and Benton Harbor.

Across the lake in Saint Joseph, John Graham, partner owner of the *Chicora* was up and about early. He saw that the barometer was falling very fast; it touched twenty-eight, an exceptional low, which most surely forecast violent weather. Quickly he ordered the steamer *Petoskey,* then at a local dock, not to sail. He also sent a wire to Captain Stines aboard the *Chicora* in Milwaukee, to remain in that port. This message was received at the dock, but the *Chicora* had sailed. Although she was only three or four ship's lengths away, it was not possible to attract the attention of anyone aboard, and the steamer sailed away into the breaking dawn. The lake was mild and if all went well, the *Chicora* should reach Saint Joseph shortly after noon.

But the sturdy ship was doomed to be struck by a howling winter gale. It began only a couple of hours after she had left port. The wind, first from the southwest, shortly swung to the northwest. It increased quickly, and the thermometer began to fall. Snow squalls covered the choppy lake waters. It must have struck the men aboard the *Chicora* as a complete surprise and a quick challenge. The mercury plunged below the zero mark, and the snow came in a blinding swirl. The waves swelled into great walls of water and buffeted the steamer about like a chip.

The ship was never seen again. What actually occurred aboard will never be known. It is believed that the *Chicora* reached within ten miles or so from the eastern shore of Lake Michigan. Marine men speculate that she may have tried to turn about in the storm, fearful of being dashed against the lee shore, only to broach-to and capsize in the valley between mountains of water that swept the lake.

At Saint Joseph and Benton Harbor the word quickly spread that the crack *Chicora* was overdue. Men familiar with Lake Michigan offered various guesses as to when she might arrive. Some were more foreboding. Captain Bert Wilson had brought his ship, *Tramp,* into the harbor as the storm began. Maybe Captain Stines would do the same, they reasoned. Other lake ports were contacted for information as to the missing craft, but no word was forthcoming. All that night watchers ashore mounted the highest vantage points hoping for a glimpse of the lights of the *Chicora.* But only the blackness of the storm was to be seen.

The following day the vigil ended. Definite reports were received from along the shore between South Haven and Saugatuck that wreckage identified as coming from the missing steamer had been found. The *Chicora* was then given up for lost. There was no insurance on the vessel or cargo; winter shipping risks ran high.

Not much salvage floated in from the *Chicora.* Month after month passed and spring turned into summer, but never a body was recovered from the sunken steamer. Twelve years later fishermen brought up fragments of a chair believed to have been on the *Chicora.* Thirty fathoms is a lot of water.

Yes indeed, thirty fathoms is a lot of water! Under it on the dark and cold sandy floor of the lake lie the new DC-4 airplane and the old steamboat, possibly nearby—both examples of man's transportation endeavors. Shifting floor currents will most likely cover both ships with the sands of time and in so doing will completely bury the victims, and shroud the mysteries of those two disasterous disappearances in the two storms over a half century apart, out there on deep Lake Michigan. Yes, thirty fathoms is a lot of water!

CHAPTER EIGHTEEN

THE ELMA AND THE PICTURED ROCKS

—1895—

The shores of Lake Superior are rugged. Much of the northern, or Canadian, side of the big lake is still wilderness with neither road nor railroad. The southern shore, on the United States side, is more settled, though it also has many miles of untraveled shore line. The few roads that do reach the lake come mostly at right angles to it from the main highways some twenty or more miles to the south. In some sections the roadways skirt the shore, and the automobile tourist has an excellent opportunity to enjoy the rustic and scenic beauty of the land, the lake, and the sky.

One of Lake Superior's most picturesque spots, and possibly one of its greatest tourist attractions of today are the Pictured Rocks that stretch along the shore east of Munising, Michigan. These interesting rocks are a series of sandstone bluffs extending along the lake shore for about five miles, and rising, in most places, vertically from the water, without any beach at the base, to a height varying from fifty to nearly two hundred feet. There are two outstanding features about the Pictured Rocks. The first is the curious manner in

160

which the cliffs have been excavated and worn away by the action of the lake, which for centuries has dashed a pounding surf against their base.

The second feature is the unusual manner in which large portions of their surface have been colored by bands of brilliant hues. The prevailing tints consist of deep brown, yellow, and gray-burnt sienna and French gray predominating. There are also bright blues and greens, though less frequent. All the colors harmonize with one another which, when viewed in connection with the grandeur of the arched and caverned surfaces on which they are laid, and the deep and pure green of the water which heaves and swells at the base, and the rich foliage above, produces an effect truly wonderful.

Two United States geologists, J. W. Foster and J. D. Whitney, cruising along the south shore prior to 1851, were early admirers of the Pictured Rocks. One spot in particular entranced them. Later, when making their report to Congress, they had this to say about it, "The coast makes an abrupt turn to the eastward, and just after, at the point where the rocks break off and the friendly sand beach begins, is seen one of the grandest works of nature in her rock-built architecture. As we could not learn that it had received a distinctive appellation, we gave to it the name of Miners' Castle, from its singular resemblance to the turreted entrance and arched portal of some old castle. The Gothic gateway which may be recognized, is about seventy feet, while that of the main wall forming the background is about one hundred and forty."

Needless to say Miners' Castle stands today just as it did when the two geologists admired and named it. For a few autumnal days in 1895 this odd rock formation became the shelter for six shipwrecked lake sailors, and at its base a seventh was dashed to his death.

The wreck of the schooner-barge *Elma* is today a forgotten story of the Great Lakes. But in the oddity of the situation, and in the fortitude, strength, and the determination of the sailors to live, the tale ranks high.

The *Elma* was a twenty-two year old vessel at the time she was wrecked. She wasn't so very large, just one hundred sixty-five feet long, and thirty feet beam, with eleven feet draft, but when she slid down the builder's ways in 1873, at Marine City, Michigan, she was considered a big craft. At first she carried canvas on her tall masts and she sailed by the winds alone, but subsequently her rig was reduced and her masts were shortened. Though she could still hoist some sail with this reduced rig, her principal duties were to trail behind a steamboat in the capacity of a barge.

It was early Saturday, September twenty-eighth, 1895, when the wooden lumber steamer, *P. H. Birck-head*, with three barges, the *Commodore*, the *Chester B. Jones*, and the *Elma*, left Whitefish Point behind them. Great Lake Superior lay ahead. Whitefish Point was the last shelter until the ships would reach Grand Island, one hundred miles along the wild and rocky south shore. The little fleet of vessels, all of wood construction, moved very slowly. To a person standing on the land, watching their progress, it seemed that the ships hardly moved. One hundred miles was a long stretch for the *P. H. Birckhead* and her consorts. The now light vessels were to load lumber at a Lake Superior port and then carry it back down the lakes to Tonawanda, New York.

As the day wore on, a dangerous nor'wester set in. The wind increased steadily until it reached gale proportions. The lake surface was churned into huge rolling waves which crested into immense white caps. The *Birckhead* had considerable difficulty in making any headway, so great became the wind and seas. The steamer would wallow in the trough of each wave and be tossed about violently. The same treatment was accorded each of the three towbarges.

The captain of the *Birckhead* decided that it was safer to return to the shelter of Whitefish Point and await better weather. So late in the afternoon he swung the steamer around in a great half circle and headed back over the route he had just traveled, hoping to reach Whitefish Point.

But the strain of breasting the huge waves in making the turn proved too much for the towlines, and they parted. The vessels became widely separated. The

Birckhead was in much the same situation as a mother duck with her brood in the storm. She did her best to pick them up and to reorganize the tow, but this orderly arrangement was now entirely impossible. The gale was howling out of the northwest and darkness was not far off.

The steamer did manage to get a line to the schooner-barge *Elma,* but that was the best she could do. Sensing this, the captain of the *Commodore* decided to attempt to sail his vessel by wind alone back to Whitefish Point and to Sault Ste. Marie, if possible. Fortune favored the plucky skipper; after a very strenuous trip he tied up in the safety of the Saint Marys River.

The third barge, the *Chester B. Jones,* under the command of Captain Nelson, also hoisted sail and maneuvered to a spot one and one half miles off Whitefish Point. Fearing he might be blown ashore and wrecked, the skipper ordered the anchor run down, intending to ride out the storm where he stood. His position was still very much exposed, as he was not able to work his ship behind the point, and the *Jones* took a dreadful pounding as the gale bore down on her from the northwest and north.

Meanwhile the *Birckhead,* with the *Elma* in tow, had set out in the open lake, heading for the shelter of Grand Island. It was evidently the captain's intention to proceed on the original course, now that he had but one barge to haul. It gave him a somewhat more secure feeling to be underway and a safe distance off the land. He might be able to ride out the storm with his single tow, rather than try to return to Whitefish Point.

All Saturday night the *Birckhead* and the *Elma* plugged along. They managed to make headway despite the storm. Things went along fairly well the next day, and it began to look as if the two vessels might at last reach the long-sought shelter of Grand Island by late Sunday evening. Their hopes increased as ahead of them could be seen the low outline of the forest-clad island.

But the *Elma* was doomed never to reach shelter. Two unfortunate things happened: first, the towline between the *Elma* and the *Birckhead* again parted; and second, the barge's steering apparatus broke. The *Elma* was then at the mercy of the gale, which increased in fury. The *Birckhead,* herself having trouble to stay afloat, reluctantly left the *Elma* and proceeded alone toward Grand Island.

In the heaving seas the *Elma* rolled and pitched unmercifully. Her masts and rigging were carried away by the storm. With a tremendous crash, heard even above the gale, the spars hit the water. Every sea swept over her. The crew worked furiously at the pumps trying to relieve her of the water that was gaining in the hold, but it was of no use.

On Sunday afternoon, September twenty-ninth, the helpless schooner-barge struck a rock about one hundred feet from shore. She was almost waterlogged at the time. The *Elma* grounded hard upon the rock and never moved afterwards. Directly ahead of her on the rocky shore stood Miners' Castle!

The situation of the schooner-barge was very dangerous for the men aboard her. She might break up at any moment. The water was deep around the rock upon which the *Elma* struck. Giant seas were still sweeping over the wreck. The men realized that they must get off the *Elma* as quickly as possible. But the one hundred feet between them and Miners' Castle was a surging maelstrom, and the rocks rose perpendicularly out of the water.

One of the sailors, George M. Johnson, decided to attempt to make the crossing in the yawl-boat. The boat, with Johnson alone in it, was launched with great difficulty on the leeward side of the *Elma*. Johnson tied lines to the yawl and the men on the wreck payed out the ropes as he battled the seas toward Miners' Castle. It was hoped that he would be able to make the lines fast on shore, so that the others marooned aboard the wreck could then use them as safety ropes or life lines to help them gain access to the rocky shore.

The wind being off the water, helped the yawl bearing Johnson to quickly cover the distance to the shore. Then the same strong wind dashed his craft against the rocky cliff of Miners' Castle. In a matter of moments the yawl was beaten to pieces and the lines were tangled and lost in the water. Johnson however managed to cling to the various small projections of outcropping rock and using these as a ladder, he cautiously climbed upward out of the reach of angry Lake Superior. He slowly continued his laborious climb until he reached one of the larger openings in the rocks. Dragging himself into this haven he was secure for the moment.

For the men still aboard the wreck it was very disheartening. Finally another sailor, Rudolph Yack, offered to swim ashore with lines tied about his body. So equipped, he plunged into the lake and was soon carried shoreward. Upon reaching the rocky cliff Yack was unable to grasp anything to hang on to. He was beaten against the rocks and soon gave up and died. The crew aboard the *Elma* tried to retrieve his body by hauling in on the ropes fastened to him, but the lines parted as they attempted to lift his body out of the water. He was never seen again.

The weary and discouraged storm-tossed crew then tried to float lines ashore to Johnson, who climbed down to the water's edge to grab them. Just as darkness settled he managed to catch hold of one of them and held on to it as he climbed back to his refuge higher in the cliff. It was too dark to continue the rescue work and all attempts were abandoned until daylight. Johnson sat all that night with the line tied about him, not knowing the intentions of those on the wreck.

As the first rays of daylight spread over Lake Superior, the crew began to complete their rescues. Each man in his turn tied the line to shore about his body, and also tied another line about himself which was left dragging from the wreck, the sailors holding fast to it. By clever and lucky manipulating of these lines each crew member was hauled up the rocky cliff to the opening haven and safety. Captain Thurston's three year old son was saved by drawing the line taut and rigging a "traveler" on it, by which the youngster was brought, high and dry, from the *Elma* to the shore haven. Thoughtful crew members managed to take with them two loaves of bread and a few blankets. This was all they had to sustain life, for how long they knew not.

Above the opening the men had first reached, they found a larger and better protected opening. Again they climbed higher, and soon all hands were temporarily safe in the larger haven. Here they built a fire of some logs that had somehow found their way into the opening. Thus in their stony refuge they made themselves as comfortable as possible until something else might turn up. The bread was apportioned, and it was soon eaten. The men suffered greatly from exposure, fatigue and the cold.

By Tuesday morning, October first, the storm had abated. The weary men decided to attempt to build a raft from the wreckage floating in the lake at the base of their cliff. With this raft they planned to return to the *Elma,* which was all but gone, and try to obtain

168

some food. It was a very hazardous and discouraging task, but the men were in a desperate plight. They gathered together the most suitable planks from the debris and were in the process of binding them together with ropes, when one of their number shouted that a boat was coming their way.

A lighthouse keeper was rowing his boat directly toward them. He had sighted smoke from their fire some days earlier, and later he saw the wrecked schooner-barge. As soon as the lake had quieted sufficiently he came out to them. The steamer *Birckhead* lay just around a corner of jutting rocks, just out of sight of the survivors. The lighthouse keeper ferried the men out to the ship and shortly they were enroute to Sault Ste. Marie.

Meanwhile, the crew of the *Chester B. Jones* had had another thrilling rescue. After she had dropped anchor off Whitefish Point the wind had shifted and, as she was in an exposed position, the waves beat against her terrifically, and it was feared she might break up under the heavy pounding.

The life-saving crew at Whitefish Point, augmented by another crew which came to assist, had watched the *Jones* through their glasses as she tossed in the gale, and they were standing by in the event the crew decided to attempt to come ashore. But the seas were too great for either the life-saving men or the schooner-barge's crew to attempt to launch a boat.

169

SHIPWRECKS OF THE LAKES

By Monday night the life-savers decided to make a break for the ship. After a hazardous trip in which their boats capsized several times, the government men reached the side of the *Jones*. The crew of the *Jones* decided to abandon their vessel, after making certain that she was as well anchored as possible. It was a desperate struggle against the wind and waves to get the ship's crew on shore, but the life-savers accomplished this daring feat. Not a man of the *Jones* was lost, although Captain Nelson came very near being drowned. The survivors acclaimed the United States Life Saving Service for its daring and heroic men, and were loud in their praises.

As the storm subsided, the tug *Boynton* started out from Sault Ste. Marie in search of the missing *Chester B. Jones*. She found her riding at anchor just where the crew had abandoned her. They got a line aboard her and brought her into port, not too much the worse for her thrilling experiences out on raging Lake Superior during a severe northwester.

⚓ ⚓ ⚓ ⚓ ⚓ ⚓ ⚓ ⚓

CHAPTER NINETEEN

THE C. J. KERSHAW, MOONLIGHT, AND HENRY A. KENT
— 1 8 9 5 —

It was four o'clock in the morning of Sunday, September twenty-ninth, 1895. The darkness was intense. A howling gale was blowing the low-hanging clouds over Lake Superior until they seemed to touch the water. That same gale had whipped the big lake into a frenzy.

Such was the scene as the steamer *C. J. Kershaw* was trying to make the port of Marquette, on the upper peninsula of Michigan. Behind the *C. J. Kershaw* were two schooners, the *Moonlight* and the *Henry A. Kent,* which the steamer had in tow. They had sailed together from the lower lakes without cargo, with orders to load iron ore at Marquette and return with it to the lower lakes. Their upbound destination was but four miles distant. The three vessels were at the moment off the mouth of the Chocolay River, which flows from the south and empties into Lake Superior.

A government Bulletin has this to say about Marquette Harbor: (located) "at the north end of Marquette Bay and, by steamer track, about 143 miles from the head of St. Marys River, and about 40 miles from Grand Island, the nearest safe natural shelter." It also says, "From Shot Point to Marquette, about 10 miles, is generally deep-to, with sandy beach. In this stretch, just southeast of Marquette, there are detached rocks extending 800 feet in a WNW and ESE direction; the easterly end nearly awash . . . and the exposed westerly about 4,100 feet from the mouth of Chocolay River. There are two detached rocks lying 1,400 feet ENE and 1,100 feet ESE from Marquette Light, with a rock nearly awash about 600 feet east of the light; a very shallow bank connects the southerly rock with the main shore, and extends about 600 feet to the eastward beyond it."

In the wildness of the storm and the blackness of the night, the steamer *C. J. Kershaw* struck hard upon this rocky reef, about a mile from shore. A steam pipe is reported to have burst and put the ship out of control.

The two schooners, *Moonlight* and *Henry A. Kent,* broke loose from their towing ship, and completely out of control, were sent scudding before the storm and were dashed high on the sandy beach at the mouth of the Chocolay River, just four miles east of their destination, Marquette.

As daylight came that Sunday morning, the three ships presented a sorry sight. The great wooden hulls of the *Moonlight* and the *Kent* loomed large on the low flat sandy beach. Each vessel was about two hundred

172

feet in length, thirty-five feet beam, and fourteen feet depth. Each carried three tall masts. The waves pounded them and drove each vessel broadside to the shore. They remained upright, as the sand quickly filled in around their curved hulls. Though sadly out of their element, the schooners were quite safe from the storm.

But the ill-fated steamer *C. J. Kershaw* stranded out on Chocolay Reef was indeed a pitiful sight. The severe pounding of the storm caused the ship to rise and fall with terrific force, each time striking her keel on the treacherous rocky reef. The forward half of the steamer broke away and was lost in the deep water surrounding the rocks.

The after half of the *Kershaw* remained fast on the reef; since the hold was filled with water she quit pounding herself to pieces. The crew managed to escape the foundering of the forward half by hurrying to the boiler house aft. Their safety was in grave question, as the remaining half of the steamer might suddenly slip off the reef and also go down in the deep water. A furious sea still beat against the wreck. The men were for the moment trapped.

Then occurred one of those heroic rescues performed by the United States Life-Saving Service— rescues that dot the history of Great Lakes shipping like jewels in a crown. The *Kershaw* had been on the reef about one hour when the life-saving crew pulled their heavy rescue boat alongside. They took off nine of the crew—all that they could handle. It had not been an easy task to launch the rescue boat in the raging waters, nor to breast the huge combers that swept between the shore and the stranded steamer, nor to avoid the hidden treacherous rocks. The wind was biting cold, and the men were thoroughly drenched, but they did reach the shore with their precious cargo of shivering survivors.

There were still four men left on the *Kershaw* to be removed. The weary life-savers started back to the wreck. When they were a short distance from shore, their boat capsized and dumped the unfortunate men into the cold waters of Lake Superior. It was a narrow escape from death for each of them, but they did manage to reach the shore. Half of their number were so battered and exhausted that they were forced to quit the rescue work. One of them nearly died. Their boat was broken badly with a large hole in the bow rendering it unfit for further service.

Another boat was brought out from the life-saving station and made ready for the trip out to the wrecked *Kershaw*. This time local men volunteered to man the boat along with whatever regular personnel were still able. The boat left the shore and headed for the wreck. It was two o'clock in the afternoon before they reached the *Kershaw*. They found the four remaining men of the steamer's crew in the yawl-boat, which they had launched and had attached to the wreck by a stout line. Evidently the men feared that the wreck might slip below the waves and carry them with it, so they repaired with great difficulty and risk to their yawl. Even in the small boat life was none too secure; the men were drenched and exhausted. They welcomed the sight of the life-saving crew and their volunteer helpers. They all reached land safely.

Word of the triple shipwrecks quickly spread through the Iron Range towns of Marquette, Negaunee, Ishpeming and smaller villages, and for many days Chocolay Beach was crowded with sightseers and souvenir hunters.

The after end of the *Kershaw* remained on Chocolay Reef for several days. Wreckers believed her engines might be salvaged, but nothing was attempted on this project. However, work was started on salvaging the two schooners, *Moonlight* and *Kent,* and an endeavor to haul them both back into the water got under way soon after they grounded.

One wrecking concern spent considerable money and time on the project. As success was in sight, another northwest storm hit the Chocolay River district and all their efforts were completely washed out. Discouraged, they left the job, but subsequently another wrecker succeeded in getting both of the heavy schooners back into the water.

The same northwester that ruined the first salvaging attempt also ruined what was left of the *Kershaw* out on the reef. In a blinding snowstorm and a howling

175

gale the wrecked half of the steamer was dislodged and it slipped off the rocks and sank into the deep water that surrounds the reef. The steamer *C. J. Kershaw* was no more.

After the schooners *Moonlight* and *Henry A. Kent* were successfully refloated, they returned to the shipping lanes they had previously traversed and resumed their former trading. The *Henry A. Kent,* twenty-two years old at the time of her Chocolay wreck, ended her days in Lake Superior, two years later, on September eighteenth, 1897, when she foundered; this time she was lost forever. Her crew was saved.

The *Moonlight,* one year younger than the *Kent,* lasted six years after her Chocolay experience. She too, ended her days in Lake Superior, twelve miles off Michigan Island in the Apostle Group, on September thirteenth, 1903. She foundered with a heavy cargo of iron ore in her hold. Her crew were rescued by the steamer *Volunteer.*

Her sinking marked the end of a notable old Great Lakes windjammer. She was one of the most widely known ships of her day on the lakes. Her career began in 1874, when she slid down the builder's ways in Milwaukee, Wisconsin. She promptly took many of the top honors in record speed runs between Great Lakes ports. When her tall masts and lofty spars were fully set with billowing sails, she presented a beautiful picture as she swept across the blue lake waters.

176

C. J. KERSHAW, MOONLIGHT, HENRY A. KENT

The height of her popularity came in the mid 1880's, when she challenged the schooner *Porter* to a race. The course to be run was a long one, from Buffalo to Milwaukee, eight hundred and twenty-eight miles along the Great Lakes lanes. Captain Orv Green sailed the *Porter* and Captain Dennis Sullivan, the *Moonlight*. All the cities along the race course learned of the match and took a sporting interest in the schooner contest, though, of course, the speeding ships could not be seen except from only a few of the ports.

All went well and the two vessels stayed fairly close together on the long run up Lake Erie and Lake Huron. But after they rounded Old Mackinac Point and entered Lake Michigan their troubles really began. A tricky squall hit the racing windjammers, suddenly and fiercely. Captain Green kept sail on his vessel and steered a straight course for Milwaukee. Captain Sullivan took a more cautious turn. He cut down his canvas and took shelter under the high bluffs off Port Washington until the blow eased. Then, all in good order, he proceeded on to Milwaukee.

Not seeing the *Porter* on the lake, he believed that he had outdistanced her; that possibly she was in shelter somewhere behind him. Imagine his astonishment upon arriving in Milwaukee to find the *Porter* at a dock! How she had changed! All her rigging, sails and gear, masts, spars and all were missing. The storm had cleaned her of everything. Had it not been that the harbor tugs at Milwaukee were on the lookout for the

177

racers, the *Porter* might never have been able to reach her destination.

Anyhow, the old-timers state that, as soon as the two contesting skippers shook hands on the dock after the race, they held a large joint celebration. The argument still continues as to which schooner really won the race.

⚓ ⚓ ⚓ ⚓ ⚓ ⚓ ⚓ ⚓

Chapter Twenty

THE IDAHO FOUNDERS

— 1 8 9 7 —

The year 1897 was singularly easy on major disasters on the Great Lakes. The weather that year was
more kind to lake shipping. Only one steamer was
struck down entirely; that unfortunate ship was the
tired old propeller *Idaho*. All the men of the lakes knew
the Idaho. They termed her a "line boat," which meant
that she carried package freight for the railroad lines.
She had been in that trade for thirty-four years, serving
the larger ports of the lakes from Buffalo to Duluth and
Chicago, becoming a very familiar sight along the lake
lanes. Captain E. M. Peck had built her of stout wooden
timbers in Cleveland early in the year 1863. She was
always a trim ship for all of her two hundred and twenty
feet and, from available old photographs and records,
was always painted a dazzling white.

A glance at her in her early days is very interesting.
A popular photograph shows her with the huge longi-
tudinal arches on each side, traditional with the wooden
ships of her day. The crest of the heavy wooden arches
tops the ship's deck houses. The arches were built into
the ship to strengthen the hull lengthwise to withstand

the terrific stress and strain during heavy weather. They were designed to prevent the ship from breaking in two, or even a milder form of breaking called "hogging" in which the midship section would rise and the ends lower. Such a ship was said to have "broken her back."

The *Idaho* also boasted of the quaint old octagonal pilot house, with its ornate woodwork and embellished windows and a huge carved golden eagle mounted at the peak of the roof. There was a small platform or bridge, just aft of the eagle where the captain could stand in the open, exposed to the weather, and have an unobstructed view to direct the navigation of his craft. An unusually tall smokestack was located about three quarters of the way aft. In those days the high stacks helped accomplish what forced draft does with the shorter stacks of today.

But the crowning glory of the *Idaho* was her towering foremast—in fact it was her only mast. In her early days she carried a large sail hung from a yard about one half the way to the top of the mast. Just above the point where the yard was fastened was a sort of crow's nest barely large enough for a man to stand in and with no protection from the weather. It was necessary for the lookout to cling to the mast to retain his position in the crow's nest. Just above the crow's nest another and lighter mast was stepped, which almost doubled the height of the lower mast. A careful estimate would place the truck, or top of the mast at about one hundred feet from the main deck of the steamer. It towered three times the height of her stack. An unusually high mast! This mast with its great height played an important part later in this tale. An immense pennant flew from the masthead carrying in five-foot letters the name *Idaho*. From lesser staffs on the hurricane deck flew four large streamers with the names of the ports to which the ship traded. A large jack flew at her bow and a much larger American flag flew at her stern. The *Idaho* was well supplied with flags and banners, but, all in all, it somehow seemed to suit her.

But came the day when age caught up with the *Idaho*. Her wooden body was beginning to wear out and her engine and boilers, though always kept in excellent repair, began to show the inevitable results of time. Then too, newer ships were coming out which were safer because of their steel construction, and were more economical to operate. So the ancient *Idaho* was relieved of her regular duties and for several seasons she lay idle at a dock in Buffalo. However, she was not abandoned but was held in readiness to go out in case of a rush of business or the breakdown of newer steamers of the line.

During the summer of 1897, in anticipation of possible future sailings, the owners decided to have the *Idaho* overhauled. At the completion of this work she was given a temporary assignment as flagship during the Grand Army of the Republic encampment at Buffalo in August. After that she went back again on the lakes run in the package freight trade under the capable command of forty-one year old Captain Alexander Gillies, a well-known and well-respected master among the lake marine men.

A cargo destined for Milwaukee, Wisconsin, was loaded into the *Idaho* at Buffalo. It is reported to have consisted largely of Christmas toys and holiday supplies. Early Friday night, November fifth, the *Idaho* steamed quietly out of Buffalo Harbor and onto Lake Erie. The course was set, generally in a west-southwest direction. Sixty-one miles along that track would put the old *Idaho* directly off Long Point, Ontario.

Long Point is exactly what its name implies. It is a long point of land that juts from the Canadian shore out into Lake Erie for some twenty miles. All ships navigating the eastern end of Lake Erie must pass Long Point, and the Canadian Goverment maintains a lighthouse on the tip of the point to help mariners on their way. To the northward it forms a large bay, called Long Point Bay, which makes a haven of refuge for ships caught out on the lake in heavy weather, especially when it blows from the west or southwest. Upbound ships find it a sheltered spot even to the present time. But outside on its exposed coast it is a dangerous menace to shipping and has oft times been referred to as the "Graveyard of Lake Erie."

As the *Idaho* cleared the harbor lights of Buffalo, the breeze freshened and almost before the crew realized it, their ship was fighting a sizzling sou'wester. One of those dreaded November gales was in the making and the old *Idaho* was headed directly into it. The captain and the mate discussed their situation and neither officer was fearful. The *Idaho* could fight her way along, though naturally her speed would be greatly reduced. No great danger was forseen, only an uncomfortable run.

And so the old veteran steamboat ploughed ahead. The waves at times would leap over her bows and slosh down her decks, but still she continued slowly onward. At last the light on Long Point appeared off the starboard bow. Many times it was lost sight of in the gale, but it was possible for the storm-tossed sailors to know their position. Another consultation between captain and mate took place. Their subject this time was whether or not to seek the shelter of Long Point. It was decided to push onward.

In almost every shipwreck there comes the moment of a great decision; often, as in the case of the *Idaho*, the seriousness of the decision is not fully realized. It is made without the knowledge of what is to follow. And so the *Idaho* continued to buck the gale, her hardy officers confident that their vessel could withstand the pounding she was taking. Her forward speed was hardly anything, so great was the force of the wind and seas. But she did progress very slowly. Long Point was passed abreast and gradually slid off to starboard quarter.

When she had left the light about twelve miles

astern, trouble began aboard the *Idaho*. She was taking water in her hull and it was rising fast. Something under the water line had sprung a leak in the pounding. Captain Gillies ordered Chief Engineer William Clancy to start the pumps. For a short time that helped, but soon the water began coming in faster than the pumps could expel it. Then one of the pumps broke down.

The storm grew worse and the ship tossed about so violently that the crew had great difficulty in going about their urgent duties. A bucket brigade was formed and buckets of water were handed from man to man and thrown back into the lake. This was wasted energy as the incoming water gained steadily. Soon it bubbled around the fire boxes under the boilers. Then with a great hissing noise it drowned out the fires.

This left the *Idaho* without power to combat the fury of the elements and in a very short time the ship was doomed. Her anchors were hove out in the hope of bringing her head into the wind so that she might possibly ride out the storm. But nothing the captain or crew could do would keep their ship afloat. Lake Erie was taking over quickly.

Sensing disaster as the *Idaho* gave a sudden lurch, the men in the engine room rushed for the open deck, preferring it to being trapped below. So frantic were they that they trampled one of their comrades in the narrow passageway to the deck. He was the first of the crew to die.

THE IDAHO FOUNDERS

Midnight had passed and, as the early morning hours of Saturday wore on, the stricken men of the *Idaho* saw a watery death staring them in the face. At three that morning the ship succumbed. The water had risen so high in her hold that she lost all buoyancy. A giant wave lifted her bow high in the air, and the water in her hold rushed toward her stern. The weight of it caused her to settle beneath the waves, stern first. Gradually the whole ship slipped away and the stormy lake waters closed over the entire vessel. Somehow, somewhere, the crew perished, nineteen of the twenty-one.

Except for the remaining two men the *Idaho* would have been another of the vanished fleet of the Great Lakes. But lady luck favored these two. William Gill, a deck hand, and Louis LaForce, Jr., the second mate, found themselves close to the mast when the steamer took her final plunge. Gill had just witnessed the sickening sight of Captain Gillies being swept from the hurricane deck by a giant wave. Both the deck hand and the mate made a grab for the mast and quickly climbed upward as the ship went down. The tall mast slowly described large circles in the air as the vessel sank, then as she settled on the bottom she rolled from port to starboard and the two men were almost tossed from their perch. Finally, the *Idaho* quit the side rolling and the mast became more steady.

The storm continued in all its rage. Rain was mixed with flying spray. Then the rain turned to hail, and it pelted the shipwrecked sailors clinging to the mast. Fortunately for them the mast was tall. By climbing into the crow's nest, they were some twenty-five feet above the water. They did have some footing, but nothing except the mast itself to cling to. It was a most precarious situation. Silently the men waited while the wind howled and the waves lashed about under them. They were at least alive. Neither knew what had happened to the rest of the crew. They well knew that no life boat could stand up in that sea, although they recalled that the boats had been made ready for a quick launching before the ship went down. In the blackness of the night they could see nothing about them. They just held fast to their mast, determined to hold on until daylight.

Finally Saturday dawned and the men were at last able to look about them. What they saw was a sorry sight indeed—storm-tossed Lake Erie in its ugliest mood. Nothing else, no sail or smoke from another ship. Early in the morning they were thrilled at the sight of a freighter coming some distance off. But she sailed on, never altering her course. Evidently her officers did not see the poor souls clinging to the lone mast.

As the ship disappeared in the distance LaForce, who was above Gill on the mast, temporarily lost his reason over the disappointment. In his despair he shouted wildly, and beat his head against the mast. He threatened to jump and to push Gill into the water. Then, as Gill reasoned with him, he calmed down and began to sing. As he became more rational, he began to pray. By now their clothing was encased in ice and the two men were in a desperate plight. But they continued to clutch the mast and pray. Their arms became paralyzed in that position. It was fast becoming only a question of how much longer each one could hold his position.

Shortly after noon their prayers were answered. By this time their senses were becoming dulled, but their faces lighted up as out over the water they saw a large steel freighter bearing directly on them. The seas were still running tremendously high, and the oncoming ship rolled and pitched. The men on the mast could see her bottom some distance back from the bow as she shook off each huge wave. But she continued to come directly toward them! Their arms were now too stiff to even wave at the ship; they could only stare and hope. As she neared the mast, the survivors were able to spell out the name on her bows, *Mariposa*.

In the pilot house of the rescue steamer stood Captain Frank Root directing the wheelsman to steer for the men on the spar. The *Mariposa's* first mate, Myron Chamberlain, had spied the two forms clinging to the mast sticking up out of the water, and had promptly reported it to Captain Root. The *Mariposa* was bound from Chicago to Buffalo with a cargo of oats, but upon sighting them, the captain immediately altered his course and headed for the survivors.

What followed is considered by many lake men to

be one of the outstanding accomplishments of ship handling on the Great Lakes. The rescue freighter was at the time one of the largest on the lakes. It was a mighty big problem to bring her up to the tiny pin point of the mast sticking out of the water, as the heavy seas rolled her about, and still not hit it and crack it off, sending the two survivors to most certain death in the water. Captain Root came up on the men very carefully. An attempt to launch a boat failed and the small boat was wrecked. That method of rescue was promptly ruled out.

There was nothing else left to do but bring the big *Mariposa* right up to the spar and then remove the men, Captain Root figured. So he proceeded to do just that. The first time he tried, the big ship fell away from the mast, and so another attempt was made. The big freighter was turned around in a large circle and headed back once more to the survivors. This time she came much closer, but still too far off to do any good. La-Force and Gill were too numb now to even catch a line that might be thrown to them. The men on the *Mariposa* knew this.

"Don't give up. We'll get you off soon," shouted a man with a loud voice from the deck of the steel freighter.

To the men on the mast it seemed an eternity. Actual rescue was still going to be very difficult. Each attempt brought the *Mariposa* nearer. On the third trial

Captain Root brought her right up to the mast. His crew were lining the deck rail awaiting their chance to snatch the ice-encrusted men off their spar.

It was all over quickly. Eager hands pulled LaForce and Gill away from the mast and brought them aboard the *Mariposa*. It was necessary to force their arms from the mast, the ice and cold had fastened them so securely. Then the rescue ship headed for Buffalo, leaving behind her a pitifully small stick standing upright in the still raging lake. That stick marked the grave of the old propeller *Idaho*.

It was around midnight when the *Mariposa* arrived in Buffalo. LaForce and Gill were alive and doing as well as could be expected. The news of the loss of the *Idaho* and her nineteen men was announced to the shocked world. Statisticians have written her off as the most serious disaster of 1897 on the Great Lakes, from the point of lives and dollars lost. The monetary loss ran something like fifteen thousand dollars for the old *Idaho*, but her cargo ran up to one hundred thousand dollars.

Marine-minded Buffalo, home port of most of the men lost on the *Idaho*, hailed the rescue as a top act of bravery. This idea quickly spread over the lake cities, and before he realized it, Captain Root and his crew were heroes. All the world loves a daring rescue.

As soon as the survivors were able, they were invited to appear on a theater stage in Buffalo, along with

Captain Root. Here they were all roundly cheered, and an appreciative city bestowed its honors upon the rescue captain and the two hardy survivors. Later, Captain Root was presented with a gold watch by the Minnesota Steamship Company, owners of the *Mariposa*. A letter of commendation from the company president instructed Captain Root to reward his first mate and chief engineer with an extra month's salary, and each of the rest of the crew with one half month's pay. Lake ship owners also have hearts and a deep respect for a job well done.

⚓ ⚓ ⚓ ⚓ ⚓ ⚓ ⚓ ⚓

CHAPTER TWENTY-ONE

THE WRECK OF THE JOHN B. LYON

— *1900* —

The Great Lakes freighter *John B. Lyon* was a hard working bulk carrier. She was built of wood throughout, and made her debut into the cold clear waters in 1881 at the old Quale shipyards at Cleveland. Sailors dubbed her "The Spider Boat" because of a web-like arrangement of stays that spread between her two smokestacks which were placed athwartships and located aft. In the center of this web she carried a large letter "G," the first letter of her owner's name, J. C. Gilchrist. She was a powerful steamer and, as was the practice of most freighters on the lakes in those days, she towed a barge. The records show the *John B. Lyon* was two hundred fifty-six feet in length, with thirty-nine feet beam, and depth of twenty feet.

The Twentieth Century was only nine months old, and the *Lyon* was nineteen years old, when she met her doom on wild Lake Erie. The exact date was September eleventh, 1900, and the approximate hour, two in the morning. In her foundering one reads of stark tragedy mixed with heroism, bad luck, poor judgment, and death.

191

The first word of the sinking of the *John B. Lyon* came from the exhausted lips of four survivors: two women, one the wife of the captain, the other the wife of the steward, and two men who were wheelsmen. Lashed to a mast and floating amid debris from the wreck, they all drifted ashore, a mile or two east of the town of North Girard, Pennsylvania. They had battled raging Lake Erie for fifteen hours and were near death when found. Later another of the crew, David Brown, second engineer, was found on the beach unconscious. These five were all that were saved; eleven were lost.

The *Lyon* had cleared Marquette, Michigan, with a full load of iron ore in her hold, and astern she towed the twenty-six year old barge, *F. A. Georger,* also laden with iron ore. The freighter and consort had an uneventful run down the lakes and through the rivers into Lake Erie.

The barge was scheduled for unloading at a dock in Ashtabula, Ohio, and the *Lyon* herself was to be unloaded in Cleveland. Captain A. H. Singhas of Marine City, Michigan, was in command of the freighter. He guided his vessels into Ashtabula without incident, dropped the barge there, and proceeded out onto Lake Erie, back toward Cleveland, somewhat retracing his course.

Chief Engineer Charles Willous, of Cleveland, complained to the captain of the poor quality of coal they were using under the boilers. Captain Singhas put into

THE WRECK OF THE JOHN B. LYON

Fairport, Ohio, enroute to Cleveland to replenish his supply of coal, hoping to improve its quality. Upon his reaching a fuel dock in Fairport he learned that no coal to suit his requirements would be available for several days, but that some was available at Erie, Pennsylvania.

So the weary captain decided to sail back east to Erie, some seventy miles, for the coal, while the unloading port for his cargo was actually thirty miles west of Fairport, where he was then.

It is not likely that Captain Singhas knew of the terrible storm that was at that hour headed for his ship. Far away Galveston, Texas, had already felt that same storm where hundreds were killed by its wrath. It swept over the country, wrecking a dozen cities on its way. That night it hit Lake Erie.

The *John B. Lyon* was ploughing along some twenty-five miles east of Ashtabula, when she first felt the effects of the rising wind. It was then midnight. The ship began to roll badly and the straining of her timbers could be heard above the whining wind. Her cargo held her down and caused her to labor in the heavy seas that swept over her decks.

Then it was found that the ship had sprung a bad leak somewhere in the cargo hold and the water was coming in fast. Soon the captain realized that his ship was in imminent danger of sinking. He ordered men into the hold in an attempt to locate the leak, and if possible to plug it. The survivors believed that the men never located the leak, and that several of the crew died while trying. The vessel was heading for the Ohio shore, and the engine was run as fast as the poor quality of coal would allow. The water rising in the hold threatened to extinguish the fires under the boilers.

The wind increased to sixty miles an hour, and that spelled doom for the *John B. Lyon.* Giant seas washed over the stricken ship. A cargo hatch was dashed to pieces and the *Lyon* was then taking water through the deck as well as through the bottom.

The graphic tale is told from this point by Second Engineer David Brown of Brigden, Ontario, who was the last of the crew to be rescued, coming ashore unconscious at Miles Grove near North Girard. He was destined to live on for another forty years.

"I was on duty, coming on at midnight," related Brown. "The water was rising fast in the engine room. All hands were called. When the hatch broke open Captain Singhas left the bridge in charge of the first mate and went below to help the crew make preparations as well as could be. It was found that one deck hand had no life belt, so Captain Singhas removed the one he was wearing and fastened it on the deck hand. He never found another one. That deck hand was saved, but the heroic skipper perished.

"Having done all he could, the captain then came below to the engine room. We were trying to work her

194

toward shore before she settled. It was a losing race, and we all knew it. It was agreed that I would stay below with the engine and Captain Singhas would stand at the top of the companionway to call me when the time came. Chief Engineer Willous did the same for the firemen.

"Captain Singhas shouted fiercely to me about two in the morning, to come up at once. The ship was cracking in two. She was already down by the head and sinking fast. I could see that it was only a matter of minutes. I tore a stepladder loose that was nailed to the side of the cabin. I held onto that ladder as the ship went down. The suction spun me downward. But I came up again hanging on to my ladder. Wreckage was all around me, but I managed to push myself clear of most of it, and somehow managed to get two pieces of timber and some line that was fastened to a hammock. I pulled the dripping hammock over me to protect me from the flying spray which stung my body like hail, as I had on only overalls and no shirt. But I managed to stay afloat somehow.

"With the coming of daylight the storm began to abate, and I tried to use the hammock as a sail, but without much success, as the waves were like high hills. Twice during the forenoon I sighted a tug that was looking for survivors, but I was unable to attract their attention.

"I was very tired and often felt that it would be

easier to let go than to hang on. But later in the afternoon I sighted a big red building on a hill and I renewed my efforts to get in to shore. They say I made it about six that afternoon. It was a terrible experience. Some men from a nearby saw mill found me unconscious on the beach and took me to shelter."

As the ship went down, Captain Singhas lashed his wife and the other woman aboard, the wife of the steward, to a broken spar. They floated ashore and were saved, but both of their husbands perished. A wheelsman was trapped in the pilot house by the wind. He was unable to open a door, but climbed through a window and lived to tell the tale.

The steamer *John B. Lyon* was not the only casualty that night on rampaging Lake Erie. The schooner-barge *Dundee* foundered eleven miles west of Cleveland. The only victim, a woman cook, was drowned. The men climbed into the rigging, and after clinging there many hours were rescued.

After a terrific struggle with the elements, the wooden freighter *Alex Nimick* finally arrived in Cleveland harbor with her pilot house completely wrecked and washed overboard. The steel freighter *Cornell* also arrived in Cleveland minus her smokestack, lost in the gale.

THE WRECK OF THE JOHN B. LYON

The big steel passenger steamer *City of Erie,* bound from Buffalo to Cleveland, had a bad time of it. She arrived at her destination many hours overdue and with a large hole stove in her bow, fortunately above the water line. Her passengers were badly shaken. The fast and powerful passenger ship *North Land* was scheduled to put in at Cleveland, but did not attempt to enter the harbor, preferring to ride out the storm in the open lake.

⚓ ⚓ ⚓ ⚓ ⚓ ⚓ ⚓ ⚓

CHAPTER TWENTY-TWO

THE JOSEPH S. FAY AND THE D. P. RHODES
— *1 9 0 2* —

A tired old freighter, her wooden hull deeply scarred by thirty-one years of hard service battling ice and waves of the five Great Lakes, was wallowing along the west shore of Lake Huron a few miles northwest of Rogers City, Michigan, downbound. To add to her difficulties she was beating against an increasing gale, and her hold was heavy with iron ore, while from her stern extended a stout manila towline, to the other end of which was securely fastened the wooden schooner-barge *D. P. Rhodes*. The lead steamer was the *Joseph S. Fay,* of the old Bradley fleet, considered at one time as the largest fleet on the lakes.

Captain Charles A. Fletcher stood solidly in the center of the three windows in the front of the pilot house. It was difficult to see through the pane of glass, as Lake Huron was in an angry mood and kept slapping huge white-crested waves against the weary sides of the steamer, which threw thick spray across her windows. The progress of the freighter and consort was indeed slow. They had left Escanaba, Michigan, each vessel

198

well loaded with iron ore, and bound for Ashtabula, Ohio, on Lake Erie.

The skipper had stood many long and tiring hours at his post in the pilot house as she ploughed through the Straits of Mackinac. She was hugging the shore for protection from the gathering storm. Suddenly the wind shifted. Instead of coming off the land it whistled in off the lake. The *Fay* and the *Rhodes* were in a precarious situation, close to the shore and the wind now carrying them even closer.

Quickly the captain ordered the wheel put hard over and the freighter began to turn her bow toward open water. The towline slackened astern as the forward pull eased. The steamer was soon heading for the open water; because of the extremely long towline, the barge had not as yet begun to make the turn outward.

Slowly the towline tightened between the two vessels; then it became taut. Each ship was rolling hard in the high seas. Suddenly the two vessels rolled violently in opposite directions as the new manila towline was at its greatest strain, beginning to pull the heavy barge about.

The strain was too much for the ancient *Joseph S. Fay*. With a great ripping crash the after end of the freighter tore loose. The bit that had held the towline went into the lake with the broken wreckage. Freed of her burdensome consort, the *Fay* gained some forward movement, but it was soon learned that she was sinking by the stern; too much of the hull had been ripped away in that powerful jerk of the towline, and the water was starting to come into the bilges. Soon it would extinguish the fires under her boilers.

The captain once again gave the order to put the wheel hard over and again the *Fay* turned about, this time heading directly for the shore. Her skipper wondered if she would float long enough to reach the beach on Forty Mile Point.

Luck was with the old freighter, even in the midst of misfortune. Tremendous seas pushed the *Fay* before them and hurried her up to the shore faster than her engines ever could have. The towbarge, *D. P. Rhodes,* was at the mercy of the gale after the towline pulled out of the *Fay*. She was blown before the wind, helpless, and was driven on the shore some four miles south of Forty Mile Point.

As the *Joseph S. Fay* scurried toward shore, the crew from the after end came forward, as the damaged stern was taking water fast. A fireman hurried on deck with but few clothes to stand the biting wind of an October gale. The captain ordered him in to the master's quarters, and soon the scantily-clad fireman was resting comfortably in the captain's berth.

It was a close race for the old *Fay* to reach the shore before she went down by the stern. But she made it! Her bow grated hard upon a sandbar not far from the beach. The ship slowly washed sideways upon the bar. This caused her to take the breakers along her entire weather side and subjected the vessel to incredible punishment.

She had not been long in this position when a giant comber struck the ship and with a powerful sweep tore the entire forward cabin off the *Fay*. This included the wheel house, the Texas deck, and the mates' and captain's rooms. The entire structure was lifted bodily from the ship and carried shoreward. Eleven men went along with it, including the captain. The tremendous seas washed the cabins and wheel house right up on the sandy beach, with the men still inside. The fireman in the captain's bunk was carried safely to the beach, and survivors state, he was sound asleep when they looked in on him after the structure landed on the shore.

Two of the crew and the first mate were not in the wreckage which came ashore. They were left on the wreck. Undaunted, two of them ripped off a spar from the rigging, and aided by this, made the shore in safety. But the mate perished. He threw a long plank into the water and jumped in after it. The seas quickly carried it away from the mate's grasp. Then he struck out for shore, apparently intending to reach there by swimming with no further aid. The surging waters and the chilling temperature were too much for the valiant mate. The seamen on the beach saw him sink. He was the only fatality in the wreck of the *Joseph S. Fay*.

The survivors turned sadly away and started a six

mile trudge through the rough lakeside country to the town of Rogers City, where they reported the loss of their vessel, and the death of their mate. Later the crew of the *D. P. Rhodes* reported their situation also. None of their number had been lost, and from all appearances their vessel was not severely damaged.

It is interesting to note that the *Rhodes* was eventually salvaged from her stranding near Forty Mile Point and lived to float many more years upon the waters of the Great Lakes. She finally came to a most peaceful end lying at the foot of East Fortieth Street in Cleveland. Along with another old Bradley schooner-barge, the *Thomas Quale,* she was gradually covered over by workers reclaiming land from Lake Erie.

But for the steamer *Joseph S. Fay* it was the end. She eventually broke up on the bar she struck on, that October 19, 1902, in the gale that farmers living along the lake shore said was the worst that they had ever seen on that part of Lake Huron.

The demise of the *Fay* was but one of the steps by which the entire early Bradley fleet left the Great Lakes. It had been a grand fleet of freight ships, dating back to the days of the small sailing schooners. Their ships' hulls were painted an attractive green, and the steamers' stacks were dark red with a wide black smoke band at the top. Only one of the steamers, the *Alva,* was of steel construction, and that was built late in the career of the famous old fleet. These ships were all *built* for the Bradleys; they never bought a ship afloat. It is reported that they never carried any insurance on their vessels. A remark credited to Captain Alva Bradley, the founder of the fleet, was to the effect that he chose only the best men to man his ships, and that they were the best insurance against loss.

An unusual record in the career of the freighter *Joseph S. Fay* was that the ship was commanded by three generations of shipmasters: a grandfather, a father, and a son. Captain Merwin S. Thompson, Jr., was the next to the last master of the *Fay.* He sailed her for two years, 1900 and 1901. His father, Captain Merwin Thompson, Sr., had sailed the *Fay* during 1880, 1881 and 1882. And his maternal grandfather, Captain George Stone, had brought the *Fay* out in 1871, when she was built in Cleveland, Ohio. He then sailed her until 1875. The old freighter *Joseph S. Fay* had a lot of quaint atmosphere about her in her thirty-one years of faithful service on the Great Lakes!

NOTE: The Bradley fleet mentioned in this chapter has no connection with the present Bradley Transportation Company fleet of self-unloaders now on the lakes.

⚓ ⚓ ⚓ ⚓ ⚓ ⚓ ⚓ ⚓

CHAPTER TWENTY-THREE

THE WRECK OF THE WILLIAM F. SAUBER

— *1 9 0 3* —

Upon the master of a ship falls very heavy responsibilities. The safety of his valuable vessel, the lives of his passengers and crew, the custody of his cargo, the skillful navigation of his ship, all these major weighty burdens and many many lesser ones are assumed by the man who accepts the job of captain of a vessel. He must first satisfy the Federal Government as to his ability as a qualified master mariner. He must be sound of mind and body. He must have had plenty of experience. If he meets all these qualifications, he is granted a license as a master of ships. The tonnage of the ship and the waters in which he is to sail are clearly defined. His license is good for five years, and must be renewed at the end of that period if he is still to be eligible as a ship's captain.

After a man is granted a master's license, his next difficulty is to obtain a master's job. Here again, he must satisfy the owners of a ship that he is the man to whom they can trust their valuable investment. Is it much wonder that after a man has finally attained the station of master of a steamer he is imbued with a very deep sense of responsibility? He has his reputation and his livelihood constantly at stake, night and day, fair weather and foul.

In years gone by it was somewhat of a tradition of the sea that if a captain lost the ship that was placed in his charge, he should also be lost with his ship. Whether or not he was to blame did not enter so much into this peculiar scheme of things. He was supposed to keep his craft afloat under all conditions, and to take no unnecessary sailing risks. He was in absolute command and his word was law aboard his ship. If the ship were lost, the likely reasoning was, that the blame be placed upon the captain. There appeared to be no other way.

Many a ship captain has remained steadfastly on his bridge until the swirling waters swept him to his death, both on salt water and fresh water, although he may have had ample opportunity to escape the wreck.

One of the outstanding shipmasters who elected to go down with his ship was Captain E. J. Smith of the ill-fated North Atlantic passenger ship *Titanic* in 1912, in what is considered the world's greatest sea disaster. Survivors tell of his standing solidly on the great liner's deck after refusing to leave in a lifeboat. He met his death as the *Titanic* plunged to the bottom of the sea, taking with her some fifteen hundred passengers, officers, and crew.

Nine years earlier this self same tradition undoubtedly ran through the mind of Captain William E. Morris of the wooden bulk lake freighter *William F. Sauber* on the wild night of October twenty-fifth, 1903, some thirty miles off Whitefish Point on Lake Superior. He made his decision! He would go down with his ship! He refused to take the last seat in the departing lifeboat with the terse remark, "Not by a damn sight." The last the men in the lifeboat saw of their courageous captain he was engulfed in the giant ice cold waves amidst the wreckage of his ship. As a last attempt they threw him a line. It fell on his shoulders and then into the debris. Captain Morris made no effort to hold onto that line. When the steamer *William F. Sauber* plunged bow first into cold Lake Superior she took along with her Captain "Bill" Morris.

The events that led up to this dramatic incident are thrilling indeed, and show the stout courage and the skill and determination of those men who sail the sometimes treacherous Great Lakes.

The *William F. Sauber* had been built by F. W. Wheeler & Co., of Bay City, Michigan, in 1891. Her dimensions were, two hundred ninety-one feet keel, and forty-one feet beam. She was a typical wooden Great Lakes bulk freighter with her engines aft and her pilot house forward. She had a small deck house almost amidships for crew quarters. Three masts extended high above the ship.

It was the *Sauber's* twelfth year, 1903, the day

being Saturday, October twenty-third, when, late that afternoon, she cleared Ashland, Wisconsin, loaded with a cargo of iron ore consigned to a Lake Erie port. Lake Superior was in an ugly mood as the *Sauber* cleared the port, but the blow was not considered of sufficient intensity to delay sailing. Late fall storms on Lake Superior are rather to be expected, and the ships do not seek shelter unless it is really necessary. Captain Morris set his course to clear Keweenaw Point, many miles ahead. All that night the *Sauber* took a severe pounding, but she safely rounded Eagle Harbor and Copper Harbor lights at the tip of the Keweenaw Peninsula. Her course was then set for distant Whitefish Point.

The wind began to blow a howling gale, and the thermometer dropped fast. The prow of the freighter cut into huge waves and sent the spray dashing across the entire ship. Soon the spray began to freeze upon everything it hit. The entire steamer was encased in a heavy coating of ice. This added seriously to her weight which, along with the cargo in her hold, presented a bad situation.

While being thus pounded and tossed about and gathering ice, another very serious mishap developed. She sprang a leak in her wooden hull below the water line. The incoming water gained steadily and soon her pumps could not keep up with the rising rush of icy water. The men aboard the *Sauber* knew that their situation was becoming critical. The captain ordered distress signals flown from her mainmast and all the crew to wear life jackets.

By nightfall Sunday the plight of the *Sauber* was almost hopeless as the storm grew worse. With death staring the crew in the face, suddenly a shout of hope came from the weary souls aboard the stricken vessel. They had sighted another freighter heading toward them through the storm! It was the steel steamer *Yale,* and her captain James Jackson, had seen her distress signals and was coming over to offer assistance! The sight of the *Yale* on that wind-swept grey sea bearing toward them, encouraged the crew of the *Sauber*. They might still cheat death of a miserable ending in that frigid water.

Captain Morris aboard the *Sauber* knew that his vessel was doomed. His only hope was to reach the shelter of Whitefish Point. And to this end he continued to force his ship. The ill-fated *Sauber* sloshed along through the huge waves, whipped up by a sixty mile an hour wind, struggling to gain protection of the land before she settled altogether. Maybe he could beach her before she sank! He encouraged his crew to stick to their posts and to keep the ship moving.

Captain Jackson aboard the *Yale* saw that the *Sauber* could not last long under the terrific beating she was forced to take. Communication was impossible between the vessels. It was also impossible to get a small boat across the water between them. The blackness of night settled over the storm-lashed lake. Captain Jackson realized that his own ship was taking a bad beating from the storm, but he stood by throughout the night, watching the lights of the *Sauber*. He maneuvered his big steamer as close to the *Sauber* as he dared, adjusting his speed to keep always to windward of the stricken ship, thus protecting her from the beating of the huge waves. So for many long hours the *Yale* broke the force of the seas before they hit the *Sauber,* hoping to keep her afloat until they might encounter smoother seas.

Great courage and skillful navigation of both ships was necessary. Long tiring hours of watching and waiting were experienced. The wheelsman on the *Sauber* remained at his post with a life preserver about him. The entire crew of the ship did likewise. Many of the men below deck were working in water up to their waists.

At three the next morning those aboard the *Yale* saw that the *Sauber* could not last much longer and that her crew must be taken off shortly or they would likely perish. Captain Jackson then brought his steamer *Yale* almost alongside the *Sauber*. It was impossible to come into direct contact as the two vessels would strike each other and both might sink. The yawls of both ships were lowered. The *Yale* afforded a sort of break-water for the *Sauber,* and the water between the two ships was much quieter than on the open lake. Reluctantly, Captain Morris ordered his crew to abandon the *Sauber*. The men did not rush to the yawls. Instead, each man went quietly over the side and into the small boats. There was no disorder.

Chief Engineer Butler was the last man except Captain Morris to go over the side. He offered the captain the last seat in the yawl. Then came the skipper's emphatic refusal.

In the transfer of the men from the *Sauber* to the *Yale* one man, an oiler, was lost, but all the others were safely hauled aboard the *Yale*. As they looked back toward the *Sauber* they heard a muffled explosion. Timbers and planks rose upward. The *Sauber's* bow slipped beneath the seas as her stern rose, lifting her propeller out of the water. The men could see it still turning. They had the satisfaction then of knowing that each man had stuck to his post until the last possible moment, and had kept everything aboard the *Sauber* in operating condition.

Captain Jackson then sailed the *Yale* into Sault Ste. Marie, and reported the loss of the steamer *William F. Sauber,* with her captain and oiler.

During the winter that followed, Captain Jackson learned that the men of the lakes admire such acts of heroism as were displayed on Lake Superior in rescuing the crew of the sinking *Sauber*. He was presented with a medal for his action, and a purse of money collected by the crews of the lake ships, was sent to him also as a reward for his gallant actions. He continued to sail as master on Great Lakes freight steamers for another quarter century or so. He passed away in Watertown, New York, at the age of seventy-six years.

⚓ ⚓ ⚓ ⚓ ⚓ ⚓ ⚓ ⚓

CHAPTER TWENTY-FOUR

SEVONA—PRETORIA—IOSCO—OLIVE JEANETTE
— *1 9 0 5* —

The three hundred foot steel freighter *Sevona* first took to the fresh waters of the Great Lakes at the Wheeler Shipyards in Bay City, Michigan, in 1890. She was christened the *Emily P. Weed*. Atop her pilot house was the first electric searchlight to be installed aboard a ship on the Great Lakes. Today even the humblest motorboat carries such a light. The searchlight placed on the *Weed* was expected to revolutionize navigation in a fog. It was claimed that the rays would penetrate one half mile into the densest fog. Step by step the improvements on shipboard were coming.

But the *Emily P. Weed* was due to undergo three important changes all within the first few years of her existence. First, she changed owners, becoming a ship in the McBrier fleet, with headquarters in Erie, Pennsylvania, although her hailing port was Cleveland, Ohio, probably because of some taxation angle. Then her name was changed to *Sevona*.

The third change was in her length. In 1905, she entered a Buffalo shipyard where she was cut in two amidships, pulled apart, and a new section seventy-two feet long, was built into her hull. This operation increased her net tonnage from one thousand eight hundred eighty-nine tons to two thousand two hundred fifty-eight tons. Quite a substantial increase.

In 1896 her master was Captain Donald Sutherland McDonald, of North East, Pennsylvania. He had spent his entire working life aboard ships. At seventeen he went sailing with his uncle, Captain John Burgess, on the Canadian steamer *Georgian.* Later he shipped out of New York City on salt water. While so employed on the Norwegian brig, *Hilding,* he was shipwrecked off the coast of Ireland. He and another sailor were the only survivors. In 1883 he returned to the Great Lakes and sailed on many vessels. He became master of the steamer *Ohio,* and in 1894 of the freighter *Nyanza.* His next command was the *Sevona.* So great were his hopes for the success of his ship that Captain McDonald invested his own savings in the vessel.

It was Friday, September first, 1905, at six o'clock in the late afternoon, that Captain McDonald piloted the *Sevona* out of the harbor of Superior, Wisconsin, and out onto broad Lake Superior. The lake was choppy. Four women passengers were aboard the freighter: three were guests of the owners, and the fourth was the wife of the steward.

The weather station had storm warnings flying as the *Sevona* cleared Superior. Captain McDonald saw them, but as he interpreted the duties of a good ship-master were to make the best time possible, he began the long trek down the lakes. He considered the *Sevona* quite capable of weathering whatever blow might come up—if one should. Then too, there were the few island shelter spots along the route. It was a chance, but the captain would take the risk. A ship lying in harbor runs up a lot of needless expense sometimes. Good skippers keep the expenses down.

Captain McDonald was a good skipper. He wanted to deliver those five thousand tons of iron ore, which lay deep in the hold of his ship, to a dock at some Lake Erie port with as little delay as possible. As the *Sevona* headed out onto Lake Superior, the captain set the course for the first leg of the voyage. That was the run of sixty-eight and one half miles over the choppy seas from Superior to Devil's Island Light. It all seemed simple enough when broken up into sections. At Devil's Island the course would change; it would then be an eleven mile run to Outer Island Light. Then on to the Portage Ship Canal Light, which course Captain McDonald had elected to take, rather than go out around Keweenaw Point in the open waters of the lake. Likely the weather would not get too bad until he could make the protection of the Portage Canal which cuts across the Keweenaw Peninsula. This waterway was used as a haven of refuge by many a storm-tossed ship around the turn of the century.

But those storm warnings back in Superior did mean

214

something this time. The weather men had prognos- ticated correctly. With sudden fury the wind whipped the choppy lake into giant combers. The *Sevona* was along her course too far to turn back to Superior. She had made the first leg of the run to Devil's Island Light without mishap, and was six miles beyond Outer Island when the going became too tough for the *Sevona*. She could make no headway in the storm. Heavy squalls of rain pelted the wheel house windows and a mist rose from the lake making it very difficult to see ahead.

Captain McDonald then decided to turn back and seek the shelter of one of the Apostle Islands. Turning the ship in the heavy seas was no easy task, but luck was with her, and the *Sevona* came about and was headed back over the same course she had traveled, this time in search of shelter. All hands in her pilot house were scanning the lake for the nearest light, that of Raspberry Island. This light, seventy-seven feet above the surface of the water would easily have been seen from the ship, had it not been for the rain and mist that covered the lake. Raspberry Island Light was never sighted by the men on the *Sevona*.

Instead, at five forty-five in the morning, Sand Island Light was picked up close by. The waters around Sand Island are very dangerous; stony reefs lie close to the surface. The *Sevona* was too close. The captain frantically tried to put about, but the storm drove his ship onto the rocks. A gaping hole was quickly torn in her bow, and in thirty minutes the pounding had severely crippled her. A great crack in the hull appeared. On the deck the break was too wide for a man to jump across, and it soon widened. Some of the men believed that the hull was breaking at a point where the ship had been lengthened.

All of the ship's lifeboats were aft. Captain McDonald, two mates and four men were caught in the forward part of the ship and could not get aft. The four women were fortunately aft when the ship struck. One of the lifeboats was wrecked by the storm before any of the men had a chance to attempt to launch it.

This left only two lifeboats. Captain McDonald shouted through his megaphone to the men aft and ordered the remaining lifeboats lowered away, and the women placed in them. The boat on the starboard side was lowered, but it required two men in it to keep it from being dashed to pieces against the side of the *Sevona*. Seventeen persons in all were in the after end of the ship. The four women were lowered into the lifeboat which was kept in the lee of the steamer.

The second and only remaining lifeboat was on the windward side of the *Sevona* and could not be launched from that side. Second engineer Adam Fiden then called for assistance, and this boat was dragged across the deck of the steamer, from the port to the starboard side, and then launched. It was necessary to cut away a water tank and several of the stays holding the stack in order to clear the path for the lifeboat across the deck. At this point one of the men tied down the cord to the *Sevona's* huge whistle, and it continued to blow until the final wisp of steam left the boilers. Fortunately, Captain McDonald had held frequent lifeboat drills aboard the *Sevona* and the men now used this drilling practice to actual advantage.

While all this was going on in the after end of the ship, the seven men up forward who were cut off from the lifeboats were loosening the wooden hatch covers between the forecastle deck house and the pilot house, and throwing them overboard with lines fastened to them. These men marooned in the forward end made no attempt to get aft.

Chief Engineer William Phillipi was in command of the after end. He decided that it was better for all hands to remain where they were as long as they possibly could. He believed this was safer than to try leaving in the small lifeboats, at least until absolutely necessary. So the women were hauled back on the *Sevona's* deck again and sent to the dining room to dry out and get what rest they might. The water was icy cold and the women were thoroughly drenched. Occasionally a great wave would crash over the entire after end of the ship, drenching all the men as they went about their hurried tasks. They suffered much, as they were not properly clothed for such exposure.

Charles Scouller, a deck hand who later became a captain, rigged lines to keep the lifeboats in the water from striking against the side of the ship. Thus snugged down for the moment all hands went into the *Sevona's* dining room to await developments. They had not long to wait. The crack in the ship's hull grew gradually wider. By eleven o'clock that morning everything on the after end of the *Sevona* seemed to go to pieces. The skylight crashed down into the dining room.

Chief Phillipi decided it was time to abandon ship. All hands, including the women, were forced to crawl through the windows on the lee side of the dining room, as the heavy seas held the entrance door closed. The women were again lowered into the larger lifeboat and seven men took their places in the same boat, eleven in all. Chief Phillipi took charge. The tossing lifeboat was dangerously run up alongside the *Sevona* to the forward end and the men in the lifeboat cupped their hands to their mouths to make their voices carry, as they tried to attract the attention of the seven men trapped in the forward part of the ship.

But they could not be heard above the noise of the ship's whistle and the roar of the storm. Evidently not one of the men forward had seen the people that were aft leave the ship. Their rescue was so close at hand, and yet they could not hear or see the lifeboat! They remained huddled in the forward cabin awaiting the subsiding of the gale. It did not subside for many long hours; instead it increased.

The second lifeboat, smaller than the first, was

manned by six men. Charles Scouller took charge of it, being the most experienced at handling small craft. Upon leaving the wrecked *Sevona,* the two lifeboats became separated. At first Scouller tried to land his boat on nearby York Island, thinking that was where Chief Phillipi intended landing his craft. But Scouller soon saw that landing on York Island was out of the question. Continually in great danger of capsizing, he decided to run with the sea to the more distant Sand Island. He was well aware of the rocky and dangerous coast of the island upon which he intended to land, and had considerable apprehension. But it was his only chance; he must make it.

He steered the boat perilously close to a jagged up-thrust rock and one of the men shouted to beware of the rocks. It was necessary to pass the rockhead close in order that the boat not be driven beyond the island where he hoped to land. Scouller steadfastly held onto his tiller oar as he skillfully made for Sand Island.

At last they rounded a rocky point and were swept into a small bay. Here a huge breaker carried the small lifeboat and its crew right up onto the shore. The men scrambled through the remaining breakers and at last were able to stand upright on solid land—safe.

Scouller found a deserted fisherman's shack, and discovered an old blanket which he wrapped around himself. Then he climbed to a high point, hoping to locate the larger lifeboat and possibly direct it to his landing place. But he saw nothing of the other craft, and feared it was lost.

In the meantime, the drenched and shivering survivors had built a fire in the log shack and were attempting to dry out their clothing. Not far away was another log cabin in which lived a Norwegian fisherman and his family, who gave them food. The fisherman claimed that this was the worst storm in the nine years he had lived on Sand Island. He left shortly to see if he could sight the *Sevona,* and returned about dusk saying that the forecastle and all her houses had disappeared.

On the following afternoon, Sunday, the body of their shipmate, Nels Salverson, one of the men trapped forward on the *Sevona,* washed ashore.

By Monday morning the storm had ceased. A ship's whistle was heard close to the island. The survivors rushed down to the bay. Imagine their elation when they saw that it was the tug *R. W. Garrie* sent out to search for them! They lost no time in getting on board. Their delight upon being rescued was quickly dimmed when the tug crew informed them that the body of Captain McDonald had washed ashore a short distance away. The *Garrie* took the six survivors to the port of Bayfield, Wisconsin.

Meanwhile, the larger lifeboat in charge of Chief Engineer Phillipi had a trip of stark terror and suffering. After leaving the wrecked *Sevona,* Phillipi lost sight of the smaller lifeboat in the giant seas. His greatest concern was to keep his craft upright and to prevent it from capsizing. It was blown before the storm past Sand Island, where the other boat had landed, and on over the water until, many hours later, it reached the forest-clad mainland of Wisconsin.

All that Saturday afternoon, the men in the boat had fought the elements in a desperate struggle to reach the shore, which was but five miles away. It was a harrowing experience. One minute it seemed that death was inevitable, then the next there was a ray of hope. Their boat filled with icy water which the women frantically bailed out. Women and men alike, in the storm-lashed lifeboat prayed fervently to be spared. The storm persisted. It carried the survivors' boat parallel to the shore. Finally, after an exhausting struggle, the men at the oars managed to get the boat into the broiling surf. A huge comber then tossed the craft high in the air and spilled all the eleven occupants sideways onto the beach. They all scrambled out of the water with what little strength they had left.

Most of the eleven were too exhausted to move. Phillipi and a fireman managed to reconnoiter about the spot where they were cast up and were delighted to find a deserted lumber camp about a quarter of a mile up the beach. Providence had left an old cookstove, with a generous supply of dry wood and matches, in one of the shacks of the camp. This greatly heartened the weary searchers. Phillipi left the fireman there to build a fire, while he trudged back to the sorry group huddled near their landing spot.

The eleven shipwrecked persons found their haven of refuge a true godsend. They huddled over the roaring cookstove trying to get a little of its warmth into their shivering bodies.

From out of the storm another man wandered into the small cabin. He was a homesteader in that wild and almost unpopulated stretch of shore line. His cow had strayed in the storm, and while seeking her he noted smoke coming from the deserted cook's shack; thus he found the survivors.

Two of the women decided to start off with the homesteader to another lumber camp, which was active. After a two mile trek inland, they arrived at the camp where they received food and dry clothing in the form of whatever mens' attire could be found by the lumberjacks. Other lumberjacks returned to the deserted camp on the shore and assisted the remaining survivors to their inland camp. When they arrived they were so completely exhausted they could scarcely stand.

They learned that the nearest town was Bayfield. One of the lumberjacks walked the half mile to the nearest telephone to notify the Bayfield authorities of the shipwreck, but he returned, saying that the telephone wires were blown down by the storm and that the instrument was not working.

At seven the next morning, Sunday, the chief engineer obtained a team of horses and a driver who knew the path through the wilderness to Bayfield, and together they set off. It was a rugged trek. They had to chop their way along, as large trees had been blown down in the terrible windstorm and had fallen across the men's path. By two-thirty that afternoon, the two men and their team reached Bayfield. Phillipi still believed that his boat was the only one of the two to reach land, as nothing had as yet been heard from Scouller and his men, who were at that moment still on Sand Island.

The chief engineer wired the owners of the *Sevona* the news of the wreck, and then obtained the services of the tug *Harrow* to search the vicinity of the wreck for the others of the crew. Along with fifteen other men aboard the tug they left Bayfield, even though the hour was five in the afternoon. The storm was still raging, but the *Harrow* reached the wreck site about seven.

Only a few spars floated near the demolished after section of the *Sevona*. The freighter had split entirely in two and the forward part had slid out of sight beneath the waves. The *Sevona* was no more. Careful search of the near-by waters brought no sign of any persons, living or dead. The tug returned to Bayfield Monday, where Phillipi was joined by the Scouller boat load of survivors, as the tug *R. W. Garrie* arrived in that port.

The seven men who remained on the forward section of the freighter all perished. It is believed that, as the ship continued to break in two, the forward end was tilted and rolled about, spilling the heavy cargo of iron ore into Lake Superior. Relieved of this weight, the forward end then slid gradually into deep water around the fatal rock upon which she had struck.

A lighthouse keeper, unable to reach the wreck, kept his binoculars trained upon it. He reported later that, as the forward part of the wreck began to slide beneath the water, he could see the captain and the six other men crawl onto the improvised raft that they had made from the wooden hatch covers. They had nearly reached Sand Island when their raft flipped over and tossed them all into the raging seas. He never saw them again.

Later, soundings around the wreck made by local fishermen, showed that had the *Sevona* been fifty feet either way, she would have avoided the fatal rock upon which she crashed.

Another fatal casualty of that same storm on Lake Superior was the wooden schooner *Pretoria* of Bay City, Michigan. She also had left Superior, Wisconsin, with a cargo of iron ore in her hold. She was in tow of the iron steamer *Venezuela*. Both ships were owned by Bay City capital. The *Venezuela* and the *Pretoria* had cleared the port somewhat ahead of the *Sevona,* but because their speed was slower due to the tow, all three ships were caught in the same storm area.

The *Pretoria* was a trim craft, three hundred thirty-eight feet long, forty-four feet beam, and twenty-three feet in depth, and was listed as two thousand seven hundred ninety gross tons, and classed as A-1 in marine ratings. She had been built in 1900 at West Bay City, Michigan. She carried a crew of ten men.

The two vessels were bound for South Chicago, the steamer having iron ore also. They were churning their way down Lake Superior in the heavy seas on Sunday morning about seven, some twenty miles off Outer Island, when the *Pretoria* suddenly foundered. The towing line to the steamer was quickly dropped, and Captain Smart and his nine men took to the lifeboat. Rather than take chances of being dashed to pieces against the sides of the *Venezuela,* the men decided to head for Outer Island.

Their progress was very slow and difficult. They had neared the island shore by late afternoon, when their boat capsized, throwing the ten men into the water. Giant waves separated the forms struggling in the lake. The captain and four men managed to right the overturned lifeboat and crawl back into it. The other five men drowned.

By sheer chance the exhausted men were beached upon Outer Island, a mile from the lighthouse. Here the *Venezuela* found them the following day.

Another pair of doomed ships sailed away from the harbor of Duluth, Minnesota, on Thursday noon, the last day of August, 1905. That was the day before the *Sevona* cleared the head of the lakes on her last trip. The doomed pair were the steamer *Iosco,* in charge of Captain Nelson Gonyaw, and the schooner *Olive Jeanette,* in tow. Both ships carried cargoes of iron ore, and were bound for Lake Erie ports.

The *Iosco* and *Olive Jeanette* were substantial wooden vessels. Both had been built at West Bay City, Michigan. The steamer was fourteen years old, and the schooner, fifteen. They were good-sized ships for their day, the *Iosco* measured two hundred ninety-one feet long, and forty-one feet beam, with twenty feet draft, while the schooner was two hundred forty-two feet in length and thirty-nine feet beam, with sixteen feet draft. Well-kept and well-officered, they presented a fine commercial picture as they left the lakehead together.

Despite her attractive sounding name, the *Olive Jeanette* had a sinister past. Seven years previous, she was being towed regularly by the steamer *L. R. Doty.* The two ships had sailed from Chicago, with cargoes

226

of corn, bound for a lower lake port. When in mid Lake Michigan, the two were struck by a furious gale and became separated. The steamer *L. R. Doty* was never heard from again. Wreckage was picked up later twenty-five miles off Kenosha, Wisconsin. Her entire crew of seventeen perished. The *Olive Jeanette* rode out the storm and was later picked up and brought into port. Her crew could throw no light on the disappearance of the *L. R. Doty*. Subsequently, the *Olive Jeanette* was assigned to the steamer *Iosco* to tow. Oftimes sailors were superstitious about such ships.

The *Iosco* and *Olive Jeanette* plodded their way across Lake Superior meeting several upbound vessels. The last to report seeing them was the crew of the steamer *William A. Paine*. They reported meeting the two downbound craft off Stannard Rock Light early Saturday morning, September second. Nothing seemed amiss with the two vessels, as far as those aboard the *Paine* could see.

What happened to the *Iosco* and her consort after meeting the *Paine* will never be known. Records tell of a severe sudden northeast gale on Lake Superior in the vicinity of where the ships were sailing. The two must have become separated in the storm and both foundered.

Watchers on the Huron Islands in Lake Superior on Sunday afternoon, about four, saw the wrecked hulk of the *Olive Jeanette* wash up on the shore. The schooner was barely able to float, and would have

227

sunk, were it not for her grounding on the beach. All the crew had perished. There was no steamer in sight then. Nor has the *Iosco* ever been seen. She evidently carried her cargo and crew to the deep bottom of the lake; nineteen sailors died with their ship. Seven more men, the crew of the *Olive Jeanette,* never lived to tell of what had happened out there on stormy Lake Superior.

⚓ ⚓ ⚓ ⚓ ⚓ ⚓ ⚓ ⚓

CHAPTER TWENTY-FIVE

THE CYPRUS DISAPPEARS

—1907—

Twenty-five days service and one cargo delivered is the full extent of the life of the big steel freighter *Cyprus*. Her launching took place on September 17, 1907, and her disappearance in Lake Superior on October 11th, the same year, is the astonishing record of the short-lived steamer, sparkling new just out of the shipyards. Only one man of her crew when she went beneath the waves, lived to talk with folks ashore and to tell of the loss of the new ship. Twenty-two others perished with the vessel.

The short life of the *Cyprus* was strenuous and she seemed to be under an unfortunate sign. As she stood on the ways in the shipyard at Lorain, Ohio, under construction, one of the curses of American industry fell upon her—a strike. Labor difficulties in the early part of the Twentieth Century were sometimes long and bloody. This one was. Other workers were brought into the plant in an effort to keep the construction of the ship continuing, and so the *Cyprus* grew slowly under the extreme handicap of the labor trouble.

SHIPWRECKS OF THE LAKES

The *Cyprus* was the fifth of six ships, all exactly alike, being built at the same yard. The other five were the *Hemlock, Elba, Odanah, Adriatic,* and *Calumet,* all of which are still plowing the Great Lakes shipping lanes as these lines are being written in 1951. The ships are listed as four hundred twenty feet keel length, fifty-two feet beam, and twenty-eight feet depth—big ships when they came out, and still today they are not considered too small. But the *Cyprus* was the one unfortunate ship of the lot.

It was on September 21, 1907, that the *Cyprus,* under the command of Captain F. B. Huyck, steamed down the Black River at Lorain into Lake Erie, and headed up the lakes on her maiden voyage.

At the head of the lakes she loaded her only cargo. It was iron ore, and she delivered it to Fairport, Ohio. And that was the only cargo the *Cyprus* ever delivered to the intended destination.

Her next trip, the second, was to be her last. She returned light to the lakehead where another cargo, this one of seven thousand one hundred and three tons of iron ore, was dumped into her hold. It was not an excessive load for a ship like the *Cyprus.* She did not carry it far, not even out of Lake Superior. She cleared the harbor of Superior, Wisconsin, at nine o'clock in the morning of Wednesday, October 9th, 1907.

The weather was rough and the *Cyprus* rolled considerably, but nothing seriously. Other ships were out on Lake Superior runs, and though they were buffeted about, it was not considered a severe storm. The seas broke over the deck of the *Cyprus* frequently. This continued all that Wednesday and throughout the night, and into the following day, Thursday, and that night. The *Cyprus* made slow time against the storm. The big waves continued to wash over her decks.

The one probable mistake made on the *Cyprus* before she sailed from Superior was that her hatches were not "battened down." This is a safety measure which consists of placing large tarpaulins over each hatch and firmly fastening them so that they completely cover the entire hatch and fastenings, thus preventing the waves which sweep over the decks from letting water down into the cargo hold through the hatches. Subsequently this "battening down" of hatches aboard lake ships has become mandatory during certain months of the sailing season when the storms are the worst.

Possibly the men aboard the *Cyprus* did not realize that their ship was taking in water in any serious amount, as she rolled and tossed about on the lake. But, marine experts believe, each wave that swept over her deck would send some water leaking down into the hold to mix with her iron ore cargo.

After nightfall of Thursday, the *Cyprus* was about eighteen miles off Deer Park, Michigan, a small town on the south shore of Lake Superior—right on her course for Whitefish Point. The freighter *George*

Stephenson was not far off, having been running the same course with the *Cyprus* for several hours, both downbound for the Soo. Suddenly the men in the pilot house of the *Stephenson* noticed that the lights of the *Cyprus* went out. The *Cyprus* had gone down!

Aboard the stricken freighter everything was confusion. The ship had suddenly taken a severe list, and nothing could be done to straighten her. The list continued and shortly she rolled over and slid to the bottom of Lake Superior in about three hundred feet of water. It all happened very quickly after the list began, and the crew had little time to prepare to leave their vessel.

Four of the crew managed to get on a life raft and then they drifted on the rough lake waters before the wind, until two o'clock the following morning. The raft then struck the breakers and turned over several times. Three of the four men were unable to retain their hold on it and were drowned close to shore.

The second mate, Charles Pitz, was the only man left. Somehow he succeeded in reaching the shore, and here he was later found by the U. S. Life Saving Service crew. He was barely able to tell his rescuers the name of the ship he was from, and that he believed all the others aboard were lost. Then he lapsed into unconsciousness and for a while it appeared that the mystery of the *Cyprus* sinking would never be told.

But Charles Pitz lived, and he was the only survivor

of the ill-fated freighter *Cyprus*, the ship with one of the shortest careers ever to sail upon the Great Lakes of America.

♱ ♱ ♱ ♱ ♱ ♱ ♱ ♱

Chapter Twenty-Six

THE CLARION FIRE

— 1 9 0 9 —

Lake men knew the iron-hulled steamer *Clarion* as a "line boat." By this they meant that she was a package freighter operated in conjunction with a railroad line. In the case of the *Clarion* she hauled for the Pennsylvania Railroad, and her ports of call ranged all over the American cities of the Great Lakes, from Buffalo and Chicago to Duluth. She was built in 1881 at Wyandotte, Michigan, and she carried anything that could be put into a box car. Some old-timers recall that in her early days she also carried a few passengers.

The "line boats" were always trim ships. The *Clarion's* hull above the main deck was painted white, and below that to the water line she was an attractive green. All the deck houses were white and her stack a solid bright red. A tall yellow mast reached upwards from just aft of her pilot house, and a much shorter mast arose some distance forward of her rather high stack, which was located near the stern, a standard design for all of the package freight propeller steamboats on the Great Lakes. Twenty-one men usually comprised her crew. Her length was two hundred forty feet, breadth thirty-six feet, and her depth fifteen feet

For twenty-eight years the sturdy *Clarion* churned her way up and down the lakes, from the time the ice permitted in the spring until it would freeze her in in the early winter, through storm and calm, fog and clear. Many a Great Lakes freighter came and went out of existence during those years, but the *Clarion* still continued. She began to show her age, but still she remained on the active list; that is, until the year 1909, when fate stepped into the tranquil life of the *Clarion* and in a few tense terrifying hours ended the ship forever.

It was early in December of that year when the *Clarion* cleared Chicago with a full cargo of flour, feed, oil cakes and glucose. Her destination was Erie, Pennsylvania, about nine hundred water-tossed miles distant. December sailing on the Great Lakes is, and always has been, treacherous. The sudden and severe storms that sweep these lakes can change calmness into tragedy within a few hours. Crews are happy when "the last trip down" is completed. The *Clarion* was making her "last trip down" and was to have wintered at Erie after unloading her cargo.

Her trip down Lake Michigan, through the Mackinac Straits and down Lake Huron was routine. Things went along well. She steamed down the river past Detroit at one forty-five in the afternoon of Wednesday, December eighth, in company with the freighter *Denmark*. The weather was ominous and a storm was forecast. The *Clarion* had no wireless or other means of communication. She was on her own.

A treacherous spot in Lake Erie is named Southeast Shoal. It is located about six miles off Point Pelee, on the Canadian side, some thirty miles east of the mouth of the Detroit River. Today a fine modern lighthouse stands above the dangerous shoal, and ships use the light to mark their turning point to various Lake Erie harbors. But in the years around 1909 only a small lightship, the *Kewaunee,* marked the spot. Mariners watched anxiously for the light or whistle from this little vessel as their ships traveled the northerly shore of Lake Erie.

Southeast Shoal lay in the path of the *Clarion.* The weather had turned bad, high winds angered the water and snow storms filled the air. Temperatures dropped to around ten degrees above zero. About seven that evening when the *Clarion* was still some one and one half miles off the lightship *Kewaunee,* fire broke out in the hold. It gained headway rapidly. The mate, James Thompson, grabbed a fire extinguisher and went into the smoke-filled hold in the hope of locating the center of the fire. He was never seen again. Captain Thomas Bell could see that the fire was spreading rapidly, as the men came up on deck, unable to stay at their stations.

The ship drifted about in the storm as the crew turned their attentions to putting out the fire. A hose was quickly coupled and the steam fire extinguisher started, but it did no good. Furiously the flames attacked the decks and cabins. Some of the crew were caught forward with Captain Bell, while others were in the after end with Chief Engineer A. E. Welch. Suddenly the fire amidships completely separated the two groups of men, and soon they were unable even to see each other through the smoke and flames.

It was then evident that the *Clarion* was doomed. The men turned to the lifeboats. The after end group managed to lower their boat over the ship's side, but it filled with so much icy water that it began to sink. The men realized that this lifeboat was their only chance to leave the burning steamer. Believing that he could clear it of water, a young oiler, James McCauley, leaped heroically overboard and swam to the sinking lifeboat. He reached it but a huge wave struck him and he disappeared in the maelstrom.

Meanwhile, the captain and the men forward had launched their boat. Thirteen men managed to climb into it. They were last seen pulling away in the direction of the lightship *Kewaunee.* They never made it. They all perished in the stormy waters.

A passing ship sighted the burning *Clarion,* but as the wreck was then drifting into dangerously shallow waters, it is quite likely that her skipper decided not to risk his ship and crew in attempting any rescue. To the six men huddled in the stern of the blazing ship it spelled doom. There remained only two choices: to stay aboard the *Clarion* and be burned to death, or to jump into the raging lake and be drowned.

The flames had ravaged the *Clarion* for four hours, and the six souls had given up hope, when out of the wildness of the night a ship's lights glowed. It was the freighter *L. C. Hanna*, Captain Mathew Anderson in command.

Hope of rescue surged through the hearts of the men huddled on the *Clarion's* after deck. The big steel rescue ship put about upon sighting the helpless men and after making a large circle, returned. A big sea was running and it was no easy task to place the *L. C. Hanna* on the exact spot where the *Clarion's* remaining crew could get aboard. Captain Anderson tried bringing his ship's bow to the stern of the burning steamer. It was a dangerous and daring operation and required great skill in navigating. At the first try the bow fell away and missed the wreck entirely. But Captain Anderson tried again—and again his ship missed. On the third attempt he brought the bow of the *Hanna* under the stern of the *Clarion* close enough for the six survivors to jump aboard. It was a truly gallant rescue. The six rescued men were taken to Buffalo aboard the *L. C. Hanna*. They were the only ones saved from the ill-fated *Clarion*.

Three days later, on Saturday, December eleventh, the tired and battered little lightship *Kewaunee* arrived in Cleveland harbor for the winter. Her season was finished. Her captain and crew of three told vivid stories of the *Clarion* burning. At one time the flaming wreck drifted within one hundred feet of where the *Kewaunee* was anchored. Later it sank some two hundred feet away. They could hear the wild cries of the drowning men in the water near them, but were unable to help. They tried to launch a small boat, but the icy waves were surging over the decks of the tossing little *Kewaunee* and it was utterly impossible.

They further reported that it was not possible to see over the waters in the darkness as a heavy mist or steam hung over the rolling surface. Only the flaming freight ship could be seen in the storm. The best that the men aboard the lightship could do was to stand by their regular posts, keep their light burning, their fog horn blowing, and sound their submarine bell. They suffered a horrible experience hearing the last wild cries of struggling men and not be able to go to their assistance.

⚓ ⚓ ⚓ ⚓ ⚓ ⚓ ⚓ ⚓

CHAPTER TWENTY-SEVEN

WRECK OF THE RICHARDSON

— *1909* —

While the ill-fated *Clarion* lay a smoldering hulk on Southeast Shoal in western Lake Erie, another ship was tearing her heart out on another dangerous shoal in the eastern end of the same turbulent lake and five more sailors were perishing in the same storm.

The second stricken freighter was the steel steamer *W. C. Richardson,* three hundred fifty-four feet long, forty-eight feet beam, and twenty-eight feet depth. She was, like the *Clarion,* on her "last trip down." In her hold she carried a large cargo of flaxseed. This is the sailors' worst grain cargo. In bulk, flaxseed is exceedingly slippery and will slide about in the hold like so much water. This disturbs the balance of the ship and can sometimes cause it considerable difficulty to remain on an even keel.

The *W. C. Richardson* was within two miles of the end of her voyage and the close of a successful season, when disaster overtook her. Imagine almost completing a trip of nearly one thousand miles, only to be wrecked

240

within sight of her destination! Such is the tale of the wreck of the *Richardson*.

This unfortunate ship was a fine trim vessel, only seven years old. She had loaded her cargo at an upper lake port and was bound for Buffalo. All went well on the downbound trip until she entered Lake Erie. Here the storm struck her. She continued onward through the elements but having a rough time of it. Possibly the flaxseed cargo may have shifted some during her run down the lake.

Shortly before dawn on Thursday, December ninth, 1909, the *Richardson* picked up the lights of Buffalo Harbor.

Rising from the floor of Lake Erie to within eleven feet of the surface, Waverly Shoal, a dangerous rock, lies about two miles off Buffalo. Somehow in the early morning blackness, the *W. C. Richardson* struck hard upon the hidden rocks. The huge freighter listed as the flaxseed shifted. Giant seas crashed over the stricken vessel and entered every opening. Water poured through her open firehold doors and soon put out the fires under her boilers. This made her completely unmanageable and also left the ship without heat while the temperature hovered around ten degrees. The waves pounded her unmercifully. Her crew became numb with the cold.

Five of her crew, believing their ship doomed, decided to leave in a lifeboat despite the raging seas and below freezing cold. Their comrades tried to persuade them to abandon their idea, but to no avail. They put off from the ship and all were lost.

Meanwhile, rockets were fired from the slanting decks. The stern had begun to sink beneath the waves and eventually it settled on the bottom, leaving the bow protruding out of the water. No help appeared from the shore. Large fires were lighted on the steel deck, hoping to attract attention to their sorry plight. The whistle was of no use since the steam was gone.

Destiny sent help to the suffering men on the ill-fated ship in the form of another steel freighter, the steamer *William A. Paine,* also Buffalo bound. Captain Emil Detlefs of the *Paine* had sighted the *Richardson* with her flaming distress signals. Should he sail on into the safety of the Buffalo breakwater and not stop to pick up the men on the *Richardson?* The wreck was in a perilous position on the rocks and it would most certainly place the *Paine* in jeopardy to attempt a rescue. It was a hard decision for a tired shipmaster to make, but Captain Detlefs made it quickly. He would try to take the men off the wrecked *Richardson!*

How the *William A. Paine* did save those freezing men from certain death by exposure and possible drowning, is one of the thrilling narratives of Great Lakes shipping. The rescue ship lay to until daylight before making any attempt. Then Captain Detlefs skillfully maneuvered his big ship in the howling wind and blinding snow until the bow of the *Paine* touched the *Richardson*. It entailed some damage to his ship, but the captain felt that the expense was justified. The crew of the *Richardson* were pulled aboard his ship, one by one, until thirteen men and one woman were rescued, all thoroughly soaked by spray with their clothing frozen to their bodies.

Even after all the survivors were removed from the wreck, Captain Detlefs' difficulties were not over. Getting his long ship away and clear of the dangerous rocks and the wreck presented still more skill in navigation. It required several hours, but at last, at seven in the morning of Friday, December tenth, the *William A. Paine* arrived at her dock in Buffalo. Captain Detlefs and his crew had had a thrilling "last trip down" but not a disasterous one, as had the captain and crew of the freighter *W. C. Richardson*.

⚓ ⚓ ⚓ ⚓ ⚓ ⚓ ⚓ ⚓

Chapter Twenty-Eight

CARFERRY PERE MARQUETTE 18

—1910—

At three in the morning, a grimy oiler hurried into the engine room from the after end. He was excited and almost breathless.

"A lot of water back aft, Chief," he reported to Chief Engineer Ross Leedham. "In the compartment under the flicker." (The "flicker" is carferry parlance for crew's quarters.)

"How much water?" the officer inquired.

"It's too much! Never saw it like that before. Something's sure wrong," the oiler insisted.

The chief turned to his telephone and called the pilot house. The first mate answered. Apprised of the situation, the mate said that he would come down and investigate.

He shortly reported to the chief engineer that it appeared to him as most likely "a busted deadlight." That would let in a lot of water, but nothing too serious. However, he called Captain Peter Kilty and reported the condition.

From then on things happened fast aboard the *Pere Marquette 18,* then the largest carferry on the Great Lakes. She was about in the middle of Lake Michigan on a trip from Ludington, Michigan, bound for Milwaukee, Wisconsin, across Lake Michigan. She had sailed just shortly before midnight. The date was September 8, 1910. Her cargo was twenty-nine loaded railroad freight cars. That very day the government inspectors had declared the ship to be sound and fit.

During that summer, the *Pere Marquette 18* had been used as an excursion steamer sailing out of Chicago. This was her first trip of the year as a carferry. She was a big ship, three hundred thirty-eight feet long, fifty-six feet beam, and twenty feet depth. Her open stern car deck had four tracks and she could carry thirty railroad cars. She had been built at Cleveland in 1902.

As the *Pere Marquette 18* cleared the harbor of Ludington and entered the open lake, Captain Kilty ordered his ship headed on a course for Milwaukee, which is in a general southwesterly direction. A stiff breeze from the north had kicked up a good sea and the ship began to roll as it was hit by the big waves. There were sixty-two persons aboard, including crew, passengers, and two stowaways.

Captain Kilty was an old hand aboard Lake Michigan carferries. Promptly upon receiving the mate's report, he went below to inspect the situation. As he

245

came up from the water-flooded after end, he ordered all pumps started, hoping to lower the water and, if possible, to locate the cause of the flooding.

But even with the pumps working full, the water continued to rise in the ship. There was no panic aboard. Each man continued to stand at his post. It was decided to alter the ship's course and to head her into Sheboygan, Wisconsin, on the western shore of the lake, fifty miles closer. The captain and crew believed they could make the shore before the water would engulf their ship.

In the hope of lightening the vessel, nine of her railroad cars were run off her stern into the lake. But this did not help much. The water continued to rise. The pumps were unable to check the onrush. At four that morning the wheelsman reported that the steamer would not respond properly to her wheel. He did not leave his post however, but continued his efforts to put the ship onto the Wisconsin shore.

By five o'clock Captain Kilty realized that his ship was doomed. He ordered the wireless operator to flash calls for help.

"*Carferry 18* sinking—help," was the message that crackled through the blackness of that early morning out over restless Lake Michigan. The operator stuck to his duty and tapped out the same message, time after time. He did not take time to add his signature. The message was the important thing right then. For nearly an hour he worked frantically at his key.

The message was received by several ships and also on the shore. One of the vessels was the *Pere Marquette 17,* a sister ship, in charge of Captain Joseph Russell. The *17* at once altered her course and began a search for the stricken steamer. As the faint light of a new day spread over the waters, those aboard the *18* saw the lights of the *17* steaming toward them. Help was at hand! Still all hands on the *18* continued at their posts, the wheelsman, the engineers, and all the others. If only they could keep her going until her bottom touched the shore!

But it was not to be. By half past seven, just as the *17* arrived at the scene, the *18* suddenly lurched to starboard and her stern started to go down, raising the huge bow of the ship high in the air. There was no hesitating; the *Pere Marquette 18* plunged quickly and finally to the four hundred foot bottom of the lake. A great roar cleft the air and a crashing noise accompanied the sinking.

Every officer on the ship lost his life. The engineers went down with the ship. Captain Kilty was last seen without a life jacket, although he had ordered others to don them. Those who could swim managed to reach the lifeboats which had previously been placed over the side for the emergency. The wheelsman, wearing a life jacket, remained in the pilot house until the bow shot into the air. He then leaped into the water and was carried downward by the suction of the sinking steamer. Tossed up to the surface only to again be drawn downward into the water, he managed to rise to the surface a second time and to grasp a part of the cabin roof which had broken loose in the sinking. He held on to this until rescued.

The crew of the rescue ship *17* immediately did what they could to save those struggling in the water. Their first attempt to launch a lifeboat proved fatal to two of the crew manning it. The small boat was crushed against the side of the ship. Another boat had better luck. It did heroic work in rescuing many of those in the water. A third lifeboat also did good work. In all, thirty-three persons were rescued by the *Pere Marquette 17.*

Two other carferries, *Pere Marquette 20* and *Pere Marquette 6,* had picked up the distress call of the stricken *18* and arrived on the scene. Also two tugs steamed up, the *A. A. C. Tessler* from Milwaukee, and another tug dispatched from Sheboygan with a lifesaving crew aboard.

Twenty-nine persons perished with the *Pere Marquette 18.* Among those were Captain Peter Kilty and Chief Engineer Ross Leedham. If any of those lost knew the actual cause of the sinking, they carried it down with them. It could not have been laid to the weather, which though not calm, was not unusual. Subsequent investigations failed to reveal the real cause of the disaster. To this day the foundering of the big carferry is still a mystery.

Speculation produced the following possibilities: deadlights at the water line may have been accidentally left open, water may have entered through the propeller shaft tunnel, a sea cock may have been opened, some stern plates may have become loosened in maneuvering the ship at a dock, a bulkhead between crew's quarters and the engine room may have given way, or the railroad cars may have shifted. No one will ever know.

CHAPTER TWENTY-NINE

THE BENJAMIN NOBLE

— *1 9 1 4* —

Most of the lake marine men, who were about in the years between 1909 and 1914 and who in that period chanced to see the trim steel freighter *Benjamin Noble,* agreed that she was a "handy vessel." She was built to be handy. When the Detroit Shipbuilding Company launched her in 1909 at Wyandotte, Michigan, they intended her to be capable of handling several types of specialized cargo, and of being able to go almost anywhere in the world.

Her length over all of two hundred fifty-six feet was made with the idea that she could pass through the Welland Canal and the other St. Lawrence River locks and have only a few inches to spare. She was built to withstand the stress and strains of deep sea navigation. Everything about her was termed "extra strong." Her hold was one large compartment, and her deck was so constructed as to enable her to carry heavy loads upon it without straining the ship. The principal cargo in mind in this connection was pulpwood, but the carrying of railroad iron and steel was also one of her special original items. In appearance she resembled all the other lake freighters of her day, with her pilot house forward and her engine room aft. Her other dimensions were: breadth, forty-two feet, and depth eighteen feet. Her twelve foot propeller could push her along at eleven miles per hour under normal conditions.

The *Benjamin Noble* sailed the lakes well during the years just after her launching; that is, 1910, '11, '12, and '13. 1914 was to be her last year. She was destined to disappear that year and only small parts of wreckage were to come ashore to testify of her sinking. Exactly where she went down is still a matter of speculation. Not a living person was to come through the ordeal. Lake Superior alone knows where the freighter *Benjamin Noble* lies, and that is deep and cold.

Captain John Eisenhardt, a native of Milwaukee, was in command of the *Benjamin Noble*. It was his first trip as a master of a vessel. It was also his last. The ill-fated freighter carried a cargo of railroad iron and steel, mostly rails, and was bound up the lakes for Duluth, Minnesota. She passed up the Sault Ste. Marie Locks after dark, seven o'clock in the early evening, on Saturday, April 25, 1914, and was last seen by men ashore as she headed across Whitefish Bay to Lake Superior.

Shortly after the twinkling lights of the *Benjamin Noble* faded away in the distance, the weather bureau believed that Lake Superior was in for a storm and they hastened to notify all shipping to be prepared for the blow. It is extremely unlikely that the officers of

251

the *Noble* ever received this information. The foul weather began with a fog over the lake, and for twelve hours it enshrouded the waters. Then strong winds quickly dissipated the fog. By Monday night, the twenty-seventh, the lake was a terrible sight to behold. A violent northeast gale was sweeping across the water, causing mountainous seas to rise and fall. At Duluth the wind and waves did thousands of dollars damage to the famous aerial bridge and to property along Park Point. A huge coal unloading machine on a Duluth dock was blown down and it fell upon the steamer *Champlain* tied at the dock, causing considerable damage to her forward houses, but fortunately no lives were lost in the accident. Sleet accompanied the high winds. All vessels remained in port as the gale swept Lake Superior. That was the night that lake men believe the *Benjamin Noble* was lost.

Possibly the *Noble* arrived off the Duluth pier heads sometime during the height of the storm and was wrecked trying to make the harbor. Unfortunately the south light on the Duluth entry pier went out during the storm. It was impossible for the light tenders to relight the antiquated oil lamp, as the waves were battering the pier heads and crashing high into the air. No one could possibly get even a quarter of the way out on the pier to the light without being washed into the lake.

No one will ever know just where the ill-fated *Noble* went down. Lake men can only guess, and each to his own experiences. Late in the afternoon of Tuesday, the twenty-eighth, a Duluth policeman reported the finding of two hatch covers on Minnesota Point. They were subsequently identified as from the *Benjamin Noble*. Then other wreckage washed ashore along the Point: oars, life belts, spars, all bearing the name of the unfortunate freighter. No bodies came ashore with the wreckage. Soon thereafter all hope was abandoned for the *Noble*. The wreckage continued to wash up on the beaches of Minnesota Point for several days.

Mutely these bits of flotsam told of the sad struggle of men and their ship against the sea and the storm. This battle was won by the elements, but there were other vessels in behind the protection of the Duluth breakwater that had made the port, but not without great difficulty. In these few cases the men and their ships had won over the storm and the waters. But what caused the foundering of the freighter *Benjamin Noble* and the loss of her entire crew of twenty out there on Lake Superior still remains one of the mysteries of the Great Lakes.

⚓ ⚓ ⚓ ⚓ ⚓ ⚓ ⚓ ⚓

CHAPTER THIRTY

THE WRECK OF THE OSCODA

— 1 9 1 4 —

Except for the pulpwood trade the transportation of forest products has vanished from the Great Lakes. Pulpwood is in no manner connected with the commercial lumber business, as the logs are eventually made into various forms of paper and none of it finds its way into the construction industry. Just prior to the turn of the century the commercial lumber trade on the Great Lakes was big business. Ships, built of wood, especially for that trade, numbered into the scores. The lake sailors dubbed them "hookers."

The Great Lakes freight trade never saw more quaint and romantic steamers than were those old lumber hookers. Small ships when compared with to-day's giants, but for their day they were considered of fair size. They plodded along the lake lanes, usually with a tow of one, two, or sometimes three barges. The barges were nearly as picturesque as were the steamers, all of them built of wood, and most of them cut down from former noble sailing schooners.

The lumber hooker was to be seen in almost every

port on the Great Lakes and tributaries up to the St. Lawrence River. They poked their blunt bows into the lumber mill loading docks of isolated Georgian Bay and Lake Superior and even Lake Huron. Loading the ships was usually a long and tedious task. Most all of the stowing and the unloading was done by hand except, of course, the heavier timbers, which were handled by cranes or block and tackle. The fragrant lumber was hauled to the docks of the large cities on Lake Erie and Lake Michigan. The lumber fleet never carried unhewn logs, but always the fresh-cut lumber ready for the construction trade in the cities.

The dwindling supply of lumber in the forests adjacent to the lakes brought a slowing down of the operations of the lumber carriers. A few were built of steel in the early years of the twentieth century, but finding little business these ships sought other trades. But, here and there along the lake routes, an old weather-beaten hooker would churn along, a last lingering tool of a once flourishing trade. It all combined to make a most colorful era of lake sailing days. Now, in 1951, the last lumber steamer has long since vanished from the lakes and those memorable days are all but forgotten.

One by one the old hookers dropped from the trade as the available cargoes diminished. Some went by fire, some by dismantling, and some by stress of weather, as did the old *Oscoda,* which figuratively died with her boots on, in northern Lake Michigan during a howling winter gale in November, 1914. The tale of her ending is somehow a bit different than most lake shipwrecks and it can rival in all its details the old sea yarns of fiction.

It was early in the month of November, 1914, that the *Oscoda* plowed her way slowly westward through the Straits of Mackinac. Trailing behind the tired old steamboat on long dragging tow lines, were two barges, the *A. C. Tuxbury* and the *Alice B. Norris*. All three vessels were heavily loaded with lumber. They had cleared from a Georgian Bay lumber mill and were bound for Chicago. November sailing on the Great Lakes is always a risky business, and masters watch the skies closely for any signs of quick changes in the weather.

On Saturday morning, November seventh, at ten-thirty, storm warnings were ordered up on Lake Superior, Lake Huron, and Lake Michigan. The flags flew stiff in the wind from each of the weather stations along the lakes named. It was a danger signal intended for the mariners. After their disasterous experience of the previous November, it was a warning that they did not intend to ignore.

So the *Oscoda* and her two barges put into the harbor of Saint Ignace, Michigan, for shelter and dropped their anchors. There they were safe from the gale that was then blowing from the southwest. While at anchor it was discovered that the barge *Alice B. Norris* was leaking. Pumping was begun, and it helped to get rid of some of the incoming water, but it was impossible to repair the leak. This condition naturally caused some concern to the masters of the barge and the steamboat. It would be well to get to their destination and then get the *Norris* safely unloaded. But all that day and evening the wind continued to howl out of the southwest and kept the three lumber-laden vessels at their sheltered anchorage.

By midnight the wind had shifted to the northwest. It continued strong, but the men on the *Oscoda* knew that by hugging the west shore of Lake Michigan they would escape the violence of the storm, as it would put their ships under the protecting land. There are many places where a northwest wind is very bad for shipping caught out on Lake Michigan, but in the case of the *Oscoda* and her consorts, it was an opportunity to proceed under protection.

The anchors were hove up and the *Oscoda* gathered up her brood of barges and began the long trek up the west coast of big Lake Michigan, but the weather continued to plague the trio. Blinding snow flurries swept across the water from the land, obscuring vision for often times long stretches. Then fog rolled in. It was very difficult navigating.

The course, of necessity, taken by the *Oscoda* and her consorts along the shore line was a dangerous path for a ship, dotted with boulder reefs and rocky shoals. Some thirty-five miles along the route lies Pelkie Reef, three-quarters of a mile long, with the water over it varying in depth from eleven feet at one end to one foot at the other. It lies off the shore about two and one half miles and curves with the coast. This ships' nemesis rises sheer in thirty feet of water.

At three o'clock that Sunday morning, fate steered the heavily-burdened *Oscoda* full onto Pelkie Reef. Her heavy keel grounded hard upon the hidden jagged rocks so close to the surface of the water. The ship came to a sudden stop throwing the men on duty off their balance. She had driven herself well up on the hard reef and it was impossible to budge her. She was there to stay.

The captains of the barges following, sensing immediately that their steamer had run hard aground, let go their anchors and stopped their forward progress. There was nothing to do until daylight arrived. The wind still blew strong out of the northwest but, for the time being, the three vessels were in the lee of the land. The leading barge, the *A. C. Tuxbury,* anchored unknowingly to the lake side of Pelkie Reef after the *Oscoda* had struck, and the other consort, the *Alice B. Norris,* anchored inside the reef, between it and Point Epoufette, Michigan, on the shore.

As a stormy day dawned over the waters of the wreck scene, the men aboard the three vessels began to make plans for their relief. The *A. C. Tuxbury,* though without any power of her own and only by expert handling, was hove alongside the grounded *Oscoda.* It was decided to attempt to lighten the steamer by removing some of her deck load of lumber and placing it on the *A. C. Tuxbury*. This was a back-breaking task out there in the November storm, but the men all fell to. Hour after hour the pieces of lumber were passed laboriously from steamer deck to schooner-barge.

As Sunday wore on and while the crews labored, the wind began to shift and it brought heavy waves slapping against the vessels' sides. The *A. C. Tuxbury* began to roll and at the same time to pound herself against the *Oscoda*. This made the situation much worse and, as the storm increased and the seas grew larger, the *Tuxbury* was more violently striking the *Oscoda*. At five-thirty that evening, with a terrific crashing and grinding, the *Oscoda* toppled over on her starboard side, which was the side that the *A. C. Tuxbury* was working. Much of the remaining cargo of the steamer slipped off the decks and into the lake. The smokestack crashed upon the barge's deck and then rolled off into the water. The *Oscoda* settled on her side upon Pelkie Reef, a complete wreck.

After being dealt this harsh blow by the elements, the crews of both the barge and the steamer decided that the *Oscoda* was done for and they abandoned the steamer, taking their belongings aboard the *Tuxbury*. There they spent Sunday night. The storm still continued to lash the *Tuxbury* and the *Alice B. Norris*, and the wreck of the *Oscoda*.

Daybreak Monday found things about the same as at sundown the day before. The crew and officers were anxious to get ashore and send word of their plight to the owners of the ships, also to obtain some help in getting the *A. C. Tuxbury* and the *Alice B. Norris* on their way, now that their own steamer was wrecked. A few selected men decided to launch the lifeboat and try to make the run across the two and one half miles of stormy water to the shore.

The lifeboat of the *A. C. Tuxbury* was made ready; the men took their places and pulled away from the barge. The heavy seas lifted the small boat high in the air and then dropped it quickly down into a valley of water. It was soon learned that the little craft was unmanageable in the storm, and it was with considerable difficulty that the men returned to the *Tuxbury*.

The situation aboard the *Tuxbury* was fast becoming untenable also. At any moment the barge's anchor might drag and allow the vessel to strike the near Pelkie Reef. Instead of subsiding, the storm was on the increase. It was urgent that some help be sent to the barges if they were to be spared.

Eighteen men and three women comprised the crews of both the *Oscoda* and the *Tuxbury*, and all were now quartered aboard the latter ship. It was decided next to attempt to make a raft from the lumber cargo and then to ride it over the reef to the *Alice B. Norris*, which was at anchor just inside the treacherous reef.

THE WRECK OF THE OSCODA

Timbers from the cargo were lashed together with pieces of rope, and a crude raft was built. It was decided that it could carry six men. The six, on their improvised raft, embarked on their perilous ride through the breakers that were crashing over the reef. They were picked up safely by the men on the *Alice B. Norris* on the other side.

Another similiar raft was constructed by the men remaining on the *Tuxbury,* and it too carried six more men over the reef to land safely aboard the *Norris.* After the experience of watching the two rafts make the journey over the reef, the nine remaining persons on the *Tuxbury* believed they could then make the trip to the *Norris* in the lifeboat. This they tried and made it. The entire crews of all three ships were then safely aboard the *Alice B. Norris*, inside of Pelkie Reef.

Just before leaving the *Tuxbury,* several of the men decided to float their personal belongings ashore by fastening the articles securely to pieces of timber from the cargo. They figured that the timbers would eventually float ashore and that they could claim their belongings later, if and when they landed. They feared the *Tuxbury* would not last out the gale, and to leave their things aboard might be to lose them entirely.

Late that day the seamen, huddling in the cabin of the *Norris,* trying to keep warm around the stove, were surprised to hear a deep-throated whistle from the big tug *Schenk* steaming through the tempest toward them.

Evidently the serious plight of the shipwrecked craft had been sighted from the sparsely settled shore, and word of the disaster had been sent out requesting help The *Schenk* had come all the way from Sault Ste. Marie, Michigan, in answer. The rescue tug managed to get a line on the *Alice B. Norris,* and braving the breakers, towed the leaking schooner-barge back into the safety of Saint Ignace harbor, from whence she had sailed several days previously.

The following day the tug *Gifford,* from Manistique, Michigan, arrived at the scene of the wreck and took the barge *A. C. Tuxbury* in tow. It was intended that they would go to Manistique harbor, fifty miles to the west, but the storm was not yet through with the sorely battered schooner-barge.

It was a black night with the wind howling from the northeast as the *Gifford* and the *Tuxbury* tried to round Seul Choix Point, on the north shore of Lake Michigan, enroute to Manistique. The violent pitching of the heavily-laden *Tuxbury* placed unexpected strain on the towline, and it parted.

The tug, freed of its burdensome tow, leaped forward, thus informing her crew of the accident to their towline. They immediately began a search for their lost tow, but it had disappeared into the wild night and was not to be seen.

Late the following afternoon the *A. C. Tuxbury,* drifting helplessly, was sighted by the tugs *Anabel* and

THE WRECK OF THE OSCODA

Burger, off Point aux Barques, many miles from where the *Gifford* had lost her. The two tugs quickly took the barge in tow and without further difficulty, the storm having subsided, towed her first into port, where her cargo was unloaded, and then eventually to a shipyard for repairs.

All the crews lived to again set foot on solid ground. The *Oscoda* remained a wreck on Pelkie Reef and eventually broke up there. Only one thing remained to be cleaned up for them. That was to locate their belongings that they had cast adrift during the gale.

After a long search they located their valuables. To their utter dismay they found that the belongings were considered as jetsam, having been thrown overboard or jettisoned during a storm and washed up from a wreck, and as such were being held for payment of two hundred dollars to cover the safe return of their possessions. Apparently the milk of human kindness had somehow soured into vinegar.

♙ ♙ ♙ ♙ ♙ ♙ ♙ ♙

Chapter Thirty-One

JOHN OWEN—H. E. RUNNELS—MYRON

— 1 9 1 9 —

November of 1919 found an interesting aggregation
of ships on Lake Superior. They were all intent upon
finishing up whatever business remained in the northland and then leaving for winter quarters, usually on
one of the lower lakes. Little steamboats with wooden
hulls and large new ore carriers with great steel hulls
were all of one mind—finish the season and be home
for Christmas. Most of them were destined to accomplish this feat, though for several it would be a close
race with the elements, but three, alas, would never
make port.

Communication from the ships out on the big lake
was difficult. Mainly, word of trouble came only when
a vessel that had sighted wreckage would make port.
Help could not yet be sought through the mouthpiece
of a telephone aboard ship, and her plight could seldom
be sparked over the air. There were few vessels equipped
with wireless telegraph. Each ship was on its own and
each master had to depend upon his own resources.
Effective help could come only from a ship within sight.
Often such a vessel would be in much the same precari-

ous situation as the craft requiring assistance, battling the same wind and water and temperature. True, some ships were newer and stronger and more powerful and could sometimes render effective rescue.

Such was the situation on Lake Superior in November over the week end of the eighth and ninth, 1919. Captain George "Ed" Benham of the steel steamer *John Owen* scanned the wild waters of the lake as the wind shrieked through the rigging. He was safe at an elevator dock in the Duluth Harbor. Battened tightly beneath his hatches were some one hundred thousand bushels of grain destined for Midland, Ontario. He decided to await a lull in the storm before beginning his long trek. Monday passed and the waters quieted some. Tuesday morning found things slightly better. The skipper figured that the blow was most likely over and consequently he decided to sail. By mid-morning the *John Owen* had passed under the famous Duluth aerial bridge and out the long piers and was well along on her course down the big lake.

Captain "Ed" Benham, as he was known in the lakes sailing fraternity, was an old hand aboard ship. He had played on ships' decks as a boy and sailed there as a man. His father had been an owner of ships both of sail and steam. The Chief Engineer, Ira Falconer, was also a well-known man of the lakes, and he too had brothers sailing. The *John Owen* was a well-rated vessel, well-maintained, and did not look her age of thirty years.

There were other ships on Lake Superior that day—ships that were later to report sighting the *John Owen* fighting the giant seas as she ploughed her stormy way eastward. These reports were favorable. All said that the *Owen* was doing as well as could be expected in the heavy weather. But later, ships traveling the same course as the *John Owen* arrived at Sault Ste. Marie Locks, all of them forty to sixty hours behind schedule, with no reports of sighting the *Owen*. W. C. Richardson & Company, her owners, grew apprehensive as the hours grew into days, and still the *John Owen* failed to arrive at some port on Lake Superior. One skipper told of seeing her, but later it was learned that the vessel he had seen was the steamer *Griffin* which resembled the *Owen* in appearance, and which later appeared at the locks for downbound passage.

There was nothing to do but wait. The storm had not abated. Instead it had again developed greater fury. Snow fell thickly and was swirled about over the water so that men in the pilot houses could not see a ship's length ahead. During a lull in the snowfall, one captain reported a particularly odd sky over the lake. There were five distinct rainbows! Masters later reported that the seas were smashing over the bows of their ships with terrific force and the water was crashing down the decks, taking with it everything not fastened down. Deck houses were badly damaged, as were pilot houses. Vessels scurried for the nearest shelter available on Lake Superior.

JOHN OWEN—H. E. RUNNELS—MYRON

Gradually the storm subsided and the weather-bound ships poked their noses out into the sullen angry lake to continue on toward their destinations. All were days behind their schedules. As each ship locked down at the Soo, their captains were asked if they had sighted the *John Owen,* now so long overdue. These skippers had seen nothing of the *Owen.* Neither did the upbound ships arriving in Duluth or Two Harbors or Ashland know anything of her whereabouts. She had disappeared! Something must have happened to the *John Owen* that neither man's experience nor skill could overcome. The ship had foundered!

This sad fact slowly became a realization to the families of the officers and crew of the *Owen,* and to the owners of the ship, and finally to the great mass of men who sail the lakes. The *John Owen* had gone down in Lake Superior and taken all hands and her cargo with her.

Then there steamed into port the steamers *Wilpen* and *Thomas Barlum.* They both reported sighting floating wreckage Friday afternoon off Manitou Island, near the course which the *John Owen* traveled. The wreckage consisted of a battered pilot house, an overturned lifeboat, and the body of a man still being held upright by a life preserver. Immediately the Coast Guard dispatched surfboats from Eagle Harbor to Manitou Island to investigate and identify the wreckage.

Next came a report from the master of the freighter

Edward N. Ohl which had limped into Buffalo many days late. He told of sighting the *John Owen* on Thursday afternoon on Lake Superior, between Devils Island and Eagle Harbor. He stated that at the time he was having great difficulty with his own ship and could see that the *Owen* was also in similar difficulty. However, the *Owen* had apparently turned about and was then headed into the storm, retracing her course. Possibly her captain decided his ship would weather the storm better in this way.

Next word came by wireless from the steamer *Westmount,* upbound on Lake Superior. Her captain stated that his ship had passed through wreckage twenty miles southeast of Caribou Island. The wreckage consisted of the side of a white cabin and smaller bits. He was unable to identify any of it.

Finally on Monday, November seventeenth, two tugs put into Grand Marais, Michigan, for shelter. They were the *Alabama* and the *Iowa,* and they brought in wreckage definitely as being from the *John Owen.* The worst fears of all concerned were then confirmed. The steamer *John Owen* had gone down in Lake Superior near Caribou Island with all her officers and crew, twenty-six in all, which included one woman, the wife of the steward.

The waters in which the *John Owen* foundered are both deep and cold. To this day undoubtedly there lies the remains of the ship on the rocky bottom of Lake

Superior and inside her cabins and engine room, if they still remain intact, rest most of her personnel. One body was recovered, that of the assistant engineer. It was found encased in ice by Coast Guardsmen on the beach near Crisp Point the following April. Around the body was a life preserver from the steamer *John Owen,* the only body from the ship ever to be found.

At two-thirty on the cold morning of Monday, November tenth, of the same year, 1919, a tired old lumber steamer pulled slowly into one of the great locks at the Soo. She was the wooden vessel *H. E. Runnels,* upbound with some nine hundred tons of hard coal in her hold. She had left a Lake Erie port and was bound for Duluth. Two heavily-clad deck hands scrambled over her side as she scraped against the lock walls and with the help of two lock men they made the steamer's lines fast.

For the past twenty-six years the *H. E. Runnels* had been locking up and down at the Soo. Most of the time she carried lumber directly from the camps on the upper lakes to the large cities on the lower lakes. Most of the trips she towed a barge also loaded with lumber. The lumber steamers were as a rule slow travelers, the average ship making seven or eight round trips during a full season. But on this trip the owners had sent the *H. E. Runnels* to the lakehead without a tow barge.

Of course no one could know that this was to be the last time that the *Runnels* would lock through. Twenty minutes after she entered the lock, the water had lifted her to the Lake Superior level. The deck hands climbed back aboard their steamer and she sailed out of the lock, headed for Whitefish Bay and Lake Superior.

On Tuesday the nation learned that the northwest was in the grip of a bad storm. Fierce blizzards were sweeping over Lake Superior headed eastward. Gales were forecast for all the upper lake region. The *Runnels* was headed straight into this terrific storm that at that minute was sweeping down the big lake from the west. The staunch little steamboat made fair time across Whitefish Bay, but after she entered Lake Superior things began to change. Her course was evidently set for the entrance of the Keweenaw Waterway, a much-sought haven of refuge for storm-tossed ships.

Things turned out badly for the plucky little freighter. Giant waves struck her, wracking her timbers from her stem to her stern. They crashed continually over her decks. The *Runnels* made slow headway caught as she was in the storm. All Tuesday, Wednesday, and Thursday she fought her way, inch by inch. Spray froze and soon she was coated with tons of ice. It was almost more than the old steamboat could stand.

Grand Marais, Michigan, is a small village about half the way between Whitefish Bay and Munising, Michigan, on the south shore of Lake Superior. The nearest railroad is some thirty-five miles distant. Grand Marais affords the only harbor of any kind in this stretch of almost one hundred miles of very dangerous coast, and where numerous shipwrecks have occurred It has been a harbor of refuge for ships in trouble for many years and a United States Coast Guard Station has long been maintained there.

Grand Marais was the only hope for the captain of the *H. E. Runnels,* as his ship began to go to pieces on raging Lake Superior. Maybe they would be sighted by the lookout of the surf station. Would the ship hold out until port could be made? All hands were doubtful. The men worked the pumps furiously, but it did little good. The whistle was tied open and the United States flag was run upside down, the sailors' sign of critical distress, and the brave little freighter battled onward.

Between snow squalls the men on the foundering steamer caught sight of the port of Grand Marais. They had hopes that they might yet be saved! The light structure and the fog signals on the shore at the surf station had been blown down by the wind. But in spite of these handicaps, and the fact that the officer in charge was ill and confined to his bed, the station maintained an alert lookout nevertheless. It was now daybreak of Friday, November fourteenth.

Grand Marais had been a haven of refuge for another ship the previous day. She was a new type of craft in those days, the *U. S. Submarine Chaser Number 438,*

271

on a training cruise out of Chicago. Barely making the harbor before the storm claimed her, the staunch chaser docked safely at the life-saving station. Her captain, Keeper John Anderson of the Chicago Life-Saving Station and his crew were resting after their strenuous experiences.

Their rest however was not for long. They were destined to be the principal actors in one of the most heroic rescues to be performed on the Great Lakes. By daybreak the helpless steamer *H. E. Runnels* had been sighted and reported. She had "fetched up" on a rocky shelf a little off the harbor entrance and was being pounded badly by the heavy surf. Her cargo was beginning to be washed toward shore. She was entirely encased in ice many inches thick.

With the regular officer of the surf station too ill to be about, the visiting officer from the submarine chaser took charge. Seventeen men comprising the crew of the *Runnels* shivered aboard the fast breaking-up ship, praying for their rescue. They were helpless to do anything for themselves. Their own lifeboats were so completely iced over that any thought of launching them was impossible. Their fires were out and the zero winds on the lake stung them even inside the remaining shelter aboard ship. They could not live long in such a situation. A slow death by freezing stared them gauntly in the face.

Providence had placed Keeper John Anderson at

the right place and at the right time for the doomed men aboard the foundering steamboat, and as subsequent events turned out, he was indeed the right man. He immediately took charge of the rescue work. He could easily see that in the prevailing zero temperature and smashing seas the breeches buoy would be of no avail. Ice would form on ropes and blocks making it impossible to operate.

There was only one other method of rescue. That was by the surfboat. Anderson and his men would have to man the thirty foot craft that was part of the station's equipment. The path that the boat must take was across snarling savage seas that could easily capsize the small boat, and anyone tossed into that sweeping surf would most surely be lost. It was a great risk for every man who took his place in the boat. But they did man the rescue craft. Anderson himself took the steering oar and with great difficulty they got their boat out of the small harbor onto the lake and headed for the wreck. It was a short but perilous trip. Flying spray froze on the men as they sat in the boat. The craft bobbed and dived, rolled and pitched. But it continually shortened the distance between it and the wrecked *Runnels*.

Imagine the feelings of those aboard the freighter as they watched the uncertain progress of the lifeboat struggling onward to rescue them. That was their only hope for any future. At last the rescue craft managed to contact the *Runnels*. Men thoroughly numbed and

273

stunned by the cold were placed in the surfboat and the return trip to the shore was begun.

It required four round trips of that little boat to rescue the entire crew of the *Runnels*. Most of them were nearly dead from exposure and exhaustion. By forty minutes past noon the last man from the wreck was brought safely to the surf station at Grand Marais. Every last one that was on the ship had been safely removed! A fine record.

That afternoon the *H. E. Runnels* practically fell apart in the raging seas. The rescue was not a minute too soon.

A small wooden steamer and her schooner-barge consort were loading lumber at the Lake Superior port of Munising, Michigan. The steamer's captain, Walter R. Neale, watched restless Lake Superior with apprehension. Soon it would become his duty to pilot his ship and her tow across that unpredictable water. The master weighed his responsibilities carefully. There was his thirty-one year old vessel, and the tow-barge to be considered. There were the valuable lumber cargoes that they carried, seven hundred thousand feet on the *Myron* and one million and fifty thousand feet aboard the barge *Miztec*. And most precious of all were the lives of the men in both crews, eighteen on his own steamer

274

and seven on the *Miztec*. Almost one thousand miles of cold storm-tossed waters lay between him and his destination, a lower lake port. Winter was fast setting in. Thick blue ice would soon lock these water lanes solid for many months. Time was running out. Two ships, the *John Owen* and the *H. E. Runnels*, had already been lost on Lake Superior within a fortnight. The wreck of the *Runnels* lay almost directly on his course. The shipmaster faced a tough situation.

Finally the last timber was stowed aboard and the steamer and barge were ready to cast off their lines. It was early morning of Saturday, November 22, 1919, that Captain Neale decided to sail. The little wooden *Myron,* only one hundred eighty-six feet long by thirty-two feet beam and thirteen feet draft, began swinging away from her dock. The towline tightened as the larger *Miztec* followed along. The long trip had begun!

Upon clearing the port of Munising, and while off the famous Pictured Rocks, the captain set his course for Whitefish Point, about ninety miles distant along the rugged south shore of Lake Superior.

All went well for about two hours. Then it was learned that the *Myron* was beginning to take water. The weather turned worse, the wind increasing to around thirty miles an hour with intermittent rain and snow squalls. The crew turned to the pumps and all hands worked to rid their ship of the inrushing water.

But in spite of their combined efforts the water rose

quickly until within a few more hours it threatened to put out the fires under the boilers. The *Myron* was in a desperate plight. To add to her troubles the wind increased to full gale proportions from the northwest.

The luckless little *Myron* was not alone on Lake Superior that afternoon. Steaming along through the storm, bound down with ore, appeared the steel freighter *Adriatic*. It was shortly after twelve noon when the men in the pilot house of the *Adriatic* made out what later proved to be the stricken *Myron* and her tow, the *Miztec*. At this time the *Adriatic* was some twelve miles to the northward of the *Myron*. Both ships were heading for the shelter of Whitefish Point, and their courses would eventually carry both steamers to the same spot on the lake.

Captain Neale decided it was imperative to drop his barge. In a master stroke of navigation he ran the *Myron* alongside the *Miztec*. Explaining his actions to the barge captain, the *Miztec* was cut loose and her anchors were run out, but she continued to drift before the wind.

It was nearly two that afternoon when the *Myron* let go her barge, as reported later by the *Adriatic*. The *Myron,* freed of her burdensome barge, then continued on, apparently making better weather of it and the two ships gradually neared each other.

Three o'clock found the *Adriatic* and the *Myron* abreast of Crisp Point, some six miles off, with the wind blowing fifty to sixty miles an hour out of the northwest. As the two vessels drew close to each other, the *Adriatic's* navigators noticed that the *Myron* suddenly blew four short blasts of her whistle and later they saw her hoist her flag upside down, thus asking for assistance.

The captain of the *Adriatic* then maneuvered his ship alongside the *Myron* trying to break the heavy seas from crashing over her. The *Myron* was then proceeding at about ten miles an hour and it was believed by the men of the *Adriatic* that she would be able to make the protection of Whitefish Point. But only the men on the ill-fated *Myron* knew their desperate plight. The inrushing water was rising fast in her hold. At twenty minutes past four that afternoon she stopped. The water had reached and extinguished her boiler fires! Just three miles short of Whitefish Point and comparative safety, and one and one half miles from the shore!

Captain Neale ordered his crew into the lifeboats. Within five minutes the *Myron* went down. Most of the men had made the small boats, but not Captain Neale! He remained in the pilot house. The storm struck savagely at the tiny house and shortly dashed it to pieces. Captain Neale clung desperately to the roof section which had suddenly become a floating raft. He clambered upon it and thus riding atop, was washed away from the wreck and out upon the open lake.

It was beginning to get dark and snow was falling. The heavy lumber cargo of the *Myron* floated about crashing into the bobbing lifeboats. The surface of the lake was littered with the dangerous tossing timbers. The two lifeboats struggled to get into the lee of the main body of flotsam for some scant protection from the heavy seas.

At this critical moment another large steel freighter reached the fateful scene. She was the *H. P. McIntosh,* also loaded with iron ore and bound down the lakes. Both the newly arrived ship and the *Adriatic* began attempts to rescue the men in the boats and upon the floating wreckage. But with the wind howling at sixty miles an hour and whipping giant seas over their decks and with only one mile in which to maneuver their long and heavily-laden vessels, the rescue ships had great difficulties. The *McIntosh* managed to get close enough for her crew to throw lines to some of the men on floating wreckage, but these unfortunates were not able to reach the offered ropes.

The *Adriatic* pulled ahead to alongside the wreckage and to windward of it thinking to break the seas so that the lifeboats could pull up to her, or that a line could be thrown to them. But the wind was too strong for the small boats to pull against and they remained tossing violently in the giant waves. Again the master of the *Adriatic* tried to come about and effect a rescue but the wind had carried the wreckage nearer the shore and the rescue steamer all but hit bottom herself. There

278

was nothing left to do but pull away and leave the struggling souls in the boats and on the wreckage to their fates. Not one of those men survived.

Both the *Adriatic* and the *H. P. McIntosh* reported the wreck upon their arrival at the Sault Ste. Marie Locks. The Coast Guard patrolled the shore line for forty-five miles where cargo and wreckage floated in hoping that the lifeboats with the men would be blown ashore. The itinerant sub-chaser *438* under command of Keeper John Anderson, which had figured so prominently the week previous in the rescue of the crew of the wrecked steamer *H. E. Runnels* at Grand Marais, also put out, but made a fruitless search of the waters of the *Myron* disaster.

The gale continued throughout the night and the probabilities are that the boats were either swamped by the giant seas or were stove in by the heavy floating timbers from the cargo.

On Monday, November twenty-fourth, following the wreck, the big freighter *W. C. Franz* steamed into Port Arthur, Ontario, at the Canadian lakehead. She brought with her Captain Walter R. Neale, the fifty-nine year old skipper of the ill-fated lumber carrier *Myron.*

The master of the wrecked freighter had been sighted lying atop his ship's pilot house roof in an unconscious condition some twenty miles from the scene of the wreck. He had floated thus for twenty hours. The captain of the *W. C. Franz* at first believed the castaway was dead, but a slow movement of the shipwrecked man's hand was noticed and a boat was lowered, since the sea had calmed. Captain Neale was brought carefully aboard the *Franz*—the only survivor of the unfortunate steamer *Myron*.

The fate of the schooner-barge *Miztec* proved better. She was picked up by the freighter *Argus* which towed her into shelter under Whitefish Point. Her deckload of lumber had been carried away and she had lost her rudder. The tug *Iowa* brought the battered vessel into port at Sault Ste. Marie the following Monday evening.

⚓ ⚓ ⚓ ⚓ ⚓ ⚓ ⚓ ⚓

CHAPTER THIRTY-TWO

THE FERRY STEAMER OMAR D. CONGER

— *1 9 2 2* —

"Did you ever hear of the steamer *Omar D. Conger?*"
I inquired of several persons recently in Port Huron,
Michigan. Almost all replied in the negative. One or
two said that the name sounded familiar, but they
could not recollect at the moment anything very definite about the vessel.

All of which bears out the statement so often made,
that the general public soon forgets. Folks move about
from city to city and to and from the farm lands; some
newcomers arrive as settlers from foreign lands, some
die and others are born. What made headlines thirty
years ago is today all but forgotten in the quickening
tempo of the rush of time.

On March twenty-sixth, 1922, the name of the large
ferry steamer *Omar D. Conger* was on the lips of everyone in Port Huron and her Canadian neighbor, Sarnia,
Ontario, just across the Saint Clair River. News services were quickly spreading the name of the ship across
the country. The steamer had blown itself to bits, right
in the heart of the city of Port Huron.

It was a spring afternoon—a Sunday, and the city was quiet. Church-goers had returned to their homes, many sat at their mid-day meals or were relaxing with their Sunday newspapers. The streets were almost deserted. Here and there could be seen a person or couple strolling the sidewalks.

But down on the Black River at the ferry docks things were humming. Folks were waiting for the ferry to Sarnia. Alongside of the dock lay the propeller steamer *Omar D. Conger*.

There were no passengers aboard as yet. She was due to start her day's run at three that afternoon and it was then about twenty minutes after two. Not all the crew were aboard, except those in the engine room and stokehold, where men were preparing the machinery for the start. Split timing saved the lives of the waiting passengers.

Without warning, at exactly twenty-two minutes past two, the big ferry exploded. With a terrifying blast the ship blew apart. Debris filled the air. In one quick flash the ship became flying pieces of wood and metal.

Her boiler was blown out of the hull and went in pieces skyward. Some parts of it sailed through the sky and landed on a frame residence over three hundred feet away from the dock, demolishing the house and setting fire to the rubble. Fortunately all the occupants were out of the place, thereby missing almost certain death.

THE FERRY STEAMER OMAR D. CONGER

Utility poles and wires along Quay Street were torn down by the force of the explosion. Plate glass windows were broken in business places within four blocks of the river. A man walking on Water Street some distance from the scene was struck on the head by flying wood. Others on streets blocks away were stunned, and some were thrown to the ground.

Services were being held in a nearby chapel of a funeral home. A piece of a radiator from the *Conger* crashed through the side wall of the building, injuring several of the mourners and causing a small panic. A lifeboat cleared the top of a dock building and crashed on the pavement of Quay Street. Waterfront folks across the wide Saint Clair River at Sarnia reported hearing and feeling the effects of the explosion, but no actual damage was reported there.

The steamer *Omar D. Conger* was, of course, no more. Her wooden hull quickly filled with water and sank alongside the dock. Firemen and police roped off the scene of the disaster, as hundreds of curious citizens crowded the riverfront.

Another ferry steamer, the *City of Cheboygan,* was fortunate to have missed the explosion, although just by minutes. She was steaming slowly up the Black River toward the ferry dock on her return trip from Sarnia with about one hundred passengers. She was some two hundred yards away when the *Conger* blew up. Her passengers were badly frightened but otherwise unhurt.

A smaller ferry steamer, *Hiawatha,* was lying immediately south of the *Conger* at the wharf and was badly damaged at the stern.

Four members of the *Conger* crew were killed; her chief engineer, R. A. Campbell, was later found buried in the wreckage, as was a fireman. One deck hand's body was found on a nearby pile of coal, and another deck hand died on the way to a hospital. Several others were injured by flying debris.

The exact cause of the terrific explosion of the *Omar D. Conger* is still a mystery. Possibly one of the men killed may have known the cause, but marine engineers believe this is unlikely. Her boiler and equipment had been inspected and approved by the regular government inspectors only three weeks previously.

The *Omar D. Conger,* or what remained of her, was eventually removed from the waters of the Black River and the ship was written off as a total loss. She had been a very popular excursion and ferry steamer in the Saint Clair River territory for many years. Twenty years before her fatal accident she had been seriously damaged by fire, but had been completely rebuilt. She had been built new in 1882 by the firm of Runnels and Moffett.

⚓ ⚓ ⚓ ⚓ ⚓ ⚓ ⚓ ⚓

CHAPTER THIRTY-THREE

THE KEWEENAW COLLECTS

—1922 TO 1927—

Every sailor in the Great Lakes ore fleet knows the Keweenaw Peninsula. Most of them have never set foot on it but they have learned to watch for the flashing lights of Eagle Harbor, Copper Harbor, Manitou Island, and Gull Rock, which dot the blunt end of the peninsula as it drops off into the waters of Lake Superior.

In the early days of sailing, the Keweenaw was a port of call for vessels trading on Lake Superior. Copper mines were flourishing, bringing prosperity to the wilderness. Today no large ships stop there. The copper mines are quiet and the tourist takes over during the summer months. Nature went all out when she decorated the Keweenaw. She covered the land with great forests and dotted it with lakes and small rivers. The shore line is famous for its ruggedness. Today several fine highways carry thousands of automobiles the entire length of the peninsula. Old Fort Wilkins, a rebuilt frontier post manned by United States troops in early days, now rests quietly at the tip of the peninsula.

285

SHIPWRECKS OF THE LAKES

While the Keweenaw Peninsula delights the tourist, it is a distinct annoyance to the lake mariner. It protrudes almost one third the way across Lake Superior and thus blocks the course of vessels running the full length of the big lake. Sailors have dubbed it "the horn," likely because of its similarity in shape to a horn, and they must take their ships "round the horn" each time they traverse Lake Superior.

Years ago, a twenty-five mile waterway was constructed across the Keweenaw to assist navigation, and for many years it was a well-traveled route. But as the lake vessels became larger and faster, and the copper cargoes became fewer, the captains gave up coaxing their long ships through the narrow confines of the waterway and preferred the open lake.

Today the Keweenaw Waterway is still navigable but only occasionally does a freighter nose her way through. The heaviest ship traffic is during the months of October and November when captains seek the sheltered waters of the canal to avoid the frequent storms of those months that whip Lake Superior into unpleasant sailing. It affords a safe haven of refuge for storm-tossed ships, particularly in its wide sections such as Lily Pond and Portage Lake. One freighter, the *Maplehurst,* met with disaster when within sight of the lights that mark the entrance to the Keweenaw Waterway.

It was late evening of November thirtieth, 1922. A

violent storm had caught the Canadian steamer on the open lake enroute to Fort William, Ontario. The *Maplehurst,* two hundred thirty-five feet long and thirty-six feet beam, and fifteen feet depth, of steel construction, was thirty years old when fate decided that her sailing days were over. She had loaded coal at Lorain, Ohio, and had fought her way through winter seas across Lake Erie and up Lake Huron, had steamed through the Sault Ste. Marie Canal Locks and had entered Lake Superior, and was a few miles off Keweenaw Peninsula when the gale beat down on her unmercifully. There yet remained the run across the lake, some fifty or sixty miles and the *Maplehurst* would have been behind Isle Royale, where another twenty or thirty miles would have brought her to her destination.

The tempest increased rapidly as the *Maplehurst* rounded the horn of Keweenaw. The wind shrieked through her rigging and as she plunged and rose, giant waves swept over her decks. Everything not firmly lashed had long since gone overboard. The freighter shuddered and groaned as she labored in the howling gale.

The captain decided to seek the shelter of the Keweenaw Waterway rather than attempt to sail across the raging lake. He ordered the ship headed in a general southwesterly direction following the upper coast of the peninsula.

Fate then struck in the engine room of the *Maple-*

287

hurst. Her power plant became disabled! The staunch ship was then at the complete mercy of the elements. Caught as she was only a short distance off the jagged rocks of the entry breakwater, it was impossible to run down an anchor and expect it to hold. The stricken freighter pitched and rolled heavily in the great combers that swept over her and struck angrily at her deck houses. It was certainly evident that the *Maplehurst* was approaching her destiny.

Now out of all control, the freighter with her cargo hold full of coal was beaten mercilessly by the raging elements. One wave bigger than the others tore away most of her superstructure. Distress signals shot into the midnight gale and her whistle was blown constantly to warn all concerned of the impending great danger.

From between the harbor lights came another vessel. It was moving out to sea! It bobbed at first, then as it left the fixed shore lights behind, it rose and dipped in turn as the craft headed directly for the stricken *Maplehurst*. It was the power surfboat of those hardy heroes of the sea, the United States Coast Guard. The plight of the *Maplehurst* had been watched by the lookout of the station located at the Portage Entry. Its crew was standing by and put to sea as soon as it was evident that the freighter was in danger.

The dauntless small boat of the rescue crew breasted the waves and made gradual headway toward the disabled steamer. Icy water swept into the craft and stinging hail hit the resolute men, but the incoming water was bailed out and the small but seaworthy boat at last reached the wallowing *Maplehurst*. By now the steamer's cargo had shifted and she was listing badly.

It was almost one o'clock in the morning when the lifeboat reached the ship. Boatswain Charles A. Tucker in charge of the rescue party, ran his lifeboat alongside the *Maplehurst* and, clinging with one hand to the gunwhale of the surfboat, he shouted instructions through his megaphone to the twenty men who comprised the crew of the freighter. He would try to take them off. He would have to circle around and pick up the men as best he could. It was impossible to stop alongside the ship, as the seas would have crushed the surfboat.

To the men aboard the *Maplehurst* it appeared almost suicide to attempt to drop into the moving rescue boat. Even if a man gained the little craft it was a question if it would itself survive the storm, what with the additional burden of the steamer's men. It was a terrible decision to make and one which later turned out to mean life or death for each man on the freighter.

In the files of the Coast Guard is the report of Boatswain Tucker of that wild night on Lake Superior, four miles off Portage Entry. It tells the story in detail. Here it is, quoted from his report.

"It being apparent that she (the *Maplehurst*) would never weather the gale, we came up alongside and directed the crew to stand by and jump into the lifeboat each time we came about. Came about and alongside of her three times but none of the crew attempted to jump into our lifeboat—until the fourth time."

Then one sailor decided to make the attempt. He scrambled over the steamer's rail and dropped safely into the lifeboat. Somewhat encouraged by their shipmate's action, the nineteen men left on the *Maplehurst's* deck watched the lifeboat again come about. Then three of them went over the side and into the bobbing rescue craft.

For several more turns none of the remaining crew dared make the perilous transfer. But still Boatswain Tucker continued his tactics. The waves were "as high as houses" his report states, and the steamer was fast being blown toward the menacing rocks of the breakwater. The lifeboat would soon have to leave the wreck as it too might be crushed.

By the tenth time to come about, five more of the *Maplehurst's* crew had decided to leave their ship for the lifeboat. That made a total of nine. Four more times Tucker came alongside, but no one from the wreck attempted the transfer. Eleven chose to stay with the *Maplehurst*. They decided their own doom. Another monster sea struck with devastating fury and cleared the steamer of her remaining deck houses. Her lights went out. Her list increased.

The well-filled surfboat now pulled away and stood by. Her motor was missing badly and might shut off altogether. It required two men to hold her steering bar. The Coast Guard crew were exhausted by their strenuous experiences. It was imperative that they return to their base—if they could. They did make the dangerous trip back between the Entry lights and into the more quiet waters of the canal, and once again the men in that lifeboat stood safely on solid ground.

But aboard the stricken *Maplehurst* the situation became quickly worse. She was broadside to the seas and in a matter of minutes, she had struck hard upon the rocky breakwater. Further rescue was now impossible. Under the terrific pounding the steamer quickly broke up. All the eleven men that remained aboard were lost. When daylight came, only the top of the smokestack and two deck derricks were all that remained to be seen of the *Maplehurst*. She lay a short distance away from the safety of the pier heads. So often just a few feet one way or another can mean so much to a ship and her crew.

A quarter of a century later a final mention is made in a U. S. Government Bulletin to Great Lakes mariners, under the heading of Keweenaw Waterway. It reads, "The steamer *Maplehurst* was wrecked December 1, 1922, and lies in 21 feet of water in the lake about 350 feet out from the shore end of the upper entrance west breakwater. Subsequent storms have flattened the wreck out so that nothing shows above the water.

291

Soundings show depths of 5 and 7 feet over the dome and boiler. The wreck is out of the course of large vessels, but should be avoided by small craft running close inshore."

Thus endeth the good ship *Maplehurst,* veteran steel freighter of the Great Lakes.

From November fifteenth and through December second, 1926, Lake Superior was in one of her bad moods. Gales accompanied with sleet and snow beset ships caught out on the open lake. Most of the beleaguered vessels eventually arrived safely in port, some of them many days late, and with considerable storm damage to report. Three, however, were destined to end their days during that stormy period. One, the steamer *Cottonwood,* was driven hard upon Coppermine Point, Ontario, about thirty-four miles northerly from the head of the Saint Marys River. A second steamer, the *Herman H. Hettler,* was running for the shelter of Grand Island, on the south shore of Lake Superior. She was driven hard ashore on that island.

But the Keweenaw was not to be overlooked by the storm. The big steel freighter *City of Bangor* was steaming through the gale, upbound on Lake Superior. Her main deck carried a full load of shiny new Chrysler automobiles. She also had another batch of the new cars in her hold, two hundred forty-eight automobiles in all. A lake freighter when carrying all the automobiles that she can crowd aboard is still not very heavily laden. Autos are not comparable to iron ore when it comes to weight, and the ships still ride fairly high in the water with an automobile cargo. And so it was with the *City of Bangor* on that last day of November, 1926, as she struggled to reach protection behind Keweenaw Point.

The wind caught the high sides of the ship and the waves beat against them, sending tons of icy water across her decks. The surface of Lake Superior became similiar to a mountainous area, constantly changing from mountain top into deep valleys. The *City of Bangor's* hull stretched its four hundred and forty-five feet across the valleys of water as it rose to the crests of the high waves. Her chief danger lay in the ship dropping longways into one of those deep valleys of solid water. Then she would have serious difficulty in climbing up the slippery sides of the water valley to once again ride the crest of the waves.

For many long hours the steamer struggled through the tempestuous seas. The automobiles on her main deck slid about and some went overboard into the lake; finally the ones remaining were sheathed with clear thick ice, as were all her cabins and boiler house. But it was destined for the battered freighter never to reach her destination, Duluth. The gale won. Gradually the ship slipped down into one of those treacherous water valleys. She was caught in the trough of the seas and she could not climb out. The trough rushed her sidelong toward Keweenaw Point. She would roll heavily from one valley to another in a beam action, but she could not pull herself free of the fatal grip.

It was only a matter of a couple of hours after she had gone out of control before her keel grated upon the hard rocks of rugged Keweenaw. Another Great Lakes freighter had gone out of existence. She never left the spot where she grounded until she was cut up into steel scrap salvage many years later.

The rescue of the stranded ship's crew by the United States Coast Guard from Eagle Harbor Station, under Boatswain A. F. Glaza, is another of the big rescue stories still told by the old-timers on Keweenaw.

The Coast Guard crew with Glaza at the helm, had been occupied with the successful rescue of the men from still another freighter previously caught in the storm—the steamer *Thomas Maytham,* stranded on Isabell Point Reef, forty-five miles distant from their base. They were returning to their home station with the survivors of the *Maytham* in their motor surfboat, when, as they approached Keweenaw Point, to their astonishment, they found the *City of Bangor* hard aground. The ship's crew of twenty-nine were huddled on the beach, having abandoned their ship. Many of them had frozen hands and feet. The thermometer stood at ten degrees below zero.

THE KEWEENAW COLLECTS

With the crews of two ships on their hands the nine coastguards had an extremely difficult situation. They managed to get all fifty men and one woman into Copper Harbor that night. Then the *Maytham* crew were taken on to Eagle Harbor to the Coast Guard Station. Returning the next day to Copper Harbor they took the *City of Bangor* crew to the station at Eagle Harbor, taking first the men suffering from frostbite.

The old-timers will tell you that two hundred thirty of the automobiles were eventually taken ashore, eighteen having been lost overboard. The snow had drifted in many places much higher than the automobiles themselves. It was a long and discouraging task, but it was finally successfully accomplished.

The *City of Bangor* defied all subsequent attempts to salvage her. Her great steel hull and deck houses rusted for many years on the shore of Keweenaw before any further notice of the wreck was taken. Almost one year later another freighter, the steamer *Altadoc,* crashed within a few feet of where the *City of Bangor* lay forlorn and alone. The Keweenaw was collecting! But the *Altadoc* wreck is another story.

At the extreme northern end of Federal Route 41, on the very tip of the Keweenaw Peninsula, stands what is probably the most unique cabin camp in the country. It is the pilot house and captain's quarters of the wrecked Canadian freighter *Altadoc*. Here you may rent all that remains of the big steel steamer, and can roam about in the very room that once housed the steering wheel, navigation controls, and charts of a bulk ship. You may pause and contemplate the happenings in this very room on the wild night of Thursday, December eighth, 1927.

You can easily picture the darkness within the room with only a tiny glow in the compass binacle. The figure of a man stands behind the wheel guiding the big ship. The master, tired and worn, paces back and forth behind the row of curved windows at the front. Snow has almost obscured his vision. It whirls in every direction and catches in the corners of each window and then tries to build upon itself a complete covering over the entire window pane. Then the howling gale quickly sweeps it off into the blackness of the night.

The flashing beacon of Copper Harbor can be seen when the snow clears for an instant. The gust howls in and the ship and shore are all blotted out again. Another form stands close by the front windows. It is one of the mates also on duty in the pilot house. He has, for the hundredth time, studied the chart and turned out the little low light that illuminates the big sheet of paper. He too strains to catch a glimpse of the flashing Copper Harbor light, and also tries to locate through the storm another landmark—the Eagle Harbor light, some fifteen miles farther along on the ship's course.

THE KEWEENAW COLLECTS

Inside the pilot house it is comfortable. The walls below the windows are lined with heater pipes and the surging hot steam can be heard gushing through. It is a battle between those pipes and the shrieking gale outside to see which wins in the pilot house. The gale is ever ready to take over should the pipes cool. It pushes persistently in around the windows and doors, but the hot steam pipes force it back.

The hours have been long for the three men—longest for the captain. The responsibility of the ship rests upon his shoulders. His record as a master mariner must be maintained. The season is late for lake shipping. Christmas is only seventeen days away. Damn the gale! Why must it continue to rage? Why hadn't the fine weather they had on Georgian Bay upon leaving Owen Sound, held just a few days longer? Fort William was just across Lake Superior. It all began after they had left Whitefish—all this wind and snow and cold.

It is easy to picture all this as you stand in the quiet pilot house now resting solidly on dry land. But you can also picture in your mind that that very same room was anything but solid when it was the nerve center of the *Altadoc*. It rose and fell as the freighter plunged into the giant seas. Icy spray was forming on the captain's bridge just outside the pilot house door. The mate was blowing thick weather signals on the deep-toned whistle—three short blasts every minute—to warn other ships of their presence.

Suddenly the man at the wheel begins to mutter nervously. He is saying, "She ain't answering her rudder, Captain. Sumthin's not right somewhere."

The *Altadoc* is not herself. Instead of taking the huge combers in an orderly fashion and in a seamanship manner, she is rolling and pitching badly and the three men in that dark room are struck dumb with the realization that possibly their ship is doomed. The steering mechanism has failed! The ship is out of control! The captain tries his hand at the wheel. He spins it wildly, but the *Altadoc* does not respond. From now on the ship is at the mercy of the gale. Neither captain nor crew can command her. The wind and the sea take over.

All this you can picture as you stand quietly in the very room where this action took place. Already the ship is nearer the flashing light of Copper Harbor. The wind and waves are attending to that. Her sides rise sheer from the water, as the *Altadoc* is without cargo. The wind slams giant waves against these great high sides of the freighter. The men in the pilot house discuss their plight. But it really doesn't matter now, for it is only a matter of time before their ship is to be dashed against the rocky shores of the Keweenaw. Only a matter of time—just an hour or two. And then what? Will she break up quickly and will they all be drowned? Or will she take it like all sailors hope, and hold together so that they might all be saved?

THE KEWEENAW COLLECTS

Here a chattering party of tourists come into the pilot house, and your dreams of the night of the wreck of the *Altadoc* are disturbed. These newcomers want to purchase postcards and souvenirs of the Keweenaw which line the walls of the interesting room. You step outside into the pine-scented air. The pilot house of the *Altadoc* has cast its spell upon you. You must know more about her. Eventually you learn the details.

The *Altadoc* was built at West Bay City, Michigan, by the F. W. Wheeler Shipbuilding Company in 1901 for the Gilchrist Transportation Company, then operating a large fleet of freighters on the Great Lakes. She carried the name of *Lake Shore* from the time of her launching until 1912 when she was sold to the Pickands Mather interests, and her name was changed to *Indus*. The ship was subsequently sold to the Paterson Steamship Company of Fort William, Ontario, and at that time she was given the name of *Altadoc*. The ships of this Canadian fleet all have the distinctive letters *doc* ending their names. The first part of the name indicates a Canadian province or city, and the *doc* is reported to stand for Dominion of Canada. Listed today as the N. M. Paterson & Sons Limited, the line operates such steamers as the *Mantadoc, Ontadoc, Quedoc, Soodoc, Windoc,* and many others. There is also listed today another *Altadoc* which, of course, is another vessel and not the one whose pilot house rests on rugged Keweenaw.

It was six o'clock on the morning of Monday, December fifth, 1927, when Captain R. D. Simpson piloted his *Altadoc* out of his home town of Owen Sound, Ontario, on Georgian Bay, and headed her for the Canadian lakehead, Fort William, Ontario. The freighter was without cargo and was expected to load grain upon her arrival in Fort William. The captain was an old hand as master of lake ships. All his life had been spent aboard ships. Forty-two years previously he had been shipwrecked. That time, as a young man he was in the crew of the ill-fated passenger steamer *Algoma,* when in 1885, she crashed in a snow-blinding gale upon the rocks of Isle Royale in Lake Superior, and was lost. Simpson was one of fourteen survivors.

All went well aboard the *Altadoc* until she entered Lake Superior. Then she became engulfed in snow squalls, which intensified as the ship continued. When off Keweenaw Peninsula it is reported that her steering mechanism became disabled and put the vessel out of control. The violent storm tossed the ship upon the rugged rocks of Keweenaw at ten minutes after six in the morning of Thursday, December eighth, some six hours after her rudder equipment broke down. She struck the shore only a thousand feet away from where the freighter *City of Bangor* lay, a deserted wreck.

The storm continued to beat down upon the *Altadoc* after striking the shore. Water flooded her engine room. All the doors on the port side of the after cabins were torn from their fastenings. Her dining room was wrecked. All the food aboard was ruined or washed away. Three of her crew were injured, but fortunately no lives were lost.

The situation of the men was indeed critical. There was no immediate way in which their plight could be communicated to the outer world. There was only one way to find help—to set out on foot. The storm had played as much havoc on the Keweenaw as it had on Lake Superior. Trees were down; what roads there were, were blocked with huge drifts of snow. The thermometer was near zero. The men aboard the wrecked freighter could survive for only a few days without help. They would perish from exposure, exhaustion, or hunger.

Captain Simpson realized their situation fully. No time should be lost if his men were not to suffer. With four of the huskiest of his crew members, he set out afoot to seek aid and report the wreck of the *Altadoc*. Their heroic trek over the frozen marshland, up and down snow encrusted terrain, across frozen streams and through thick forest until they reached Copper Harbor, nine miles distant from the wreck, is outstanding in the annals of sailors' history on the Great Lakes.

Upon reaching Copper Harbor the five survivors learned that all communication lines were down. It would be necessary to tramp on to Delaware, the nearest town, three miles inland, to reach a telephone. They went onward and there managed to find a phone still

301

in working order. They notified the Coast Guard Station at Eagle Harbor, Michigan.

The following morning, the storm had abated somewhat and the coastguards were able to reach the stranded *Altadoc* and rescue the marooned crew. The hull of the freighter had broken in two and water had filled the boiler room and all the lower quarters by the time help arrived. The three hundred eighty-five foot freighter *Altadoc* was then abandoned to the elements as the crew sought shelter ashore. It was her last resting place. The Keweenaw had again collected.

Salvage crews located the steamer during the summer of 1928 and her engines and machinery were removed. It was at this time that her pilot house was removed also. This structure was cut away from the steel deck with acetylene torches, and with the aid of a huge derrick, it was placed upon a scow and floated ashore on Keweenaw Point where it stands at present —probably the smallest hotel in the country.

Many years later, World War II brought a big demand for steel scrap. Again salvage crews sought out the wrecked freighters *Altadoc* and *City of Bangor,* long battered by the storms of Lake Superior. The wrecks were cut up in sections and floated off to lake ports with roaring furnaces, and thus the wrecked vessels came back into usefulness in some other form.

CHAPTER THIRTY-FOUR

THE LAKELAND SINKING

— *1924* —

Not many freight steamers on the Great Lakes ever became regular passenger ships, but this transition did happen to the steel freighter *Cambria*. Upon her main deck were built long rows of staterooms, cabins, dining salon, and such other rooms as are required in a modern passenger ship. Her cargo hold was arranged to carry what is known on the lakes as "package freight" and automobiles. When the work of changing her over into a passenger ship was completed, marine men were surprised at the smartness of her appearance. She was two hundred eighty feet long, forty feet beam, and twenty feet depth, and these dimensions were not altered when she was converted from a freight vessel into a passenger ship.

When the *Cambria* slid down the ways at the yards of the old Globe Shipbuilding Company in Cleveland, she was acclaimed the largest freighter on the Great Lakes. After she entered the bulk freight trade she transported several record cargoes. She carried three lofty masts, intended for auxiliary sails. However, this practice was subsequently abandoned on all lake

303

steamers so equipped as being not practical. But the masts on the *Cambria* remained in place until she was converted for the passenger trade. After that she carried only two masts. An ample smokestack in the after part of the ship remained unchanged.

As a freighter, the hull was painted a shiny black, with a white stripe at the top and running the full length of the vessel. Her cabins, located in the forward end, and the boiler house in the after end, were painted dark red. Her early stack design was black with a large white circle painted on each side near the top. The *Cambria* had several owners, the first being The Mutual Transportation Company of Escanaba, Michigan. The Hanna interests managed the ship until she became a unit of the Pittsburgh Steamship fleet in 1901. Upon her subsequent sale by this concern, the *Cambria* left the freight trade and was converted into a passenger liner and her name was changed to *Lakeland*.

Headquarters for the *Lakeland* after her change-over was at Port Huron, Michigan. Her route lay from that port to Duluth, the head of the lakes, and she carried automobiles and package freight along with her complement of passengers. Advertising mentioned that the cruise was made in a freight ship and stressed the novel idea of such travel. However, a regular schedule was maintained during the summer season. After her passenger season closed, the *Lakeland* made special trips carrying automobiles to the lake cities.

It was while returning from one of these post-season

runs to Chicago that the *Lakeland* met her fate. She had delivered her entire cargo of new automobiles to the "Windy City" early in December, 1924. Then she sailed light (without cargo) for Detroit. December sailing on the Great Lakes is usually a cautious procedure. With this in mind the captain hugged the west shore of Lake Michigan to be in the lee of the land on his trip down the lake. In spite of this the strong northwest winds rolled the *Lakeland* considerably. On Tuesday night, December second, she sought shelter just inside the entrance of the Sturgeon Bay Canal, which is about two-thirds the distance down the big lake. There she lay to and awaited daylight.

It was Wednesday morning when the *Lakeland* ventured out again on Lake Michigan to resume her voyage to Detroit. When about ten miles off shore, it was discovered that the ship was leaking badly. She was at once turned about and headed for the Sturgeon Bay Canal entrance where she had just spent the night. All her available pumps were put to work removing the incoming water, but in spite of this effort the water continued to rise in the ship's hold.

When it was seen that the *Lakeland* would not likely make shore before she sank, her officers broadcast an S O S wireless appeal for help. Assistance came from two sources. First to arrive was the carferry *Ann Arbor No. 6,* which happened at the time to be the nearest ship to the troubled *Lakeland.* She was on her regular run westward from Frankfort, Michigan, to

Manitowoc, Wisconsin, when she picked up the radio signals of the *Lakeland*. The second to answer the distress call was a Coast Guard cutter which arrived after the carferry, as she was some distance away when the call was received. The *Lakeland* began to settle by the stern as the *Ann Arbor No. 6* started to take the crew aboard as they left the sinking steamer in small boats. Within thirty minutes the entire crew of twenty-six men were transferred to the carferry. The rescue had been completed just thirty minutes when the stern of the *Lakeland* settled deep in the water and her bow rose high in the air. She went to the bottom of Lake Michigan, thirty-five fathoms below the surface. As the big steamer took her final plunge, watchers aboard the carferry heard muffled explosions as the trapped air burst forth from various chambers in the ship, and sections of her cabins and hatch covers flew into the air an estimated forty feet.

Insurance companies holding coverage on the *Lakeland* started an investigation to learn the cause of the sinking. They brought from salt water five deep-sea divers and their specially equipped vessel, the *Chittenden*. After locating the *Lakeland*, they prepared to inspect the wreck as she lay on the bottom. It is reported that the divers found the *Lakeland* hanging over a rock ledge, with about one-third of her bow protruding over much deeper water. Had she gone down one hundred feet ahead it is quite unlikely that divers would have been able to reach her in the much deeper water over the ledge.

THE LAKELAND SINKING

A law suit was instituted in the Federal Court at Cleveland to withhold the damages. It subsequently became one of the outstanding court cases of the lake marine.

When the case was tried in October, 1925, the jury was deadlocked and discharged. Another jury was selected and the case was tried in February, 1926. This time a decision was made in favor of the owners of the *Lakeland* and the insurance companies were denied a new trial. Thus ended the career of the freighter that became a passenger steamer.

CHAPTER THIRTY-FIVE

ROCK OF AGES WRECK

— 1 9 3 3 —

This story rightfully begins with the passenger steamer *Puritan*. All the old-time steamboat fans along the shores of Lake Michigan, from Chicago to Mackinac Island, on both sides of the lake, can recall this trim craft. She had a long and honored career. Her debut into the water came at Toledo, Ohio, in 1901, when she was launched for the Graham & Morton Line. She was of steel construction, two hundred fifty-nine feet long, forty feet beam, and twenty-six feet depth, of screw propulsion, with two tall masts and a large single smokestack located almost directly amidships. She was a yacht-like ship and was a favorite of all those who sailed on her.

After leaving the Toledo shipyards, the *Puritan* took up her duties for Graham & Morton on the run across the head of Lake Michigan, from Chicago to Benton Harbor and Saint Joseph, Michigan. She continued in the service of the G & M Line until 1918 when the United States Navy acquired her and used her as a training ship for recruits. Late in 1919, the *Puritan* returned to civilian duties, this time in the Chicago,

Racine, and Milwaukee Line. But the ship is better remembered for her subsequent service in the Michigan Transit Corporation. Under her various owners, the *Puritan* became a welcome caller in the many ports of Lake Michigan and thousands of vacationers rode the ship into the resort towns and have happy recollections of the many good times aboard her.

In 1933 she was purchased by still another owner. Her erstwhile black hull was then painted a glistening white and her name was changed to *George M. Cox.* The vessel was completely refitted and made ready for an early trip from Chicago to Port Arthur, Ontario, on the north shore of Lake Superior.

The month of May is early for pleasure seekers on Lake Superior, but the newly outfitted *George M. Cox's* first trip was not alone one of cruising relaxation. It was intended that she would bring to Chicago a load of Canadians, boarding at Port Arthur. They were to visit the gigantic Century of Progress Exposition then showing in the "Windy City." The visitors were to live aboard ship while attending the exposition, and then were to be returned to Port Arthur. This necessitated the *George M. Cox* making the run up the lakes in what is termed a "dead-head" trip, that is, not a regular fare paying operation. As this was the first trip under her new name, the new owners invited friends to make the special run as guest passengers.

The trip began at Chicago. The weather was satisfactory and the Cox made an uneventful run down Lake Michigan and through the Straits of Mackinac; made the turn into the Saint Marys River at Detour Light, passed up through the Sault Ste. Marie Locks, and entered Lake Superior. She took the cut across the Keweenaw Peninsula and put in at the city of Houghton, Michigan, for a brief pause. She left there at two in the afternoon on Saturday, May 27, 1933, for the one hundred sixteen mile trip across Lake Superior to Port Arthur.

Rugged Isle Royale lies directly on the course between the two ports. It is a rocky stretch of land protruding out of the cold waters of Lake Superior for a distance of some fifty miles, and all ships crossing the lake at this point must give it a wide berth. Magnetic deposits in the vicinity sometimes effect the old style ships' compasses and make the crossing difficult. Rock of Ages is located at the extreme westerly end of Isle Royale and is marked by a lighthouse. The George M. Cox was to have rounded this lighthouse and then squared away for her destination.

It was dinner time in the evening as the Cox neared Rock of Ages, and most of her passengers were in the dining room. A low-hanging fog clung to the water, making visibility poor. The Cox continued to steam ahead. The crew of the lighthouse were tending their light as the Cox approached. The fog prevented the men, high up in the lighthouse, from seeing the hull of the oncoming steamer, but towering high above the low-hanging fog the men saw the masts of the *Cox*. They were exactly in line with their lighthouse, indicating that the ship was headed directly for Rock of Ages. Shipwreck was certain unless the pilot could be warned quickly. One of the lighthouse crew seized the cord to their fog horn, which had been blowing its usual signals, and frantically jerked the line, hoping thereby to attract the attention of the officers aboard the oncoming vessel.

But this first trip of the *George M. Cox* was destined to be her last, for as she steamed ahead at an estimated speed of seventeen knots, she crashed hard on the treacherous Rock of Ages Reef. The force of the impact was tremendous. It is said that the ship's boilers and engines were torn from their bases and that everything movable slid dangerously. Passengers were knocked from their feet and onto the decks. Of thirty-two passengers aboard only four were hurt badly enough to require special attention.

The bow of the *Cox* was driven high up on the reef and her stern settled under water. She filled at once with water and hung precariously upon the reef. The sea was calm and the crew launched her lifeboats and safely removed all aboard the stricken ship. The freighter *Morris B. Tremaine* and Coast Guard stations answered distress calls from the *Cox* and with the aid of the lighthouse crew managed to land all hands on the tiny islet. The few more severely injured were placed aboard the *Tremaine* and taken to Port Arthur for hospitalization.

The protection of the lighthouse was too small to hold all the ship's company and passengers, so they took turns standing inside. After a chilling night, a Coast Guard cutter removed the survivors on the following morning and landed them—one hundred eighteen in all—at Houghton an Sunday afternoon. A shipwreck without the loss of a single life!

The stranded *George M. Cox* remained hard on Rock of Ages with her bow out of water and her stern under water, with a crazy list to port. It was believed that the steamer might be salvaged, and a crew started for the wreck with the necessary equipment.

Nature took a hand in the final scene of the ill-fated passenger steamer before the salvage crew began work. A hard storm whipped up the lake, causing swift currents of water to swirl around Rock of Ages. The *George M. Cox* slowly slid from her precarious perch atop the reef and with a tremendous gurgle, sank easily to the deep cold rocks on the bottom of Lake Superior. And to this day lies that Toledo-built passenger ship, remembered for over thirty years of faithful service on Lake Michigan, and close by is rugged Rock of Ages Reef, her nemesis after all those miles of pleasure travel for so many thousands of pleasure seekers. Thus the curtain falls upon another of the fast-dwindling fleet of passenger steamers of the Great Lakes.

§ § § § § § § §

CHAPTER THIRTY-SIX

THE ADMIRAL AND THE CLEVECO

— 1 9 4 2 —

Most of the important shipwrecks are of many years ago. Seldom are the steamers of today wrecked. But as late as 1942, Lake Erie claimed the steam tug *Admiral* and her tanker-barge *Cleveco,* along with every one of the crew members of both ships, all within the normal range of the lights of Cleveland Harbor. Thirty-two men perished in the wrecks of the two vessels in what is considered the worst marine disaster to overtake lake freight shipping in modern times.

Heroic attempts by many craft to reach the foundering *Cleveco* during the height of one of Lake Erie's worst snowstorms, and their subsequent failures to locate the drifting barge show conclusively that men will still brave the dangers of storm and cold in the hope of rescuing distressed sailors. Even the help of radio telephone communication aboard the ships figuring in the disaster could not save the unfortunate crewmen.

It was Tuesday afternoon, December 1, 1942, when the big tug *Admiral* took the towline of the tanker-

313

barge *Cleveco* in Toledo Harbor, pulled her down the Maumee River to Lake Erie, and squared away for the ninety-six mile run along the south shore of the lake for Cleveland. The tanks of the *Cleveco* held one million gallons of crude oil. The weather was average for early December and there was nothing to forecast the doom of the two ships. On through the long night, the *Admiral* churned her way eastward. The wind began to roll up an occasional breaker against the sides of the tug and her consort, and their force became greater after midnight. The thermometer dropped suddenly. At midnight it stood exactly at the freezing mark and by early morning it registered twenty-four degrees.

It was about four that morning when the lookout on the *Cleveco* came into the wheel house and reported that the towline connecting the barge to the tug was not as it should be. It appeared to be coming up from the bottom of the lake instead of its normal position when underway. The headway of the *Cleveco* had stopped. Nothing could be seen of the lights of the *Admiral*.

Captain William H. Smith of the barge held a consultation with his officers—his brother, Edwin S. Smith, was the first mate. What had happened to their tug *Admiral*? They decided that she had capsized or foundered, and was at that very moment lying on the bottom of Lake Erie, although no one aboard the *Cleveco* had actually witnessed the accident. It was a tragic moment for the men on the tanker-barge. If their guess was true that the *Admiral* had sunk, then fourteen of their fellow sailors who comprised the officers and crew of the tug were in dire straits, or possibly were drowned. Nothing could be heard or seen of them from the *Cleveco*. Definitely the *Cleveco* was left without propulsion power. Her own predicament demanded immediate action. The storm was beginning to rise, which added some anxiety to their situation.

Captain Smith, sixty-two year old skipper, coming from a long line of lake men, turned to his radio telephone and reported his plight to his shore connections. He asked that other tugs be sent to bring in his ship, at once.

The captain gave his location then as about fifteen miles off Avon Point, fifteen miles west of Cleveland. He stated that his vessel was in no immediate danger, but needed a tug promptly, and that his situation was not good due to the increasing wind and cold. There were ample provisions aboard and the crew were not suffering, as the donkey boilers were providing ample heat for comfort.

Two husky tugs, the *California* and the *Pennsylvania,* of the Great Lakes Towing fleet left Cleveland Harbor to assist the *Cleveco,* and proceeded toward the spot indicated in Captain Smith's report. What actually happened to the towline between the *Admiral* and the *Cleveco* still remains somewhat of a mystery, but it is generally believed that the barge men let go the line and allowd their powerless vessel to drift with the wind toward Cleveland Harbor.

Upon reaching the site, the two tugs were unable to locate any sign of the *Cleveco*. The storm had increased in intensity in the meantime and was now swirling great masses of snow over the surface of the lake. The severe and sudden cold had caused a fog or steam to form on the surface of the lake which, with the swirling snow, made visibility exceedingly difficult. This condition grew worse as the day went on. The wind also increased during the day. Apparently the *Cleveco* let go both her anchors after cutting loose from the sunken *Admiral*. But both anchors were not sufficient to hold the heavily-laden tanker in the gale. She continued to drift eastward and away from the shore line.

Many craft joined in the hunt for the elusive *Cleveco*, both on the lake and in the air. Some reported spotting her for a short time, only to lose her again in the snow and mists. Telephone communication with the drifting ship was maintained throughout the morning and into mid-afternoon. The searching craft were battered by the terrific seas and high winds and stung by the cold. The Coast Guard sent out all available boats, and the cutter *Ossipee* joined in the search. The commander of the *Ossipee* contacted Captain Smith of the *Cleveco* by telephone, and details of the proposed rescue were discussed.

After a fruitless search of the waters off Avon Point,

the rescue craft decided the information was erroneous and requested that Captain Smith give better location of his ship. Her position was then established as ten miles north of the west Cleveland light. Very valuable time and energy had been lost and now the *Ossipee* carried on the search alone, being the largest vessel in the rescue fleet. Smaller Coast Guard boats were forced to return to shore. The wind howled over the lake at thirty-five miles per hour and the thermometer hovered around fourteen degrees at noon on Wednesday, the second of December.

About one-thirty that afternoon the officers of the *Ossipee* managed to get a glimpse of the ill-fated *Cleveco,* but she was quickly lost to view again. They circled the spot for hours hoping for another sight of her. About two they saw her again for a moment, then she disappeared forever. But contact was maintained between the two ships by radio telephone. At first Captain Smith said that his crew were in no danger and would prefer not to leave their ship. Subsequent messages indicated that the storm was beginning to wreak its vengence upon the luckless tanker-barge and that the men considered their situation dangerous. Final calls asked that they be taken off the *Cleveco.* By three-thirty a message was received stating that the tanker was taking water and it was feared this would kill the ship's generators, which would put out the radio telephone and also the entire electrical system of the tanker.

The wind increased to a velocity of sixty miles an

hour, with occasional gusts up to seventy. The final message came from the *Cleveco* at four-forty that afternoon. The *Ossipee* commander radioed to have the crew of the tanker pump oil onto the water, hoping thereby to calm the surface and possibly make a "slick" which might help locate the *Cleveco*. No reply came back.

The gallant Coast Guard cutter remained at the scene on wild Lake Erie all that night. The ship took a terrific pounding in the darkness as the storm had intensified into a full gale with waves eighteen to twenty feet high and visibility of zero. The gyro compass went out of order and she was forced to use her stand-by magnetic compass. Her safe was torn loose from its fastenings. Veterans of many years service became seasick. Meals could not be served because of the severe rolling of the cutter. The outside of the *Ossipee* became coated heavily with ice which eventually effected her maneuverability. It was indeed a tough round of duty for the crew of the cutter.

At last daylight came, and with it the men aboard the battered *Ossipee* were able to see two bodies floating alongside, and which they managed to bring aboard. The bodies were covered with heavy oil and wore life belts from the *Cleveco*. The *Ossipee* gave up the vigil at nightfall. Shrouded completely in thick ice, she limped into the harbor of Fairport, Ohio, after thirty-six hours of continuous duty. After clearing the coating of ice, she once more steamed out onto the lake in search of other bodies of the crew of the lost tanker. It is supposed that the *Cleveco* went down in the darkness of Thursday morning, December third. The tanker had taken the lives of her entire crew, eighteen men. Only an oil "slick" was left on the surface of Lake Erie to mark the spot where she went down. For several days Coast Guard motor lifeboats, the cutter *Ossipee,* and Coast Guard Auxiliary vessels, and other private craft, along with the tanker *Comet* of the same fleet as the *Cleveco,* and several planes, continued the search for bodies of the crews of both the *Admiral* and the *Cleveco*. Several were found from both ships. Some are believed still to be within the cabin walls of both vessels, trapped there as their ships went down.

It has been scarcely a decade since the *Admiral —* *Cleveco* disaster and even in that comparatively short space of time, scientists and marine men have overcome the direct cause of the failure to locate and possibly rescue the *Cleveco*. Today, in the pilot houses of most of the ships that ply the Great Lakes is an interesting instrument called a radar that looks through fog, snow, darkness, and thick weather, where the human eye cannot penetrate. It can locate another ship, or even smaller objects such as buoys. It shows the shore line clearly. It does even better in its service to the mariner—it shows exactly how many miles distant is the object of the search. Then it accurately indicates the direction from the searching vessel. It can even look over the horizon! What a Heaven-sent aid to the men who sail the ships today! It was unknown to sailors in the days of the *Admiral* and the *Cleveco*. Had the *Ossipee* been equipped with a radar, locating the *Cleveco* would have been but an ordinary routine matter of looking into a darkened ground glass screen, similar to a television screen, and then watching a glowing spot inside a series of circles, which would represent the other vessel.

The exact whereabouts of the sunken tug *Admiral* are still a mystery. The lake bottom has been carefully "swept" in the hope of locating the wrecked hulk of the big tug, but it still defies the efforts of the searchers. Could it be possible that within another decade scientists and mariners working together will develop an instrument with which they can look at and examine the floor of the seas from the deck of a ship? It is even now in an embryonic stage.

Better success was attained in the search for the *Cleveco*. It still lies where it sank, approximately four and one half miles out in the lake off the resort of Euclid Beach, in some sixty-five feet of water. The hull has been examined by a diver, who reports that the ship is resting bottom side up on the floor of the lake. It is thought by many that her cargo of oil might still be intact, provided that her tanks have not been strained to the point of opening at the seams, or connections broken. Salvage men have considered the possibility of raising the *Cleveco*, but up to the present time the tanker-barge is still where she came to rest after her sinking during that wild gale on Lake Erie in early December of 1942.

THE ADMIRAL AND THE CLEVECO

The sturdy Coast Guard Cutter *Ossipee* is no more. The service decided that the old veteran of many a lake gale was obsolete, and ordered her sold. After spending many long months idle in Cuyhoga River at Cleveland, the cutter was finally sold for scrap and was dismantled.

⚓ ⚓ ⚓ ⚓ ⚓ ⚓ ⚓ ⚓

CHAPTER THIRTY-SEVEN

HAMONIC, NORONIC, AND QUEBEC
—*1945* TO *1950*—

Lovers of lake cruises and vacationers traveling between the United States and Canada lost three of the finest luxury passenger liners on fresh water, within a period of five years between July, 1945, and August, 1950. So far as it is known at present the lost vessels will not be replaced. Untold thousands of persons have enjoyed sailing upon these splendid steamships since their entry of service upon the Great Lakes. The routes covered by these steamers extend from Duluth to the Saguenay River, the entire length of the Great Lakes system and well down the St. Lawrence River and its tributary.

All three ships were lost by fire, each many miles apart. They were the *Hamonic,* the *Noronic,* and the *Quebec.* All were in the large fleet of the Canada Steamship Lines. The *Hamonic* was the first of the trio to be destroyed. She burned to a wreck at Point Edward, near Sarnia, Ontario, on July 17, 1945. Her sister ship, the *Noronic,* was next to succumb to the flames. She burned to a wreck at Toronto, Ontario, on September 17, 1949. The last to burn of the three floating palaces

322

was the *Quebec* which caught fire on August 14, 1950, five miles off Tadoussac, Quebec, where the Saguenay River empties into the St. Lawrence River.

It was late in the evening, almost midnight, when the *Hamonic* left Detroit, Michigan. Here she made the southern turn around on her regular weekly cruise, and headed northward to Lake Superior. It was a slow and easy night run up the St. Clair River to her dock at Point Edward, a few miles upriver from Sarnia, and almost under the famous Blue Water Bridge.

Little did Captain Horace L. Beaton realize that this was to be the final docking of the *Hamonic,* and that disaster was to strike within a few hours. He had been on duty all that night, and it was about four-thirty in the morning of Tuesday, July 17, 1945, when he ordered the lines made fast to the dock, and the *Hamonic* was berthed quietly so as not to disturb the sleeping passengers. All was well, so the captain retired to his cabin and was soon sound asleep.

The *Hamonic* was tied up at a long dock upon which was built an equally long freight warehouse of frame construction. Coal was piled high on the dock just astern of the *Hamonic,* and a steam power shovel with a clam bucket stood nearby ready to move the coal to and from the stock pile and into ships for bunker fuel. Railroad box cars, many filled with merchandise, stood on the far side of the warehouse.

At the usual time to begin work for the day, came the men employed on the dock and in the warehouse. Some conveyer equipment powered by a gasoline motor was being repaired, it is reported, and while the mechanics were at work on the machinery, a burst of flame shot forth. Instantly the flame spread to the oily warehouse floor and other dry inflammable things. Fanned by a strong breeze the fire quickly spread through the long warehouse, feeding on packing cases, cartons, and perishable merchandise and the huge wooden warehouse itself. Almost before the workmen realized it, the fire was beyond their control.

In a very short time the warehouse was a raging inferno, and the flames engulfed the box cars standing alongside. Then the breeze sent the flames and smoke toward the steamer tied to the dock. Almost in a matter of minutes the *Hamonic* was doomed. Except for her steel hull, she was aflame on the dock side her entire length.

Captain Beaton, awakened by the commotion, came out on the bridge still clad in his pajamas, in time to see his ship a mass of roaring flames from stem to stern. He realized in an instant that the fire on shore barred his passengers from leaving the ship. He decided at once to run the vessel back along the dock to the spot where the coal was stored and where the power shovel stood, and away from the fire and outside the choking pall of smoke.

He sprang to the engine-room telegraph and rang

324

signals which would move his ship away from the burning warehouse and back to a safer spot. For only a
moment he feared that the flames might have driven
his engine crew out of their quarters, but as the propeller
began to churn and the ship to move in response to his
signals, he knew that someone was down there at the
engine controls.

The man there was Chief Engineer James D. Neilson of Point Edward. He was standing at the throttle
of his ship as the flames licked around the engine room
outer walls. Over his head the ceiling was afire. Cans
of exploding vegetables and fruit were dropping all
about him. The storage room for these supplies was
located directly above the engine controls and the
intense heat was expanding the contents of the cans,
forcing them to explode as they fell through the floor
and into the engine room. But the plucky chief stuck
to his post and much credit is due this heroic engineer
for the rescue of many of the passengers. He stayed in
this dangerous spot, working his engines in response to
the signals from the captain on the bridge, until the
flaming *Hamonic* had been placed in the most favorable
position possible along the dock. It is reported that Chief
Engineer Neilson was the last man to step off the raging
ship, and by then he was hemmed in on all sides except
one which opened on the side away from the dock and
which had a large opening almost at the water's edge.
Captain Beaton piloted a small boat to this opening
and through it he rescued his chief engineer.

Many of the passengers could get ashore after the ship had been moved away from the burning warehouse. Some slid down ropes placed over the ship's sides, while others preferred to leap into the water to be picked up by several small rescue craft which had hurried to the scene.

Quick thinking on the part of Elmer Kleinsmith, the operator of the power shovel, saved the lives of many of the passengers and crew. When the ship came to her final stop, her bow was nosed into the bank within reach of the boom of the crane. He called to the passengers trapped in the bow to climb into the bucket of his crane, which he had lowered gently to the ship's deck. Then he hoisted the ten or so people who had clambered in it to the ground and to safety. This operation was repeated many times and many lives were thus saved by this man's quick thinking and actions.

Coastguardsmen and firemen from Port Huron, Michigan, across the St. Clair River, rushed to the aid of the local fire-fighting forces and many private power boats assisted in the rescue work. Every one of the passengers and crew was saved, but many were treated for various burns.

The *Hamonic* never sailed again! She lay a smoldering wreck on the water front for a few days. She later was towed away and eventually cut up into scrap steel. It was a sudden and premature ending for a fine ship; one that was much loved by many persons on both sides of the International Boundary.

HAMONIC, NORONIC, AND QUEBEC

The *Hamonic* had been built in Canadian shipyards at Collingwood, in 1909. She was three hundred fifty feet long, fifty feet beam, and twenty-four feet depth. Her gross tonnage was seven thousand, one hundred sixty, and her registered tonnage three thousand, two hundred ninety-five. Her graceful hull was painted a glistening black and her cabins white. Her stack carried the traditional Canada Steamship Lines red and white with black smoke band.

In the thirty-six years of the *Hamonic's* career, she carried passengers and freight between Detroit and St. Clair River ports to Sault Ste. Marie, Ontario, and northern Lake Superior cities. On two previous occasions during this long period, the ship was in serious difficulties. The first occurred during the Big Storm on the Great Lakes, that fateful November in 1913, which wreaked such terrific havoc to shipping. She was one of the few passenger ships still operating that late in the season and was caught out on Lake Superior by the storm. The gale blew in all her pilot house windows and she suffered considerable storm damage throughout the ship. She was intentionally grounded in Whitefish Bay, Lake Superior, to prevent further damage. After the storm had blown itself out, the *Hamonic* made her home port of Sarnia without further incident.

Her second serious adventure with the elements was on November 6, 1925, when about eighty miles above Whitefish Point on Lake Superior, during a howling gale and snow storm. She lost her propeller and then dropped into the trough of the sea, where she wallowed and rolled dangerously, entirely out of control.

The big freighter *Richard Trimble,* herself blown around so that she was headed back over the course she had just traveled from the Soo, sighted the *Hamonic* blowing distress signals and showing a red flare. Captain George H. Banker brought the *Richard Trimble* as close to the *Hamonic* as he dared in the bleak darkness just after midnight. He decided to await daylight.

A hectic night was spent on the raging lake by both ships. Later, Captain Banker reported that he had had no food for thirty hours and no sleep for forty-eight hours. Conditions aboard the *Hamonic* were equally bad or possibly worse. By daylight the crew of the *Richard Trimble* managed to pick up a three-quarter inch messenger line tied to a life preserver floated from the *Hamonic.*

While huge icy waves broke over both steamers, the crews managed to rig a heavy ten inch towline between the vessels and the slow and perilous trip to more protected waters began. By nine that night the two ships were abreast of Point Iroquois. Here, in relatively quiet waters, the *Hamonic* let go her anchor and the *Richard Trimble* steamed on to report the affair at Sault Ste. Marie Locks.

The passenger steamer *Noronic* was the flagship of

the upper lakes fleet of the Canada Steamship Lines, being the largest of this group. After the burning of the *Hamonic,* the *Noronic* carried on the route alone. She was an impressive appearing ship, three hundred eighty-five feet over all in length, fifty-two feet beam, and twenty-four feet depth. She towered high above the water, having six decks. Her hull and cabins were painted the same as the *Hamonic,* glistening black hull and white cabins, and her large single smokestack was painted with the line's distinctive and attractive red and white, with a black smoke band at the top of the stack.

The *Noronic* was a palatial craft. The dining salon, located on the top deck, had huge observation windows affording an excellent view. Another delightful location was her observation salon which also had large windows and comfortable over-stuffed chairs. This huge room became the ballroom in the evening when the ship's orchestra entertained with dancing. There were other public rooms for the convenience of her passengers, such as: the writing room, the music room, the smoking room, a buffet bar, a barber shop, and a beauty parlor.

The *Noronic* had come out in 1913 from the ship-yards in Port Arthur, Ontario, for the Northern Navigation Company, which concern subsequently merged with the Richelieu and Ontario Line and others, to form the Canada Steamship Lines. Her name was evolved from a combination of significant letters. When the Northern Navigation Company started, it was decided to have the ships carry some distinctive names. The letters *"nic"* were decided upon to end the name. Some said that the *"ic"* was intended to stand for "inland company" in view of the pending consolidation. The fleet had therefore, among others, the *Saronic,* named for the city of Sarnia, the *Hamonic* named for a former president of the line, Mr. Hammond, the *Huronic* from the name of the lake upon which she principally traded.

When the new ship was named, it was decided to call her *Noronic,* using the *"No"* to indicate the Northern Navigation Company, the *"ro"* to honor the Richelieu and Ontario Line, and then the regular ending, *"nic"* was tacked onto the two. Thus a famous ship was named.

Her plates and boilers were actually made in Cleveland and were hauled to Port Arthur on the little steamer *Mary Boyce.* It required many trips of the antiquated *Boyce,* but eventually the *Noronic* was put together and launched at Port Arthur. Later it was decided to "bustle" the *Noronic.* This consisted of extending her beam at the water line by installing an extension of plates and frames. To many folks this addition appeared to give the *Noronic* a sort of bloated appearance to her hull. But it did actually give the vessel much greater stabilization, and proved to be a beneficial appendage.

For thirty-six years the *Noronic* served the commercial travelers and vacationists on the Great Lakes. Folks along the St. Clair River and those closely associated with the ship affectionately knew her as the "*Norrie.*" She plied a steady run from Detroit and Windsor to Port Arthur and Duluth. Nothing of any great consequence ever happened to the *Noronic* except that some years she would get caught out in a late seasonal storm, have a rough time of it and probably be delayed in her time of arrival. But, year in and year out, she was a dependable ship.

During her later years the *Noronic* laid up earlier in the season. She wintered at Sarnia. It was the custom to send her out on a couple of post-season cruises immediately after her regular trip schedule was completed. These cruises generally took her into Lake Ontario and the Thousand Islands, making calls at the various interesting ports along the route. The trips were widely advertised and were well patronized. The Great Lakes in September are usually delightful.

It was while making one of these post-season cruises that the *Noronic* ended her days. The cruise began at Detroit and then proceeded to Cleveland. Passengers embarked at each port and the ship was well filled. Leaving Cleveland the *Noronic* passed down Lake Erie and through the Welland Canal into Lake Ontario, and thence to Toronto, Ontario. She arrived at Pier 9 of the Canada Steamship Lines and tied up at six o'clock in the afternoon of Friday, September 16, 1949. She was berthed with her bow toward the land with her starboard side to the dock. She had on board a passenger list of five hundred twenty-four persons and a crew of one hundred seventy-one, and carried no freight.

Upon her arrival at the dock, many of the passengers went ashore to sightsee or visit. Subsequently during the evening, many of the crew also went ashore. The *Noronic* was scheduled to sail from Toronto at seven in the early evening on the following day, Saturday, September seventeenth. This gave the vessel an overnight stop at the dock and almost a full day in Toronto on Saturday before proceeding on her cruise.

The early evening passed uneventfully. Captain William Taylor of the *Noronic* went ashore to visit friends. Passengers and crew went to and from the ship as she laid tied to the wharf. As the hours went by some of the passengers returned to the ship and retired for the night. Others sat chatting in groups about the steamer. A crew of fifteen men assumed their assigned duties after midnight to care for the wants of the passengers.

A passenger walking along a corridor about one-fifteen that morning noticed smoke curling from around a linen locker. He tried the door, found it locked, and then hurried to call a bellboy. The two returned and after some delay, opened the door to find the closet interior aflame. From that point on, things happened quickly aboard the *Noronic*. Unable to quench the fire, the passenger and bellboy separated to get assistance and spread the alarm. Soon there was great confusion as the fire spread rapidly.

A watchman on the dock saw the flames in a window toward the after end of the ship and hurriedly telephoned the Toronto Fire Department. They responded promptly, but by that time the *Noronic* was a mass of flames.

Meanwhile the captain of the ship had returned. With the small crew on duty he was greatly handicapped in fighting the spreading blazes. He directed his attentions toward arousing the passengers, and in a hurried futile attempt manned a hose. He was soon forced to leave his flaming ship.

Crewmen on duty did their best to get the passengers off the *Noronic,* and they succeeded in seeing four hundred and six of them safely ashore, though many were injured to some extent. This left, according to a later tally by agencies of the Canadian Government, one hundred four passengers dead and fourteen missing. The entire crew escaped death. Many of them were not aboard, and those that were, being thoroughly familiar with the four gangways, found their way to the dock.

The water pumped onto the *Noronic* by the fire fighters during the night to extinguish the holocaust gradually caused the vessel to sink in the comparatively shallow water at the pier. The steamer was a total loss. A few days later she was towed out of the Toronto harbor, a sad sight indeed, and taken to the plant of a salvage wrecker to be cut up into scrap steel. A great ship of the Great Lakes had perished and with it many of her passengers. The actual cause of the fire was never established.

While the *Noronic* disaster ranks as the tenth worst in the annals of Great Lakes shipping, in the number of lives lost, statisticians point out that the number lost in this shipwreck is something less than half of the automobile crash fatalities that occurred over the Labor Day holiday upon the highways of the United States that same year.

Fire was still to strike another passenger ship of the Canada Steamship Lines. The third steamer was the palatial *Quebec*. The scene of this disaster was many miles from the Great Lakes proper, on the Saint Lawrence River, the outlet of the Great Lakes to the sea.

The *Quebec* was more a river type steamer than the *Hamonic* or *Noronic*. She was of steel hull construction, three hundred fifty feet long, seventy feet beam, and almost nineteen feet depth; her gross tonnage was seven thousand and sixteen, and her registered tonnage four thousand one hundred forty-three. She had been built in 1928 at Lauzon, Quebec. Her usual run was between Montreal, Quebec, and Bagotville, some forty miles up the Saguenay River. Most of the ship was painted white. The only other color on her hull was a jet black which formed a sort of band around her, a few feet above the water line. She had two smokestacks about amidships, both painted in the attractive colors of the line.

The *Quebec,* with a comfortable number of three hundred fifty passengers and a crew of one hundred fifty, was steaming down the Saint Lawrence River late in the afternoon of Monday, August 14, 1950, on her regular run—the popular Saguenay River cruise. Saint Simeon had been left astern. The *Quebec* was some twenty-five miles from the mouth of the Saguenay River, where it enters the Saint Lawrence, when the horror cry of "Fire" rang through the ship. This was about four-thirty in the afternoon.

Captain C. H. Burch decided to continue on to the town of Tadoussac, which nestles close to the water at the spot where the Saguenay meets the Saint Lawrence. Meanwhile the crew turned to and fought the flames, but it was a losing battle which developed into a race between the flames and the ship. The *Quebec* fortunately won this round. She was brought to a dock in Tadoussac as the fire was gaining. The local fire department promptly responded to the call for aid. There was no panic. The passengers quickly left the steamer and went ashore. Some of their automobiles were even run safely onto the dock.

Much credit for saving the lives of the passengers and crew is due Captain Burch and his hard working officers, both in the engine room and on deck, because of their calmness and lack of hysteria. A very serious disaster was averted by their actions. Only three persons were lost.

Reports conflicted as to the origin of the fire, most of those in position to know stating they believed it started in a linen closet. The *Quebec* burned well into the night. By midnight the fire fighters believed that they had the flames under control. But the *Quebec* was a complete loss, according to a report from the owners issued in the city of Quebec. A court of investigation later found that the fire was due to sabotage by a person or persons unknown. The facts of the case were then turned over to the police.

The traveling public which enjoys and patronizes the Great Lakes passenger steamers has lost three old friends in the *Hamonic, Noronic,* and *Quebec.*

CHAPTER THIRTY-EIGHT

THE WRECK OF THE JULES LA PLANTE

'Twas one dark night on Lac St. Clair,
De wind she blow, blow, blow,
When de crew of de wood scow *Jules La Plante*
Got scar't and run below.

For de wind she blow like hurricane,
Bime by she blow some more,
When de scow bust up on Lac St. Clair,
T'ree acre from de shore.

De Cap'n walk de front deck,
He walk de hind deck too—
He call de crew up from de hold,
He call de cook also.

De cook she's name was Rosa,
Was come from Montreal,
Was chambermaid on lumber barge,
On dat big Lachine Canal.

De wind she blow from de nor'east, west,
De sou' wind she blow too,
When Rosa say, "Oh, Capt'n,
What ever I shall do?"

SHIPWRECKS OF THE LAKES

De Cap he trow de hanker,
But still dat scow she driff,
De crew he can't get on de shore,
Because he lose hees skiff.

De night was dark like one black cat,
De waves rolled high and fast,
When de Captain he took Rosa,
And lashed her to de mast.

Den de Cap put on de life preserve,
An' jumped into de Lac,
An' said, "Goodbye, my Rosa dear,
I go drown for your sake!"

Next morning very early,
'Bout half past two—t'ree—four—
De Captain, de crew, and de wood scow
Lay corpses on dat shore.

For de wind she blow like hurricane,
Bime by she blow some more,
When de scow bust up on Lac St. Clair,
T'ree acre from de shore.

Now all good wood scow sailor mans,
Take warning by dat storm,
An' go marry one nice French girl,
And live on one beeg farm.

Den de wind can blow like hurricane,

THE WRECK OF THE JULES LA PLANTE

An' suppose she blow some more,
You can't get drowned in Lac St. Clair,
So long you stay on shore.

Reminiscent of the days of the French Canadian sailors on the Great Lakes, this was a favorite poem of the lake men many years ago. It is almost identical to a poem written by William Henry Drummond, being changed only in the locale and a few minor details.

CHAPTER THIRTY-NINE

A LIST OF GREAT LAKES SHIPWRECKS

The following list of wrecked vessels on the Great Lakes and tributary waters is submitted for ready reference. A long, complete, and detailed listing of the shipwrecks of the lakes is not the intended purpose of this book.

This list has been carefully compiled from a great many sources, all of which are considered reliable. However, errors may have crept into the compilation, as in some instances the source of material varied. It is, nevertheless, as authentic and reliable as it is possible to make at this time.

Not all of the vessels listed became total losses. Many were later salvaged after their difficulties and were returned to service. It might therefore be possible for the same ship name to appear in the list more than one time.

A LIST OF GREAT LAKES SHIPWRECKS

DATE	NAME OF SHIP	WHERE LOST	REASON FOR LOSS	LIVES LOST
		1679		
	Griffin	Not Known	Not Known	5
		1814		
Aug. 14	Schnr. *Nancy*	Nancy Island, Georgian Bay	Burned	
		1818		
Oct.	Schnr. *Hercules*	Off Calumet River, Lake Michigan	Stranded	Several
	Schnr. *Independence*	Off Black River, Lake Erie	Capsized	All Hands
	Schnr. *Dolphin*	Pultneyville, N.Y., Lake Ontario	By Ice	Crew Saved
		1820		
	Schnr. *Franklin*	Off Grand River, Lake Erie	Foundered	Crew Lost
	Schnr. *Asp*	Salmon River, Lake Ontario	Foundered	Several Lost
		1821		
Nov. 1	Stmr. *Walk-In-The-Water*	Point Abino, Lake Erie	Stranded	None
		1824		
	Schnr. *Sylph*	North Bass Island, Lake Erie	Wrecked	Several Lost
		1825		
	Schnr. *Good Intent*	Off Dunkirk, N.Y.	Wrecked	Not Known
		1827		
	Stmr. *Frontenac*	Niagara River	Burned	Not Known
	Schnr. *Ann*	Off Long Point, Lake Erie	Wrecked	Several
		1828		
Nov. 4	Schnr. *Alice Hackett*	Georgian Bay	Stranded	None
		1830		
Sept. 16	Stmr. *William Peacock*	Off Buffalo, Lake Erie	Explosion	15 to 30
Nov. 15	Schnr. *Emily*	Lake St. Clair	Wrecked	7
		1832		
Nov. 12	Stmr. *Martha Ogden*	Off Stony Point, Lake Ontario	Stranded	All Saved

SHIPWRECKS OF THE LAKES

DATE	NAME OF SHIP	WHERE LOST	REASON FOR LOSS	LIVES LOST
		1834		
June 16	Stmr. *(George)Washington*	Off Dunkirk, N.Y.	Burned	30
		1835		
July 21	Stmr. *Commodore Perry*	Buffalo, N. Y.	Explosion	6
		1836		
June	Stmr. *Delaware*	Off St. Joseph, Lake Michigan	Stranded	All Saved
		1837		
Dec.	Stmr. *Caroline*	Niagara Falls	Fire	None
		1839		
Oct. 11	Stmr. *DeWitt Clinton*	Off Milwaukee, Lake Michigan	Foundered	5
		1841		
Aug. 9	Stmr. *Erie*	Off Silver Creek, N.Y., Lake Erie	Burned	100 to 175
		1842		
Oct. 21	Stmr. *Reindeer*	Off Point Sauble, Lake Michigan	Foundered	21
		1843		
	Stmr. *Superior*	Lake Michigan	Foundered	
		1845		
	Stmr. *Kent*	Off Point Pelee, Lake Erie	Collision	8
		1846		
June	Stmr. *Chesapeake*	Off Conneaut, Lake Erie	Collision	13
Nov. 19	Schnr. *Lexington*	Lake Erie Islands	Foundered	13
Nov. 20	Stmr. *Helen Strong*	Lake Erie	Stranded	Several Lost
		1847		
June	Schnr. *Merchant*	Lake Superior	Disappeared	14
Nov. 21	Stmr. *Phoenix*	'tween Manitowoc and Sheboygan, Lake Michigan	Fire	190 to 250
Nov.	Schnr. *Black Hawk*	Lake Michigan	Disappeared	All Hands
	Schnr. *J. C. Daun*	Off Conneaut, Ohio, Lake Erie	Capsized	8

A LIST OF GREAT LAKES SHIPWRECKS

DATE	NAME OF SHIP	WHERE LOST	REASON FOR LOSS	LIVES LOST
		1848		
April 18	Stmr. *Niagara*	Lake Ontario	Stranded	None
Sept. 14	Stmr. *Goliah*	Lake Huron	Fire and Explosion	18
Nov. 11	Stmr. *Scotland*	Nr. Port Stanley, Lake Erie	Stranded	None
Dec. 5	Stmr. *Indiana*	Conneaut, Ohio	Fire	None
		1849		
	Stmr. *Passport*	St. Lawrence River	Scalding	14
Aug. 1	Stmr. *Chicago*	Buffalo Harbor	Burned	None
		1850		
Mar. 23	Stmr. *Troy*	Off Black Rock, New York	Explosion	22
April 18	Stmr. *Anthony Wayne*	Off Vermilion, Lake Erie	Explosion	38 to 65
May	Stmr. *Commerce*	Off Grand River, Canada	Collision	40
June 17	Stmr. *G. P. Griffith*	Off Chagrin River, Lake Erie	Fire	250 to 295
Sept. 6	Stmr. *Nile*	Milwaukee Harbor	Burned	None
		1851		
Oct. 25	Stmr. *Henry Clay*	Off Long Point, Lake Erie	Capsized	16 to 19
		1852		
Aug. 20	Stmr. *Atlantic*	Nr. Long Point, Lake Erie	Collision	150 to 250
Nov.	Stmr. *St. Louis*	Nr. Kelleys Island, Lake Erie	Foundered	
	Stmr. *Caspian*	Nr. Cleveland, Lake Erie	Foundered	None
	Stmr. *Oneida*	Lake Erie	Capsized	17
		1853		
April 30	Stmr. *Ocean Wave*	Off Kingston, Lake Ontario	Fire	28
Nov. 22	Stmr. *Independence*	Sault Ste. Marie, Michigan	Explosion	4
		1854		
Oct. 8	Stmr. *E. K. Collins*	Detroit River, Nr. Lake Erie	Fire	23
Nov. 12	Stmr. *Bucephalus*	Lake Huron	Foundered	10
Dec. 7	Stmr. *Westmorland*	Lake Michigan	Foundered	17

SHIPWRECKS OF THE LAKES

DATE	NAME OF SHIP	WHERE LOST	REASON FOR LOSS	LIVES LOST
		1855		
Nov.	Stmr. *Omar Pasha*	Lake Michigan	Disappeared	All Hands
		1856		
July 17	Stmr. *Northern Indiana*	Lake Erie	Fire	30 to 56
May 9	Stmr. *Inkerman*	Toronto Harbor	Explosion	All Hands
Sept. 24	Stmr. *Niagara*	Lake Michigan	Fire	65
Oct. 24	Stmr. *Toledo*	Lake Michigan	Foundered	40 to 55
Oct. 29	Stmr. *Superior*	Lake Superior	Foundered	35
		1857		
Aug. 30	Stmr. *Montreal*	St. Lawrence River	Fire	250
Sept.	Stmr. *Louisville*	Lake Michigan	Fire	None
Oct.	Stmr. *Sandusky*	Lake Erie	Fire	None
Nov. 27	Tug *Noah C. Sprague*	Detroit River	Explosion	All Hands
		1858		
April 5	Stmr. *Forest City*	Port Stanley, Ont.	Fire	None
Aug. 3	Schnr. *E. H. Rae*	Lake Ontario	Capsized	None
		1859		
Mar.	Stmr. *Lady of the Lake*	Lake Erie	Explosion	2
Oct. 18	Stmr. *Troy*	Saginaw Bay	Foundered	23
		1860		
July 4	Tug *A. S. Field*	Detroit River	Explosion	All Hands
Sept. 8	Stmr. *Lady Elgin*	Lake Michigan	Collision	297
Nov.	Stmr. *Dacotah*	Lake Erie	Foundered	All Hands
		1861		
Nov. 10	Stmr. *Keystone State*	Lake Huron	Disappeared	All Hands
		1862		
May 25	Tug *Zouave*	Lake St. Clair	Exposion	4
		1863		
Aug. 28	Stmr. *Sunbeam*	Lake Superior	Foundered	28
Aug.	Stmr. *Planet*	Lake Superior	Foundered	35
Nov.	Stmr. *Water Witch*	Saginaw Bay	Disappeared	All Hands
Dec. 4	Stmr. *City of Detroit*	Saginaw Bay	Disappeared	All Hands
		1864		
May 21	Stmr. *Nile*	Detroit Dock	Explosion	8
Sept. 24	Stmr. *Tonawanda*	Chicago River	Explosion	1
Fall	Bark *Western Metropolis*	Lake Superior	Stranded	Not Known

A LIST OF GREAT LAKES SHIPWRECKS

DATE	NAME OF SHIP	WHERE LOST	REASON FOR LOSS	LIVES LOST
		1865		
April 20	Stmr. *Oregon*	Detroit River	Explosion	12
Aug. 9	Stmr. *Pewabic*	Lake Huron	Collision	125
		1866		
April 23	Stmr. *Windsor*	Detroit River	Fire	30
June 4	Schnr. *Jennie P. King*	Lake Erie	Stranded	14
Oct. 22	Schnr. *Alma*	Lake Erie	Foundered	All Hands
		1867		
May 21	Stmr. *Wisconsin*	Lake Ontario	Fire	23 to 30
Oct.	Stmr. *Portsmouth*	Lake Huron	Fire	None
Oct.	Stmr. *Oswego*	Lake Erie	Stranded	5
		1868		
April 9	Stmr. *Seabird*	Lake Michigan	Fire	68 to 100
May 1	Stmr. *Governor Cushman*	Buffalo Harbor	Explosion	12
June 21	Stmr. *Morning Star*	Lake Erie	Collision	23 to 32
Sept. 8	Stmr. *Hippocampus*	Lake Michigan	Foundered	25
		1869		
Oct. 4	Schnr. *Kate Bully*	Lake Michigan	Foundered	5
Nov. 18	Stmr. *Equator*		Foundered	
Nov. 18	Stmr. *Thomas A. Scott*		Foundered	
	Schnr. *Persia*	Lake Huron	Foundered	All Hands
		1870		
Oct. 31	Schnr. *Jessie*	Lake Ontario	Stranded	All Hands
Nov. 6	Stmr. *Wasaga*	Lake Superior	Fire	All Rescued
		1871		
May 26	Tug *B. B. Jones*	Port Huron Dock	Explosion	7
Oct. 9	Stmr. *Navarino*	Chicago Harbor	Fire	None
Oct. 15	Stmr. *R. G. Coburn*	Saginaw Bay	Foundered	31
		1872		
June 18	Schnr. *Jamaica*	Lake Huron	Foundered	None
Sept.	Schnr. *George F. Whitney*	Lake Superior	Disappeared	All Hands
Oct.	Stmr. *Lac La Belle*	Lake Michigan	Foundered	8
Nov. 15	Schnr. *O. O. Brown*	Lake Superior	Foundered	6
Nov. 15	Schnr. *Griswold*	Lake Superior	Foundered	All Hands
Nov. 15	Barges *Saturn and Jupiter*	Lake Superior	Foundered	All Hands
Nov. 26	Schnr. *Souvenir*	Lake Michigan	Foundered	6

SHIPWRECKS OF THE LAKES

DATE	NAME OF SHIP	WHERE LOST	REASON FOR LOSS	LIVES LOST
		1873		
Sept. 15	Stmr. *Ironsides*	Lake Michigan	Foundered	24 to 30
Oct. 27	Schnr. *Gilbert Mollison*	Lake Michigan	Foundered	All Hands
	Stmr. *Meteor*	Detroit Dock	Fire	None
Nov. 5	Stmr. *Bavarian*	Lake Ontario	Fire	14
		1874		
Oct. 22	Stmr. *Brooklyn*	Detroit River	Explosion	16
Nov.	Stmr. *Eclipse*	Lake Huron	Disappeared	All Hands
		1875		
Aug. 26	Stmr. *Comet*	Lake Superior	Collision	10
Sept. 10	Stmr. *Equinox*	Lake Michigan	Foundered	20 to 26
Sept. 10	Stmr. *Mendota*	Lake Michigan	Foundered	12
		1876		
Mar. 24	Stmr. *City of Sandusky*	Pt. Stanley Harbor	Fire	
July 9	Stmr. *St. Clair*	Lake Superior	Fire	25
		1877		
July 24	Stmr. *Cumberland*		Foundered	
Nov. 8	Schnr. *Berlin*	Lake Huron	Stranded	4
Nov. 8	Schnr. *Kate L. Bruce*	Lake Huron	Disappeared	All Hands
		1878		
April	Schnr. *Express*	Lake Michigan	Collision	
June	Stmr. *Montgomery*	St. Clair River	Fire	
July	Stmr. *Mary Robertson*		Fire	
Oct.	Schnr. *Daniel Lyons*	Lake Michigan	Collision	
		1879		
Sept.	Stmr. *George S. Frost*	Erie Harbor	Fire	None
Oct. 28	Stmr. *Amazon*	Lake Michigan	Stranded	
Nov.	Schnr. *Two Fannies*	Grand Traverse Bay	Stranded	
Nov. 22	Stmr. *Waubuno*	Georgian Bay	Disappeared	24
		1880		
Mar. 14	Tug *George Lamont*	Lake Michigan	Foundered	All Hands-3
Aug. 29	Stmr. *Marine City*	Lake Huron	Fire	8 to 10
Oct. 15	Stmr. *Trader*	Lake Michigan	Foundered	10
	Stmr. *George L. Dunlap*	Lake Huron	Cut by Ice	
Oct. 16	Stmr. *Alpena*	Lake Michigan	Foundered	60 to 101
Nov. 7	Stmr. *Zealand*	Lake Ontario	Foundered	All Hands-16

A LIST OF GREAT LAKES SHIPWRECKS

DATE	NAME OF SHIP	WHERE LOST	REASON FOR LOSS	LIVES LOST
Nov. 24	Stmr. *Simcoe*	Lake Huron	Foundered	12

1881

DATE	NAME OF SHIP	WHERE LOST	REASON FOR LOSS	LIVES LOST
July 19	Stmr. *City of Winnipeg*	Lake Superior	Fire	
Sept. 10	Stmr. *Columbia*	Lake Michigan	Foundered	
Nov. 12	Schnr. *Carlingford*	Lake Erie	Collision	1
Nov. 12	Stmr. *Brunswick*	Lake Erie	Collision	3
Nov. 24	Stmr. *Lake Erie*	Lake Michigan	Collision	
Nov. 24	Stmr. *Northern Queen*		Foundered	

1882

DATE	NAME OF SHIP	WHERE LOST	REASON FOR LOSS	LIVES LOST
April 10	Schnr. *Clayton Belle*	Lake Huron	Collision	4
May 18	Stmr. *Manitoulin*	Georgian Bay	Fire	25 to 40
Sept. 15	Stmr. *Asia*	Georgian Bay	Foundered	123

1883

DATE	NAME OF SHIP	WHERE LOST	REASON FOR LOSS	LIVES LOST
May 20	Schnr. *Wells Burt*	Lake Michigan	Foundered	All Hands-10
Nov. 13	Stmr. *H. C. Akley*	Lake Michigan	Foundered	6
Nov. 16	Stmr. *Manistee*	Lake Superior	Foundered	All Hands-30

1884

DATE	NAME OF SHIP	WHERE LOST	REASON FOR LOSS	LIVES LOST
July 27	Stmr. *John M. Osborn*	Lake Superior	Collision	4
Sept. 24	Schnr. *Golden Rule*	Lake Superior	Capsized	2
Oct. 26	Schnr. *New Dominion*	Lake Erie	Foundered	6

1885

DATE	NAME OF SHIP	WHERE LOST	REASON FOR LOSS	LIVES LOST
Mar. 20	Stmr. *Michigan*	Lake Michigan	Foundered	
Nov. 7	Stmr. *Algoma*	Lake Superior	Stranded	37
Dec. 17	Schnr. *Orphan Boy*	Lake Michigan	Foundered	All Hands-12

1886

DATE	NAME OF SHIP	WHERE LOST	REASON FOR LOSS	LIVES LOST
April	Stmr. *Africa*	Owen Sound, Ont.	Fire	
Oct.	Schnr. *Belle Mitchell*	Lake Erie	Foundered	8
	Stmr. *Oregon*	Lake Erie	Collision	
	Schnr. *Lucerne*		Disappeared	All Hands
	Stmr. *Reutan*	Lake Michigan	Stranded	
Nov. 18	Schnr. *Two Wallaces*	Lake Superior	Stranded	None

1887

DATE	NAME OF SHIP	WHERE LOST	REASON FOR LOSS	LIVES LOST
June 17	Stmr. *Champlain*	Lake Michigan	Fire	22
Oct. 3	Schnr. *City of Green Bay*	Lake Michigan	Stranded	6
Oct. 3	Schnr. *Havana*	Lake Michigan	Foundered	3
Oct. 3	Schnr. *C. L. Hutchinson*	Lake Erie	Foundered	

SHIPWRECKS OF THE LAKES

DATE	NAME OF SHIP	WHERE LOST	REASON FOR LOSS	LIVES LOST
Oct. 4	Stmr. *California*	Lake Michigan	Foundered	9 to 14
Oct. 23	Schnr. *James F. Joy*	Lake Erie	Foundered	
Oct. 29	Stmr. *Vernon*	Lake Michigan	Foundered	36 to 41
Nov. 18	Stmr. *Arizona*	Lake Superior	Fire	

1888

DATE	NAME OF SHIP	WHERE LOST	REASON FOR LOSS	LIVES LOST
Aug. 20	Schnr. *Walter H. Oades*	Lake Erie	Collision	
Oct. 1	Barge *St. Clair*	Lake Huron	Foundered	5
Nov. 11	Barge *Banner*	Lake Erie	Foundered	
	Stmr. *City of Owen Sound*		Stranded	

1889

DATE	NAME OF SHIP	WHERE LOST	REASON FOR LOSS	LIVES LOST
Oct. 23	Stmr. *Quinte*	Bay of Quinte	Fire	4
Nov. 27	Barges *Midnight & Mears*	Lake Huron	Stranded	1
Nov. 30	Schnr. *David Dows*	Lake Michigan	Foundered	
	Schnr. *Bavaria*	Lake Ontario	Foundered	8

1890

DATE	NAME OF SHIP	WHERE LOST	REASON FOR LOSS	LIVES LOST
April	Stmr. *Chenango*	Lake Erie	Fire	
	Stmr. *Bruno* and Barge *Louisa*	Lake Superior	Foundered	
	Stmr. *Annie Young*	Lake Huron	Fire	9

1891

DATE	NAME OF SHIP	WHERE LOST	REASON FOR LOSS	LIVES LOST
May 21	Schnr. *Thomas Hume*	Lake Michigan	Disappeared	All Hands-6
Sept. 26	Schnr. *Frank Perew*	Lake Superior	Foundered	6
Oct.	Stmr. *Winslow*	Duluth Harbor	Fire	None
Nov. 17	Schnr. *Hattie A. Estelle*	Lake Michigan	Stranded	3
	Schnr. *Atlanta*	Lake Superior	Foundered	All Hands

1892

DATE	NAME OF SHIP	WHERE LOST	REASON FOR LOSS	LIVES LOST
Aug. 30	Stmr. *Western Reserve*	Lake Superior	Foundered	26
Sept. 26	Schnr. *John Burt*	Lake Ontario	Foundered	2
Oct. 4	Stmr. *Nashua*	Lake Huron	Foundered	All Hands-15
Oct. 28	Stmr. *W. H. Gilcher*	Lake Michigan	Foundered	All Hands-21
Oct. 28	Schnr. *Ostrich*	Lake Michigan	Foundered	All Hands-8
Oct. 28	Schnr. *A. P. Nichols*	Lake Michigan	Foundered	None
Oct. 31	Schnr. *Zach Chandler*	Lake Superior	Foundered	1

1893

DATE	NAME OF SHIP	WHERE LOST	REASON FOR LOSS	LIVES LOST
Oct. 14	Stmr. *Dean Richmond*	Lake Erie	Foundered	All Hands-15 to 23
Oct. 14	Stmr. *Wocoken*	Lake Erie	Foundered	14
Nov. 7	Stmr. *Philadelphia*	Lake Huron	Collision	
Nov. 7	Stmr. *Albany*	Lake Huron	Collision	24

A LIST OF GREAT LAKES SHIPWRECKS

DATE	NAME OF SHIP	WHERE LOST	REASON FOR LOSS	LIVES LOST
	Schnr. *Newell A. Eddy*	Lake Huron	Foundered	All Hands
	Schnr. *Minnehaha*	Lake Michigan	Stranded	6

1894

DATE	NAME OF SHIP	WHERE LOST	REASON FOR LOSS	LIVES LOST
May 18	Schnr. *M. J. Cummings*	Lake Michigan	Foundered	6
May 18	Schnr. *Myrtle*	Chicago Waterfront	Stranded	All Hands
May 19	Schnr. *William Shupe*	Lake Huron	Stranded	4
Oct. 11	Schnr. *Hartford*	Lake Ontario	Foundered	7

1895

DATE	NAME OF SHIP	WHERE LOST	REASON FOR LOSS	LIVES LOST
Jan. 21	Stmr. *Chicora*	Lake Michigan	Foundered	All Hands-24
June 7	Stmr. *St. Magnus*	Cleveland Harbor	Capsized	None
Sept. 5	Stmr. *Baltic*	Collingwood, Ont.	Fire	
Sept. 29	Stmr. *C. J. Kershaw*	Lake Superior	Stranded	None
Sept. 29	Schnr. *Henry A. Kent*	Lake Superior	Stranded	None
Sept. 29	Schnr. *Moonlight*	Lake Superior	Stranded	None
Sept. 29	Schnr. *Elma*	Lake Superior	Stranded	1
Oct. 6	Schnr. *Henry C. Richards*	Lake Michigan	Foundered	
Nov. 1	Stmr. *Missoula*	Lake Superior	Foundered	None
	Stmr. *Africa*	Lake Huron	Foundered	All Hands-13

1896

DATE	NAME OF SHIP	WHERE LOST	REASON FOR LOSS	LIVES LOST
May 17	Schnr. *Mary D. Ayres*		Collision	5
Oct.	Stmr. *Australasia*	Lake Michigan	Fire	
Nov. 7	Schnr. *Waukesha*	Lake Michigan	Foundered	6
Nov. 26	Stmr. *J. H. Jones*	Georgian Bay		26
	Barge *Sumatra*	Lake Michigan	Foundered	4

1897

DATE	NAME OF SHIP	WHERE LOST	REASON FOR LOSS	LIVES LOST
May 20	Stmr. *Florida*	Lake Huron	Collision	
June	Stmr. *Southeastern*	Prescott, Ont. Harbor	Fire	
Sept. 18	Schnr. *Henry A. Kent*	Lake Superior	Foundered	All Saved
Sept. 25	Stmr. *C. B. Wallace*	Toledo, O., Harbor	Fire	None
Oct. 9	Stmr. *E. B. Hale*	Lake Huron	Foundered	
Nov. 5	Stmr. *Idaho*	Lake Erie	Foundered	19
Nov. 30	Stmr. *Nahant*	Escanaba, Michigan Harbor	Fire	2

1898

DATE	NAME OF SHIP	WHERE LOST	REASON FOR LOSS	LIVES LOST
Oct. 13	Schnr. *Churchill*	Lake Michigan	Foundered	2
Oct. 26	Stmr. *L. R. Doty*	Lake Michigan	Disappeared	17
Oct. 27	Schnr. *St. Peter*	Lake Ontario	Foundered	8
Nov. 3	Stmr. *Pacific*	Collingwood, Ont.	Fire	

SHIPWRECKS OF THE LAKES

DATE	NAME OF SHIP	WHERE LOST	REASON FOR LOSS	LIVES LOST
Nov. 10	Schnr. S. *Thol*	Lake Michigan	Foundered	5

1899

DATE	NAME OF SHIP	WHERE LOST	REASON FOR LOSS	LIVES LOST
June 3	Stmr. *R. G. Stewart*	Lake Superior	Stranding and Fire	1
July 21	Schnr. *John Breden*	Lake Huron	Foundered	3
Sept. 28	Stmr. *R. J. Gordon*	Chicago Harbor	Fire	None
Oct. 14	Schnr. *Typo*	Lake Huron	Collision	4
Dec. 5	Stmr. *Niagara*	Lake Erie	Foundered	12
	Stmr. *Margaret Olwill*	Lake Erie	Foundered	8

1900

DATE	NAME OF SHIP	WHERE LOST	REASON FOR LOSS	LIVES LOST
Sept. 11	Stmr. *John B. Lyon*	Lake Erie	Foundered	11
Sept. 11	Schnr. *Dundee*	Lake Erie	Foundered	1

1901

DATE	NAME OF SHIP	WHERE LOST	REASON FOR LOSS	LIVES LOST
May 10	Stmr. *Bon Voyage*	Lake Superior	Fire	4
May 24	Stmr. *Baltimore*	Lake Huron	Foundered	14
July 29	Barge *Sagamore*	Lake Superior	Collision	3
Sept. 16	Stmr. *Hudson*	Lake Superior	Foundered	All Hands-24
Sept. 20	Stmr. *Fedora*	Lake Superior	Foundered	None
Oct. 17	Stmr. *City of Cleveland*	Lake Huron	Fire	None
Nov. 11	Schnr. *Marine City*	Lake Huron	Foundered	4

1902

DATE	NAME OF SHIP	WHERE LOST	REASON FOR LOSS	LIVES LOST
June 29	Stmr. *George Dunbar*	Lake Erie	Foundered	7
Oct. 13	Barge *129*	Lake Superior	Collision	
Oct. 19	Stmr. *Joseph S. Fay*	Lake Huron	Foundered	1
Nov. 21	Stmr. *Bannockburn*	Lake Superior	Disappeared	All Hands-20
Nov. 23	Stmr. *Sylvanus J. Macy*	Lake Erie	Foundered	All Hands-14
Nov. 29	Schnr. *Celtic*	Lake Huron	Disappeared	All Hands-8
Dec. 2	Schnr. *Jessie Drummond*	Lake Ontario	Foundered	None
Dec. 14	Stmr. *John E. Hall*	Lake Ontario	Stranded	All Hands-9
	Stmr. *C. B. Lockwood*	Lake Erie	Foundered	10

1903

DATE	NAME OF SHIP	WHERE LOST	REASON FOR LOSS	LIVES LOST
Aug. 13	Stmr. *Pittsburgh*	Sandwich, Ontario	Burned	
Aug. 20	Stmr. *Queen of the West*	Lake Erie	Foundered	1
Sept. 13	Schnr. *Moonlight*	Lake Superior	Foundered	None
Oct. 3	Stmr. *Erie L. Hackley*	Green Bay	Foundered	11
Oct. 9	Stmr. *John N. Glidden*	St. Clair Ship Canal	Collision	None
Oct. 25	Stmr. *William F. Sauber*	Lake Superior	Foundered	2
Nov. 10	Stmr. *Atlantic*	Georgian Bay	Burned	

1904

DATE	NAME OF SHIP	WHERE LOST	REASON FOR LOSS	LIVES LOST
Mar. 11	Carferry *Shenango No. 1*	Lake Erie	Burned	1

A LIST OF GREAT LAKES SHIPWRECKS

DATE	NAME OF SHIP	WHERE LOST	REASON FOR LOSS	LIVES LOST
April 11	Tug *Frank Canfield*	Lake Michigan	Stranded	
Oct. 25	Stmr. *Eliza H. Strong*	Lake Huron	Foundered	
Nov. 4	Stmr. *Germanic*	Stag Island, Ont.	Stranded and Fire	
Nov. 21	Stmr. *W. C. Franz*	Lake Huron	Collision	
Nov. 25	Barge *Massasoit*	Niagara River	Stranded	

1905

June 19	Stmr. *City of Collingwood*	Collingwood, Ont.	Burned	
Sept. 2	Stmr. *Sevona*	Lake Superior	Foundered	7
Sept. 3	Stmr. *Iosco*	Lake Superior	Foundered	All Hands-19
Sept. 3	Schnr. *Pretoria*	Lake Superior	Foundered	All Hands-5
Sept. 3	Schnr. *Olive Jeanette*	Lake Superior	Foundered	All Hands-7
Oct. 19	Stmr. *Kaliyuga*	Lake Huron	Disappeared	All Hands-16
Oct.	Schnr. *Minnedosa*		Foundered	All Hands
Nov. 24	Stmr. *Argo*	Lake Michigan	Stranded	None
Nov. 28	Stmr. *Ira H. Owen*	Lake Superior	Foundered	19
Nov. 30	Stmr. *Mataafa*	Duluth Harbor	Stranded	9
Nov. 30	Stmr. *LaFayette*	Lake Superior	Stranded	
Nov. 30	Barge *Madeira*	Lake Superior	Stranded	
Nov. 30	Stmr. *Crescent City*	Lake Superior	Stranded	
Nov. 30	Stmr. *Vega*	Lake Michigan	Stranded	
Nov. 30	Stmr. *Monkshaven*	Lake Superior	Stranded	None
Nov. 30	Barge *Olga*	Lake Huron	Stranded	None
Nov. 30	Barge *H. Bissell*	Lake Huron	Stranded	
Nov. 30	Stmr. *Point Abino*	Lake St. Clair	Stranded	
Nov. 30	Schnr. *George Herbert*	Lake Superior	Foundered	5

1906

Mar.	Stmr. *Atlanta*	Lake Michigan	Burned	1
Sept. 16	Stmr. *Charles B. Packard*	Lake Erie	Foundered	
Dec. 6	Stmr. *Monarch*	Lake Superior	Stranded	All Saved

1907

April 14	Stmr. *Arcadia*	Lake Michigan	Foundered	14
Sept. 21	Stmr. *Alex Nimick*	Lake Superior	Foundered	6
Oct. 11	Stmr. *Cyprus*	Lake Superior	Foundered	22

1908

Nov. 1	Stmr. *Telegram*	Georgian Bay	Foundered	
Nov. 30	Stmr. *D. M. Clemson*	Lake Superior	Foundered	24
	Stmr. *Naomi*	Lake Michigan	Burned	7
	Stmr. *Soo City*	Gulf of St. Lawrence	Foundered	All Hands-20

351

SHIPWRECKS OF THE LAKES

DATE	NAME OF SHIP	WHERE LOST	REASON FOR LOSS	LIVES LOST
		1909		
April 7	Tug *George A. Floss*		Disappeared	All Hands-9
May 9	Stmr. *Adella Shores*		Disappeared	All Hands-27
June 7	Stmr. *Campana*	St. Lawrence River	Foundered	
July 12	Stmr. *John B. Cowle*	Lake Superior	Collision	14
Oct. 13	Stmr. *George Stone*	Lake Erie	Stranded	6
Dec. 8	Stmr. *Clarion*	Lake Erie	Burned	15
Dec. 9	Stmr. *W. C. Richardson*	Lake Erie	Stranded	5
Dec. 9	Carferry *Marquette* and *Bessemer No. 2*	Lake Erie	Disappeared	36
	Stmr. *Russia*	Lake Huron	Foundered	None
	Stmr. *Tempest No. 2*	Georgian Bay	Burned	6
	Stmr. *Badger State*	Lake Huron	Burned	15
	Schnr. *Charles Spademan*	Lake Erie	Foundered	
		1910		
Mar. 7	Carferry *Ann Arbor No. 1*	Manitowoc Harbor	Burned	
May 23	Stmr. *Frank H. Goodyear*	Lake Huron	Collision	18
Sept. 9	Carferry *Pere Marquette No. 18*	Lake Michigan	Foundered	29
Oct. 2	Stmr. *New York*	Lake Huron	Burned	None
Oct. 6	Stmr. *Muskegon*	Michigan City Harbor	Burned	None
Oct. 18	Stmr. *W. C. Moreland*	Lake Superior	Stranded	None
Nov. 16	Stmr. *Wasaga*	Lake Superior	Burned	None
		1911		
April 15	Tug *Silver Spray*	Lake Erie	Disappeared	All Hands-9
June 3	Stmr. *North West*	Buffalo Harbor	Burned	
July 9	Stmr. *John Mitchell*	Lake Superior	Collision	3
Sept. 22	Stmr. *Joliet*	St. Clair River	Collision	
Oct. 25	Schnr. *Azov*	Lake Huron	Foundered	None
		1912		
Aug. 7	Stmr. *James Gayley*	Lake Superior	Collision	None
Oct. 21	Stmr. *Pine Lake*	Lake St. Clair	Collision	2
Oct. 26	Stmr. *Keystorm*	St. Lawrence River	Stranded	None
Nov. 9	Schnr. *Hattie Wells*	Lake Michigan	Foundered	None
Nov. 12	Stmr. *South Shore*	Lake Superior	Stranded	None
Nov. 24	Schnr. *Three Sisters*	Green Bay	Foundered	4
Nov.	Stmr. *Flora*	Chicago Harbor	Burned	None
		1913		
April 19	Stmr. *Uganda*	Mackinac Straits	Foundered	None

A LIST OF GREAT LAKES SHIPWRECKS

DATE	NAME OF SHIP	WHERE LOST	REASON FOR LOSS	LIVES LOST
Oct. 21	Stmr. *C. W. Elphicke*	Lake Erie	Stranded	None
Nov. 8	Stmr. *L. C. Waldo*	Lake Superior	Stranded	None
Nov. 8	Stmr. *Turret Chief*	Lake Superior	Stranded	None
Nov. 10	Stmr. *Louisiana*	Lake Michigan	Stranded	None
Nov. 11	Stmr. *Charles S. Price*	Lake Huron	Foundered	All Hands
Nov. 11	Stmr. *Isaac M. Scott*	Lake Huron	Foundered	All Hands
Nov. 11	Stmr. *Henry B. Smith*	Lake Superior	Foundered	All Hands
Nov. 11	Stmr. *James Carruthers*	Lake Huron	Foundered	All Hands
Nov. 11	Stmr. *Wexford*	Lake Huron	Foundered	All Hands
Nov. 11	Stmr. *Regina*	Lake Huron	Foundered	All Hands
Nov. 11	Stmr. *Leafield*	Lake Superior	Foundered	All Hands
Nov. 11	Stmr. *John A. McGean*	Lake Huron	Foundered	All Hands
Nov. 11	Stmr. *Argus*	Lake Huron	Foundered	All Hands
Nov. 11	Stmr. *Hydrus*	Lake Huron	Foundered	All Hands
Nov. 11	Barge *Plymouth*	Lake Michigan	Foundered	All Hands
Nov. 11	Lightship *82*	Lake Erie	Foundered	All Hands
Nov. 11	Barge *Halsted*	Lake Michigan	Foundered	All Hands
Nov. 11	Stmr. *H. M. Hanna, Jr.*	Lake Huron	Stranded	
Nov. 11	Stmr. *Major*	Lake Superior	Stranded	
Nov. 11	Stmr. *Matoa*	Lake Huron	Stranded	
Nov. 11	Stmr. *William Nottingham*	Lake Superior	Stranded	None
Nov. 24	Barge *Parsons*	Lake Ontario	Foundered	
Nov. 26	Stmr. *I. W. Nicholas*	Lake Huron	Stranded	
Nov. 26	Schnr. *Rouse Simmons*	Lake Michigan	Disappeared	All Hands-17
	1914			
April 27	Stmr. *Benjamin Noble*	Lake Superior	Disappeared	All Hands-20
May 22	Stmr. *W. H. Gilbert*	Lake Huron	Collision	None
May 29	Stmr. *Empress of Ireland*	St. Lawrence River	Collision	1,024
Aug. 30	Stmr. *City of Chicago*	Lake Michigan	Burned	None
Nov. 8	Stmr. *Oscoda*	Lake Michigan	Stranded	None
Nov. 19	Stmr. *C. F. Curtis*	Lake Superior	Foundered	All Hands
Nov. 19	Barge *Annie M. Peterson*	Lake Superior	Foundered	All Hands
Nov. 19	Barge *Seldon E. Marvin*	Lake Superior	Foundered	All Hands
	1915			
June 27	Stmr. *Sydney C. McLouth*	Lake Michigan	Burned	
July 11	Stmr. *Choctaw*	Lake Huron	Collision	None
July 24	Stmr. *Eastland*	Chicago Harbor	Capsized	835
Aug. 13	Stmr. *Alexandria*	Lake Ontario	Foundered	
Sept. 15	Stmr. *Onoko*	Lake Superior	Foundered	
Oct. 8	Stmr. *James B. Neilson*	Lake Superior	Stranded	None
Nov. 1	Tug *Frank C. Barnes*	Lake Ontario	Disappeared	All Hands-6
Dec. 15	Stmr. *Majestic*	Sarnia, Ontario	Burned	None

SHIPWRECKS OF THE LAKES

DATE	NAME OF SHIP	WHERE LOST	REASON FOR LOSS	LIVES LOST
		1916		
Mar. 17	Stmr. *City of Midland*	Collingwood Ont.	Burned	
May 10	Stmr. *S. R. Kirby*	Lake Superior	Foundered	20
Aug. 20	Stmr. *Saronic*	Georgian Bay	Burned	
Oct. 20	Stmr. *James B. Colgate*	Lake Erie	Foundered	21 to 23
Oct. 20	Stmr. *Merida*	Lake Erie	Foundered	23
Oct. 20	Stmr. *Marshall F. Butters*	Lake Erie	Foundered	None
Oct. 20	Schnr. *D. L. Filer*	Lake Erie	Foundered	
		1917		
April 5	Stmr. *Germanic*	Collingwood, Ont.	Burned	
May 11	Stmr. *Lloyd S. Porter*	Lake Ontario	Burned	
May 11	Stmr. *Conger Coal*	Lake Ontario	Burned	
June 6	Stmr. *Isabella J. Boyce*	Lake Erie	Burned	
Oct. 14	Stmr. *George A. Graham*	Georgian Bay	Stranded	
Dec. 8	Schnr. *Desmond*	Lake Michigan	Foundered	6
	Stmr. *Goodreau*	Lake Huron	Stranded	
		1918		
June 17	Stmr. *Jay Gould*	Lake Erie	Foundered	None
June 17	Barge *Commodore*	Lake Erie	Foundered	None
July 2	Stmr. *Cream City*	Lake Huron	Stranded	
Aug. 27	Stmr. *Tempest*	Lake Erie	Foundered	1
Oct. 29	Stmr. *Rising Sun*	Lake Michigan	Stranded	
Oct. 30	Stmr. *Vulcan*	Lake Superior	Stranded	None
Nov. 8	Stmr. *Chester A. Congdon*	Lake Superior	Stranded	None
Nov. 24	Mine Sweeper *Cerisoler*	Lake Superior	Disappeared	38
Nov. 24	Mine Sweeper *Inkerman*	Lake Superior	Disappeared	38
Nov. 28	Stmr. *North West* (Bow Section)	Lake Ontario	Foundered	2
		1919		
May 16	Stmr. *D. R. Hanna*	Lake Huron	Collision	None
June 10	Stmr. *Ferd. Schlesinger*	Lake Superior	Foundered	None
Sept. 13	Barge *Chickamauga*	Lake Huron	Foundered	None
Sept. 22	Stmr. *T. J. Waffle*	Lake Ontario	Foundered	8
Oct. 28	Stmr. *Muskegon*	Lake Michigan	Stranded	21 to 29
Oct. 28	Stmr. *Homer Warren*	Lake Ontario	Foundered	9
Nov. 12	Stmr. *John Owen*	Lake Superior	Foundered	22
Nov. 14	Stmr. *H. E. Runnels*	Lake Superior	Stranded	None
Nov. 23	Stmr. *Myron*	Lake Superior	Foundered	17
Nov. 26	Stmr. *Tioga*	Lake Superior	Foundered	None

A LIST OF GREAT LAKES SHIPWRECKS

DATE	NAME OF SHIP	WHERE LOST	REASON FOR LOSS	LIVES LOST
		1920		
Mar. 7	Carferry *Pere Marquette No. 3*	Lake Michigan	Crushed by Ice	
Aug. 20	Stmr. *Superior City*	Lake Superior	Collision	29
Aug. 28	Stmr. *Mary A. McGregor*	Lake Huron	Stranded and Burned	
Nov. 12	Stmr. *Francis Widlar*	Lake Superior	Stranded	
Nov. 13	Stmr. *John F. Eddy*	Lake Erie	Foundered	
		1921		
Oct. 30	Schnr. *Rosebelle*	Lake Michigan	Foundered	All Hands
	Stmr. *J. H. Shrigley*	Lake Ontario	Foundered	
		1922		
Mar. 26	Stmr. *Omar D. Conger*	Port Huron, Mich.	Explosion	4
Aug. 10	Stmr. *Annie Laura*	St. Clair River	Burned	None
Oct. 29	Stmr. *Mecosta*	Lake Erie	Foundered	None
Oct.	Stmr. *Arrow*	Put-in-Bay, Ohio	Burned	None
Nov. 26	Schnr. *Horace Taber*	St. Lawrence River	Stranded	None
Nov. 30	Stmr. *Maplehurst*	Lake Superior	Stranded	11
Dec. 21	Tug *Cornell*	Lake Erie	Foundered	8
		1923		
Feb. 14	Carferry *Ann Arbor No. 4*	Lake Michigan	Stranded	None
May 18	Stmr. *Orinoco*	Lake Superior	Foundered	5
July 11	Stmr. *Philetus Sawyer*	Toledo, Ohio	Burned	
Nov. 28	Stmr. *Linden*	Tawas Bay	Burned	
		1924		
May 20	Stmr. *State of Ohio*	Cleveland, Ohio	Burned	1 or 2
Aug. 6	Stmr. *Miami*	Lake Huron	Burned	
Sept. 8	Stmr. *P. J. Ralph*	Lake Michigan	Foundered	
Sept. 22	Stmr. *Clifton*	Lake Huron	Disappeared	All Hands 27 or 28
Oct. 27	Stmr. *Kansas*	Manistee, Mich.	Burned	
Nov. 2	Stmr. *Niko*	Lake Michigan	Foundered	
Nov. 2	Stmr. *Turret Crown*	Lake Huron	Stranded	
Dec. 3	Stmr. *Lakeland*	Lake Michigan	Foundered	None
		1925		
June 9	Stmr. *Oakwood*	Lake Ontario	Stranded	
Aug. 19	Stmr. *Penobscot*	Marine City, Mich.	Burned	
Sept. 1	Stmr. *Colonial*	Lake Erie	Burned	3
Nov. 5	Stmr. *J. F. Crane*	Lake Superior	Foundered	7
	Stmr. *Kelley Island*	Lake Erie	Capsized	9

SHIPWRECKS OF THE LAKES

DATE	NAME OF SHIP	WHERE LOST	REASON FOR LOSS	LOST LIVES
		1926		
May 31	Stmr. *Nesbit Grammer*	Lake Ontario	Collision	
June 8	Tug *John B. Breyman*	Toledo, Ohio	Burned	
July 1	Stmr. *North Wind*	Georgian Bay	Stranded	None
Aug. 21	Stmr. *Howard S. Gerkin*	Lake Erie	Foundered	3
Aug. 21	Stmr. *Saronic*	Cockburn Island	Stranded and Burned	
Nov. 21	Stmr. *Herman Hettler*	Grand Island	Stranded	
Nov. 30	Stmr. *Thomas Maytham*	Lake Superior	Stranded	None
Nov. 30	Stmr. *City of Bangor*	Lake Superior	Stranded	None
		1927		
Dec. 6	Stmr. *Kamloops*	Lake Superior	Disappeared	All Hands 20 to 22
Dec. 7	Stmr. *Agawa*	Manitoulin Island	Stranded	
Dec. 8	Stmr. *Altadoc*	Lake Superior	Stranded	None
Dec. 8	Stmr. *Lambton*	Lake Superior	Foundered	
	Stmr. *United States*	Sarnia, Ont.	Burned	
	Stmr. *Pere Marquette No. 8*	Lake Michigan	Burned	
	Stmr. *Quedoc*	Lake Superior	Foundered	
		1928		
Mar. 23	Stmr. *Sachem*	St. Clair River	Burned	
June 7	Stmr. *America*	Isle Royale	Stranded	
June 25	Stmr. *Marysville*	Belle River, Mich.	Foundered	
Sept. 20	Stmr. *W. H. Sawyer*	Lake Huron	Foundered	
Oct. 4	Stmr. *M. J. Bartelme*	Cana Island	Stranded	
Dec. 9	Stmr. *Harbinger*	Lake Erie	Burned	
		1929		
May 16	Stmr. *Ralph Budd*	Lake Superior	Stranded	None
Sept. 10	Stmr. *Andaste*	Lake Michigan	Foundered	25 to 28
Oct. 22	Carferry *Milwaukee*	Lake Michigan	Foundered	46 to 52
Oct. 23	Stmr. *Chicago*	Lake Superior	Stranded	None
Oct. 23	Stmr. *N. J. Nessen*	Lake Erie	Foundered	13
Oct. 29	Stmr. *Wisconsin*	Lake Michigan	Foundered	16
Oct. 31	Stmr. *Senator*	Lake Michigan	Collision	10
		1930		
July 29	Stmr. *George J. Whelan*	Lake Erie	Foundered	15
Sept. 26	Schnr. *Our Son*	Lake Michigan	Foundered	None
Sept. 26	Stmr. *Salvor*	Lake Michigan	Foundered	6
Sept. 26	Stmr. *North Shore*	Lake Michigan	Foundered	6

A LIST OF GREAT LAKES SHIPWRECKS

DATE	NAME OF SHIP	WHERE LOST	REASON FOR LOSS	LIVES LOST
		1931		
Oct. 8	Stmr. *Charles H. Bradley*	Portage Lake	Burned	
		1932		
Oct. 5	Stmr. *John J. Boland, Jr.*	Lake Erie	Foundered	4
		1933		
May 27	Stmr. *George M. Cox*	Isle Royale	Stranded	None
Aug.	Schnr. *Lyman M. Davis*	Toronto, Ont.	Burned	None
		1934		
Nov. 21	Stmr. *W. C. Franz*	Lake Huron	Collision	4
Nov. 30	Stmr. *Henry Cort*	Lake Michigan	Stranded	1
		1935		
Dec. 5	Stmr. *Petoskey*	Sturgeon Bay, Wis.	Burned	None
Dec. 5	Schnr. *Lucia A. Simpson*	Sturgeon Bay, Wis.	Burned	None
Dec. 5	Schnr. *E. G. Crosby*	Sturgeon Bay, Wis.	Burned	None
		1936		
June 18	Stmr. *Tashmoo*	Detroit River	Hit Obstruction	None
July 29	MS *Material Service*	Lake Michigan	Foundered	15
Oct. 17	Stmr. *Sand Merchant*	Lake Erie	Foundered	19
Nov. 13	Tug *Frederick A. Lee*	Lake Huron	Foundered	5
		1937		
July 19	Stmr. *Frontier*	St. Marys River	Foundered	2
Aug. 10	MS *B. H. Becker*	Lake Huron	Foundered	None
Sept. 19	MS *C. E. Redfern*	Lake Michigan	Foundered	None
Sept. 24	Stmr. *Neebing*	Lake Superior	Foundered	2
Nov.	Stmr. *Calgadoc*	Newfoundland	Foundered	20
		1938		
Mar. 20	Stmr. *City of Buffalo*	Cleveland, Ohio	Burned	None
		1939		
Sept. 12	Stmr. *Hydro*	Cleveland, Ohio	Foundered	None
Oct. 28	Tug *R. P. Reidenbach*	Lake Erie	Capsized	2
Nov.	Tug *Badger State*	Lake Michigan	Foundered	1
		1940		
May 1	Stmr. *Arlington*	Lake Superior	Foundered	1
June	Stmr. *Sidney O. Neff*	Menominee, Mich.	Foundered	None
Nov. 11	Stmr. *Novadoc*	Lake Michigan	Foundered	2

SHIPWRECKS OF THE LAKES

DATE	NAME OF SHIP	WHERE LOST	REASON FOR LOSS	LIVES LOST
Nov. 11	Stmr. *Anna C. Minch*	Lake Michigan	Disappeared	All Hands
Nov. 11	Stmr. *William B. Davock*	Lake Michigan	Disappeared	All Hands
		1941		
Mar. 7	Stmr. *Maplecourt*	Atlantic Ocean	Enemy Action	All Hands
Oct. 23	Tug *America*	Detroit River	Capsized	6
		1942		
Sept. 2	MS *Steel Vendor*	Lake Superior	Foundered	1
Sept. 26	Tanker *Transoil*	Toledo, Ohio	Burned	2
Dec. 2	Tug *Admiral*	Lake Erie	Foundered	All Hands-14
Dec. 3	Barge *Cleveco*	Lake Erie	Foundered	All Hands-18
		1943		
April 29	Tug *Marions*		Explosion	3
June 15	Stmr. *George M. Humphrey*	Straits of Mackinac	Collision	None
July 27	Stmr. *Bruce Hudson*	Chicago, Ill.	Explosion	4
	Stmr. *Sarnian*	Lake Superior	Stranded	
		1944		
Jan.	Stmr. *Nevada*	Atlantic Ocean	Foundered	
April 27	Stmr. *James H. Reed*	Lake Erie	Collision	10
April 27	Stmr. *Frank E. Vigor*	Lake Erie	Collision	None
		1945		
July 17	Stmr. *Hamonic*	Sarnia, Ont.	Burned	None
		1946		
July 4	Ship *Success*	Port Clinton Bay	Burned	None
		1947		
June 4	Stmr. *Emperor*	Lake Superior	Stranded	12
Sept. 24	Stmr. *Milverton*	St. Lawrence River	Collision and Fire	15
Nov.	Stmr. *Wm. C. Warren*	Lake Huron	Stranded	
		1949		
Sept. 17	Stmr. *Noronic*	Toronto Harbor	Burned	118
	Coaler *West Shore*	Buffalo Harbor	Capsized	
		1950		
Aug. 14	Stmr. *Quebec*	St. Lawrence River	Burned	3
Oct. 16	Stmr. *John M. McKerchey*	Lake Erie	Foundered	1
Dec. 18	Tug *Sachem*	Lake Erie	Disappeared	12

A LIST OF GREAT LAKES SHIPWRECKS

DATE	NAME OF SHIP	WHERE LOST	REASON FOR LOSS	LIVES LOST
		1952		
Aug. 30	Stmr. *Hamiltonian*	Hamilton, Ont.	Burned	None
		1953		
May 11	Stmr. *Henry Steinbrenner*	Lake Superior	Foundered	17
June 20	Stmr. *Scotiadoc*	Lake Superior	Collision	1
		1954		
Oct. 14	M. S. *Prins Willem V*	Lake Michigan	Collision	None
		1958		
Sept. 18	Stmr. *Ashtabula*	Lake Erie	Collision	None
Nov. 18	Stmr. *Carl D. Bradley*	Lake Michigan	Foundered	33
		1959		
June 26	Stmr. *Monrovia*	Lake Huron	Collision	None
		1960		
Nov. 29	Stmr. *Francisco Morazan*	Lake Michigan	Stranded	None
		1962		
Dec. 9	Stmr. *Bayanna*	Lake Ontario	Striking Obstruction	None
		1964		
Sept. 5	Stmr. *Leecliffe Hall*	St. Lawrence River	Collision	3
		1965		
May 7	Stmr. *Cedarville*	Mackinac Straits	Collision	10
July 31	Tkr. *Cedarbranch*	Montreal Harbor	Fire & Explosion	1
Sept. 14	M. V. *Fort William*	Montreal Harbor	Explosion	5
Nov. 16	M. V. *Lawrencecliffe Hall*	St. Lawrence River	Collision	None
		1966		
Nov. 19	M. V. *Nordmeer*	Lake Huron	Stranding	None
Nov. 29	Stmr. *Daniel J. Morrell*	Lake Huron	Foundered	28
		1967		
Sept. 14	Stmr. *North American* (under tow)	North Atlantic	Foundered	None
Oct. 26	Barge *Wiltranco*	Lake Erie	Stranded	None

SHIPWRECKS OF THE LAKES

DATE	NAME OF SHIP	WHERE LOST	REASON FOR LOSS	LIVES LOST
		1968		
Oct. 23	Stmr. *Norman P. Clement*	Georgian Bay	Explosion	None
		1970		
July 14	m/v *Eastcliffe Hall*	Massena, N.Y.	Struck Crysler Shoal	9
		1972		
June 5	Stmr. *Sidney E. Smith, Jr.*	Port Huron, Mi.	Collision	None
August 7	m/v *Transbay*	Sept Iles, Que.	Capsized & Sank	None

Corrected to 1974

SHIPWRECKS OF THE LAKES

ACKNOWLEDGMENTS

Many persons over many miles have helped with this book —far too many to list herein. Particularly valuable inspiration of a general nature came from my family and friends.

Much helpful detailed technical information was received from the following masters of Great Lakes ships: Captain William P. Benham of Coronado Beach, Florida; Captain E. F. Burke of Midland, Ontario; Captain Richard W. England of Lakewood, Ohio; Captain Frank E. Hamilton of Kelleys Island, Ohio; Captain H. C. Inches of Westlake, Ohio; Captain Reginald Jarman of Victoria Harbor, Ontario; Captain Charles F. Meyers of Ashtabula, Ohio; Captain John C. Mier of Daytona Beach, Florida; Captain Robert Mitchell of Port McNicoll, Ontario; Captain John C. Murray of Cleveland, Ohio; Captain N. F. Peltier of Mt. Clemens, Mich.; Captain C. O. Rydholm of Cleveland, Ohio; Captain J. Oscar Spjut of Holland, Michigan, and Captain Merwin S. Thompson of Cleveland, Ohio, also the late Captain Warren C. Jones of Lakewood, Ohio, and the late Captain Varn L. Hosner of Daytona Beach, Florida.

I also greatly appreciate the helpful assistance received from the following persons: Nina Clifton Allbritten formerly of Marquette, Michigan; Mr. A. H. Amhaus, Fleet Engineer of Bethlehem Transportation Corporation; Mr. Harry S. Brown of Chatham, Ontario; Mr. Oliver Burnham of the Lake Carriers' Association; Alice B. Clapp, Librarian of Carnegie Public Library at Sault Ste. Marie, Michigan; Cleveland Public Library; Chicago Historical Society; Mr. Tom Cheney of Ashtabula, Ohio; Detroit Public Library; Rev. Edward J. Dowling, S. J. of the University of Detroit; Mr. Rollo Every of Clark Lake, Michigan; Mr. Julian Griffin of the Cleveland Press; First

SHIPWRECKS OF THE LAKES

Mate Walter L. Goodlet of the steamer *Andrew S. Upson;* Commander A. F. Glaza, Retired, U. S. Coast Guard; Dr. Frank Ward Holt of Grosse Pointe, Michigan; Chief Steward Murray Hoschel of the steamer *Edward Y. Townsend;* Mr. Bertram B. Lewis of the Cleveland Plain Dealer; Dorice E. Loveland of St. Clair, Michigan; Mr. William A. McDonald of Detroit, Michigan; Mr. Robert J. MacDonald of North East, Pennsylvania; Mr. H. G. MacLean, City Editor of The Canadian Observer, Sarnia, Ontario; Mrs. Robert Needham, Sr. of Corunna, Ontario; Mr. Gordon M. Potter of St. Joseph, Michigan; Mr. William D. Preston of the Cleveland Plain Dealer; Dr. W. M. Prentice of Toronto, Canada; Donna L. Root of the Cleveland Public Library; Mr. William O. Rainnie of Ashtabula, Ohio; Mr. Fred Roberts of Roberts Landing, Michigan; Mr. Austin I. Smith of Pacific Palisades, California; Ruth Hosner Shuck formerly of Ashtabula, Ohio; Mr. Gerald S. Wellman of Case Institute of Technology of Cleveland, Ohio; Mr. Warren S. Weiant, Jr. of Newark, Ohio; Mr. Richard G. Wendt of Sandusky, Ohio; Mr. A. E. Williams of Lorain, Ohio; Mrs. E. A. Worrell of Pentwater, Michigan, and Mrs. White of the Western Reserve Historical Society of Cleveland, Ohio.

Many of these persons provided basic information from family records, while others furnished helpful informative photographs. For special courtesies extended by Mr. A. B. Kern of The M. A. Hanna Company and Mr. John T. Hutchinson and Mr. Gene C. Hutchinson of Pioneer Steamship Company, I am also grateful.

To all these named, and to the many others not mentioned but who also helped in many ways, I extend my sincere appreciation and heartfelt thanks.

The Author

INDEX OF SHIPS

Note: * Indicates illustration.

INDEX OF SHIPS (Continued)

Note: * Indicates illustration.

364

INDEX OF SHIPS (Continued)

Note: * Indicates illustration.

365

INDEX OF SHIPS (Continued)

Note: * Indicates illustration.

INDEX OF SHIPS (Continued)

Note: * Indicates illustration.

INDEX OF SHIPS (Continued)

Note: * Indicates illustration.